AFRICA AND PREFERENTIAL TRADE

AFRICA AND PREFERENTIAL TRADE

*An Unpredictable
Path for Development*

RICHARD E. MSHOMBA

STANFORD UNIVERSITY PRESS
Stanford, California

Stanford University Press
Stanford, California

Library of Congress Cataloging-in-Publication Data

Names: Mshomba, Richard Elias, 1954- author.
Title: Africa and preferential trade : an unpredictable path for
    development / Richard E. Mshomba.
Description: Stanford, California : Stanford University Press, 2024. |
    Includes bibliographical references and index.
Identifiers: LCCN 2024012241 (print) | LCCN 2024012242 (ebook) |
    ISBN 9781503614611 (cloth) | ISBN 9781503640429 (ebook)
Subjects: LCSH: Tariff preferences—Africa. | Economic development—Africa. |
    Africa—Commerce—European Union countries. | European Union
    countries—Commerce—Africa. | Africa—Commerce. | Africa—Economic
    conditions—1960.
Classification: LCC HF1733.A35 M84 2024 (print) | LCC HF1733.A35 (ebook) |
    DDC 382/.914096—dc23/eng/20240412
LC record available at https://lccn.loc.gov/2024012241
LC ebook record available at https://lccn.loc.gov/2024012242

Cover design: George Kirkpatrick
Cover art: iStock
Typeset by Newgen in Source Serif Pro 10/15

To my wife, Elaine

CONTENTS

LIST OF TABLES

LIST OF ABBREVIATIONS

ACP	African, Caribbean, and Pacific countries
AfCFTA	African Continental Free Trade Area
AGOA	African Growth and Opportunity Act
ATPA	Andean Trade Preference Act
ATPDEA	Andean Trade Promotion and Drug Eradication Act
CAP	Common Agricultural Policy
CAR	Central African Republic
CCA	Corporate Council on Africa
CDP	Committee for Development Policy
CEMAC	Economic and Monetary Community of Central Africa
CEN-SAD	Community of Sahel-Saharan States
CETs	common external tariffs
CMA	Common Monetary Area
CN	Combined Nomenclature
CNL	Competitive Need Limitations
CPI	Corruption Perception Index
COMESA	Common Market for Eastern and Southern Africa
DFQF	duty-free and quota-free

DRC	Democratic Republic of the Congo
DSU	Dispute Settlement Understanding
EAC	East African Community
EBA	Everything But Arms
ECA	Economic Commission for Africa
ECCAS	Economic Community of Central African States
ECGLC	Economic Community of Great Lakes Countries
ECOSOC	Economic and Social Council
ECOWAS	Economic Community of West African States
ECU	European Currency Unit
EDF	Economic Development Fund
EEC	European Economic Community
EPA	Economic Partnership Agreement
EPZs	export processing zones
ESA	Eastern and Southern Africa
EU	European Union
FOCAC	Forum on China-Africa Cooperation
GAF	Globalization Adjustment Fund
GATT	General Agreement on Tariffs and Trade
GDP	gross domestic product
GNI	gross national income
GPT	General Preferential Tariff
GSP	Generalized System of Preferences
HDI	Human Development Index
HFI	Human Freedom Index
HS	Harmonized System
ICAC	International Cotton Advisory Committee
ICGLR	International Conference on the Great Lakes Region
IGAD	Intergovernmental Authority on Development
IMF	International Monetary Fund
IOC	Indian Ocean Commission
IPRI	International Property Rights Index
LDCs	least developed countries
MFA	Multi-Fiber Agreement
MFN	most favored nation

MRU	Mano River Union
NAFTA	North American Free Trade Agreement
OAMCE	Organisation Africaine et Malgache de Coopération Économique (Brazzaville Group)
OAU	Organization of African Unity
OCTs	Overseas Countries and Territories
OPEC	Organization of the Petroleum Exporting Countries
OTEXA	Office of Textiles and Apparel
PTA	Preferential Trade Area
ROOs	Rules of Origins
SACU	Southern African Customs Union
SADC	Southern African Development Community
SAPs	Structural Adjustment Programs
SPLM	Sudanese People's Liberation Movement
SSA	Sub-Saharan Africa
STABEX	Export earnings stabilization program for agricultural products
SYSMIN	Export earnings stabilization program for minerals
TAA	Trade Adjustment Assistance
TDCA	Trade, Development, and Cooperation Agreement
TPLF	Tigray People's Liberation Front
TPP	Trans-Pacific Partnership
UCMP	Uganda Chamber of Mines and Petroleum
UEMOA	West African Customs and Economic Union
UMA	Union of Arab Maghreb
UN	United Nations
UNCTAD	United Nations Conference on Trade and Development
UNDP	United Nations Development Program
VAT	value added tax
WAMZ	West African Monetary Zone
WRC	Worker Rights Consortium
WTO	World Trade Organization

ACKNOWLEDGMENTS

The Lord is kind and merciful.
—Psalm 103:8

First and foremost, I thank God with all my heart. When I was in my last two years of elementary school at Sinon Primary School (Arusha, Tanzania), my best friend, Alphonce Marandu, and I went to Mass every morning at St. Theresa of the Child Jesus Parish in Arusha. Our mothers would wake us up at 5:00 a.m. and we would walk (past our school) for an hour to get to church, which was four miles away. After Mass, we would walk two miles back, to our school. Alphonce was praying that he would be accepted into the junior seminary and become a priest; I was praying that I would be admitted into secondary school. Less than 5 percent of students who finished elementary school at the time (the 1960s) were admitted into secondary school. The national exam I took at the end of primary school was the most important exam I ever took in my life. Our prayers were answered a millionfold! It was beyond my wildest dreams that one day I would go to college, let alone become a college professor and write scholarly books. But with God, all things are possible.

I am also profoundly indebted to my parents, who were very loving and caring. They taught me and my siblings the importance of working hard. Although they did not have formal education themselves and were only subsistence farmers, barely able to make a living, they saw the value of education. My immediate family and my extended families—the Durnings, the Kavishes, the Mshombas, and the O'Hallorans—have all been a constant source of support for me with their love, words of encouragement, and prayers.

I had great professors and mentors at the three universities I attended, La Salle University, the University of Delaware, and the University of Illinois Urbana-Champaign. I thank them for guiding me and instilling in me a passion for research.

I will forever be grateful to La Salle University for offering me a full-tuition scholarship for my undergraduate studies and later giving me a job. La Salle also gave me a course reduction to work on this book. I am very grateful. I also sincerely thank my colleagues in the Economics Department for their friendship and support.

Like any other book, my work has certainly benefited from the work of others, as the bibliography clearly reveals. My thanks to all those who conduct research on Africa and also to organizations that produce and publish data. In conducting my own research for this book, I spent time in Botswana, Kenya, and Tanzania. I consulted with business executives, government officials, and ordinary factory workers. I also consulted with an executive of a textile company in Ethiopia through email. I am thankful for their time and information. I learned a lot from them. I have also benefited from frequent discussions on Africa with my friends, including Philip Balele, Paul Fisso, and Daniel Ole Njoolay.

My students have always inspired me with their interest in issues pertaining to African countries. Guiding them on their research papers on international economics and the political economy of Africa has always motivated me to learn more about Africa in the global economy. I especially want to thank Brian Murphy. Brian volunteered to be my research assistant for this book. He helped me with data collection and analysis and also read and commented on my drafts.

I owe special thanks to anonymous reviewers for their extremely useful suggestions and constructive criticism. My thanks also to my editors at Stanford University Press, Steve Catalano and Daniel Lo-

Preto, for their guidance and assistance. I am also indebted to my former editor, Scott Parris, for his friendship and support.

I am grateful to my sons, Alphonce, Dennis, and Charles, and my daughter-in-law, Kelley, for their unwavering support. My grandchildren, Mary Elaine and Richard Elias, also give me energy and help me find joy in my work. I most certainly could not have completed this manuscript in a timely manner without the loving and ever-present support of my wife, Elaine. She is a gifted editor. With her legal background and more than twenty-five years of experience as a language teacher, she is very attentive to detail, language, and organization. I don't know what I would have done without her. It is my sincere pleasure to dedicate this book to her. Of course, I still take full responsibility for any errors, omissions, and other shortcomings.

Richard E. Mshomba

FIGURE 1. Map of Africa. Bruce Jones Design, Inc.

AFRICA AND PREFERENTIAL TRADE

INTRODUCTION

ACCORDING TO A FAMOUS PROVERB, "Give a man a fish, and you feed him for a day. Teach a man to fish, and you feed him for a lifetime." Nonreciprocal preferential trade arrangements neither "give a man a fish" nor "teach a man how to fish." Rather, they offer the promise of a market in which to sell one's fish. That is, these arrangements encourage preference-receiving countries to "teach themselves how to fish" and to "go fishing on their own," with the nonbinding promise that they will have a market for the fish they are able to catch and sell. Nonreciprocal preferential trade arrangements are thus a form of foreign aid—aid through trade. In addition, a preference-receiving country might receive some assistance to buy a boat and nets as part of "aid for trade," but it cannot count on such assistance.

Nonreciprocal preferential trade arrangements have been a defining feature of the relationship between developed and developing countries, dating back to the colonial era for African countries. In the late 1950s, preferential trade arrangements started to take a multilateral form when the European Economic Community (EEC) was founded and its members, collectively, decided to establish special trade arrangements with their colonies. Since then, a number of preferential trade agreements have featured African countries among the preference-receiving countries.

It is often taken for granted that preferential trade arrangements are important stimuli for African development. They are seen as a positive form of "aid"—not a handout, but rather aid that takes advantage of the strengths of the preference-receiving countries. Countries such as Lesotho and Mauritius have indeed benefited considerably from preferential treatment (ECA, 2007; Belay, 2007).

Yet it is not always clear: (a) how preferential these arrangements actually are; (b) to what extent African countries are able to take advantage of them; and (c) whether these arrangements in fact help African countries or instead lead them to perpetual dependence on specific markets and products. Moreover, preferential trade agreements are often unpredictable, since the duration and magnitude of preferences are at the discretion of the preference-giving countries.

This book explores the impact of trade on development and the salient features of nonreciprocal preferential trade programs. Special attention is given to the trade relationship between the EU and African countries. In addition to considering the history and objectives of preferential trade arrangements, the book examines systems and procedures used in African countries to take advantage of these programs.

African countries receive preferential treatment for their exports to developed countries and some middle-income countries. In part, this special favor has its background in Africa's colonial history, but it continues to be provided and justified by the relatively poor economic development of most African countries. As of 2023, 33 of the 46 least developed countries (LDCs) in the world were in Africa.

The most widely used program under which developed countries provide a nonreciprocal preferential reduction of trade barriers for goods coming from developing countries is the Generalized System of Preferences (GSP). This program was established in 1971 under the auspices of the General Agreement on Tariffs and Trade (GATT), and it continues to operate under its successor, the World Trade Organization (WTO). It is important to note that the GSP program is not one collective program in which preference-giving countries join together to give uniform preferential treatment. Rather, there are thirteen independent GSP programs, established by Australia, Belarus, Canada, the EU, Iceland, Japan, Kazakhstan, New Zealand, Norway, Russia, Switzerland, Turkey, and the U.S. (UNCTAD, 2015). As such, preference-receiving countries engage with many GSP programs, each with its own unique features and requirements. Table 0.1 shows African beneficiary countries for five of those programs.

In addition to the GSP programs, other special trade arrangements have also given nonreciprocal preferential treatment to African and other developing countries. These include the transient Cotonou Agreement between the EU and the African, Caribbean, and Pacific (ACP) countries, the EU Everything But Arms (EBA) program between the EU and LDCs, the U.S. African Growth and Opportunity Act (AGOA) between the U.S. and Sub-Saharan African countries, and the preferential tariff schemes of China and South Korea for LDCs.

It would be naïve to assume that nonreciprocal preferences are extended by preference-giving countries based purely on altruistic motives. Consumers in those countries benefit from imported goods (from the preference-receiving countries) that cost less, due to the reduction or removal of tariffs altogether. However, there is more to it than that. These nonreciprocal preferences enhance the global political power and leverage that large economies already have. They serve as an important diplomatic "currency" that can be used to advance alliances and mitigate the influence of rival powers.

As pointed out by an anonymous reviewer, nonreciprocal preferential trade arrangements are "intimately bound up with questions of power and agency." The distinction between "agency" and "power" is rather subtle. Some sociologists describe agency as "an actor's ability to initiate and maintain a program of action while [power is] an actor's ability to act independently of the constraining power of social structure" (Campbell, 2009: 407).[1] The discussion in this book uses the term *power* in its broadest sense to mean all the ways in which a nation is able to act and react independently.

Since nonreciprocal preferential trade arrangements are voluntary, African countries have hardly any power in the negotiations.

TABLE 0.1. Beneficiary countries of five GSP programs, GSP+, EBA, and AGOA (as of 2023)

LDCs in italics	Australia	Canada	EU GSP	EU EBA	EU GSP+	Japan	US GSP	US AGOA
Algeria	X					X	X	
Angola	X	X		X		X	X	X
Benin	X	X		X		X	X	X
Botswana						X	X	X
Burkina Faso	X			X		X	X	X
Burundi	X	X		X		X	X	
Cabo Verde	X	X			X	X	X	X
Cameroon	X	X				X	X	X
Central African Republic	X	X		X		X	X	X
Chad	X	X		X		X	X	X
Comoros	X	X		X		X	X	X
Congo, Democratic Republic	X	X		X		X	X	X
Congo, Republic	X	X	X			X	X	X
Côte d'Ivoire	X	X				X	X	X
Djibouti	X	X		X		X	X	X
Egypt	X	X				X	X	
Equatorial Guinea	X			X		X		
Eritrea	X	X		X		X	X	

(continued)

LDCs in italics	Australia	Canada	EU GSP	EU EBA	EU GSP+	Japan	US GSP	US AGOA
Eswatini	X	X				X	X	X
Ethiopia	X	X		X		X	X	X
Gabon	X					X	X	X
Gambia	X	X		X		X	X	X
Ghana	X	X				X	X	X
Guinea	X	X		X		X	X	X
Guinea-Bissau	X	X		X		X	X	X
Kenya	X	X	X			X	X	X
Lesotho	X	X		X		X	X	X
Liberia	X	X		X		X	X	X
Libya	X					X		
Madagascar	X	X		X		X	X	X
Malawi	X	X		X		X	X	X
Mali	X	X		X		X	X	X
Mauritania	X	X		X		X	X	X
Mauritius	X					X	X	X
Morocco	X	X				X		
Mozambique	X	X		X		X	X	X
Namibia						X	X	X

(continued)

TABLE 0.1. (*continued*)

LDCs in italics	Australia	Canada	EU GSP	EU EBA	EU GSP+	Japan	US GSP	US AGOA
Niger	X	X		X		X	X	X
Nigeria	X	X	X			X	X	X
Rwanda	X	X		X		X	X	X
Sao Tomé and Principe	X	X		X		X	X	X
Senegal	X	X		X		X	X	X
Seychelles	X							
Sierra Leone	X	X		X		X	X	X
Somalia	X	X		X		X	X	
South Africa						X	X	X
South Sudan		X		X			X	
Sudan	X	X		X		X		
Tanzania	X	X		X		X	X	X
Togo	X	X		X		X	X	X
Tunisia	X					X	X	
Uganda	X	X		X		X	X	X
Zambia	X	X		X		X	X	X
Zimbabwe	X	X				X	X	

Sources: U.S. Congressional Research Service (2022), EU's EBA, and GSP websites of respective countries.

Negotiations are usually conducted within the confines of the domestic constituencies in the preference-giving countries. Even when African representatives are invited to these discussions, they come from a weak position because of their dependence on foreign markets and insufficient knowledge of all the intricacies involved in the negotiations. A few African countries have business associations in the capitals of the rich economies in order to stay abreast of any developments that could impact their countries and to advocate for their countries' interests. For example, Mauritius and South Africa have business associations in Washington, D.C., the Mauritius-U.S. Business Association, and the South African Business Council, respectively. These associations usually seek the support of importing companies in the U.S. to build their case for easier access to the U.S. market.

Kragelund and Carmody (2015) explain how the long-term dependence on resources has made some African countries vulnerable and, therefore, weakened their negotiating powers, except at times when resource prices are on the rise. At the same time, economic differences and interests within African regional economic blocs, which are magnified at the continent-wide level, limit the capacity of African countries to participate and negotiate as a unified group.[2]

It is important to point out that the emergence of China as an economic power has changed the dynamics of global power. The competition for alliances between China (and other emerging markets) and the West has given African countries alternatives and some leverage in negotiations. Still, this point must not be overstated. As Taylor (2011:101) cautions:

> Africa's leadership has, in general, promoted and fostered dependent relationships with Western capitalist powers and there is a danger that FOCAC [the Forum on China-Africa Cooperation] may simply reproduce this dependency. An Africa where external actors consume the continent's resources and add little to Africa's self-development is something which has staked out much of post-colonial Africa's trajectory. In these circumstances, African elites attending forums such as FOCAC can, from a particular perspective, be seen as characters reduced to beggars angling for

some Chinese largesse, rather than development-conscious participants, and certainly not partners.

Given that most African countries are relatively poor, they are inherently predisposed to being seen as "beggars," even at times when they are simply asking rich countries for a level playing field. For example, the colonial system and the global trading system subjected some African countries to being overly dependent on exporting raw natural resources. To free them from this, they do need assistance. Thus one can describe nonreciprocal preferential trade arrangements as a form of affirmative action.

In many ways, it is easy to make strong arguments for nonreciprocal preferential trade policy toward African countries. African countries suffered under the exploitation of colonialism by European countries for eight decades. They were also affected in negative ways by the Cold War. During the Cold War era, many African dictators were given protection and financial "aid" to maintain their allegiance. The so-called "development aid" often went into the personal accounts of those dictators and their cronies, instead of helping to grow their economies. This apparently happened with the full knowledge of the donor countries, some of which are now the ones with preferential trade policies.[3] Even where there was no outright misappropriation of public funds, there were still issues:

> [F]or much of the period between independence and 1994, African governments were more directly responsible to external donors, in setting public sector priorities and delivering public services, than they were to their own populations. For practical purposes, the prioritization and delivery of collective goods was either absent or in external hands. (O'Connell and Dolan, 2012)

In addition, during GATT's entire existence (1948–94), two sectors important to developing countries, (1) agriculture and (2) textiles and apparel, were excluded from multilateral rules and were highly protected in developed countries. Although they are now included in the WTO surveillance and negotiations, domestic support and protection of these sectors in developed countries are still substantial. The preferential trade policy in favor of LDCs is a way to give these countries a reprieve from such obstacles.

Nonreciprocal preferential trade policy is also seen as a more effective form of aid than direct financial aid. Growth in the export sector as a result of easy market access can increase jobs and incomes in the broader economy. It essentially becomes a form of aid disbursed to millions of people, unlike direct financial aid that can easily be misappropriated.

Notwithstanding these arguments for potential benefits, nonreciprocal preferential trade policy can raise significant concerns. First, there is the question about whether the beneficiary countries have the administration and production capacity to utilize the market access. Can preferential trade policy be effective without supplementary direct aid? The impetus for the "Aid for Trade" initiative in the WTO was mainly to address domestic supply constraints in African and other developing countries and thus enable them to take advantage of market opportunities.

Second, a preferential trade policy may make beneficiary countries overly dependent on a few markets and products and thus unmotivated to explore other markets and diversify their export sector. Preferential arrangements may also be biased in favor of raw materials, thus discouraging industrialization in the preference-receiving countries.

Third, by its very nature, preferential trade policy is nonbinding. Because it is voluntary, it is unpredictable and temporary. As can be expected, negotiations between the preference-giving and preference-receiving countries are common. However, the ultimate decisions as to which countries and which goods will receive preferential treatment, what level of preferential treatment will be given, and how long the preferential treatment will last, rest on the donor country. Even when the motive is to help a developing country to grow, the donor country is informed and constrained by its own self-interest and values. A preferential trade policy can be suspended for any reason deemed legitimate by the preference-giving country. For example, Central African Republic, Cote d'Ivoire, the Democratic Republic of the Congo, Eritrea, Eswatini, Ethiopia, the Gambia, Guinea, Madagascar, Mauritania, Rwanda, and South Sudan have been removed from the U.S. African Growth and Opportunity Act (AGOA) at one point or another.

Fourth, like any other forms of aid, preferential trade policy reduces whatever little leverage a preference-receiving country might have had in negotiating in other areas, for fear of losing the benefit. This is especially true because the preference-giving country or region is the one that sets the criteria for eligibility. It is partly because they are aid recipients that African countries have been relatively passive in the dispute settlement system in the WTO.

Fifth, none of the programs that provide nonreciprocal preferential trade treatment cover all African countries. This is due in part to the economic diversity of African countries in terms of their economic development and their structures of exports. It is also due to the discretion enjoyed by the donor countries. As such, these programs can create tension among African countries and hurt their efforts to strengthen regional economic integration. These tensions have become even more apparent as the Cotonou Agreement, signed in 2000, is being replaced by Economic Partnership Agreements (EPAs), that is, reciprocal preferential trade agreements between the EU and ACP countries.

These issues are addressed to various degrees in this book. Nonreciprocal preferential trade arrangements can be likened to lending a tool to relatively poor neighbors or acquaintances to help them grow their economic capacity. You determine the size and quality of the tool to lend and how long they can have it, aware that the tool can increase their potential to compete against you. The usefulness of the tool depends on what other tools they have.

A borrowed tool is just what it is, even when one is allowed to use it for a long time. You cannot make long-term projections of your economic development based on it. As such, nonreciprocal preferential trade arrangements cannot be used to plan or predict long-term paths for development. They provide short-term opportunities that, when used effectively, can enable a country to develop a more diverse economic structure that is less dependent on preferential treatment. But the fact that many African countries are still dependent on preferential trade arrangements, and seem startled every time the margin of preference decreases, suggests that these arrangements have not strengthened African economies to the point of giving them adequate resilience.

Of course, even under the best circumstances, nonreciprocal preferential trade arrangements alone cannot be expected to be a panacea for the many challenges that developing countries face in growing their export sectors, let alone their economies in general. The challenges include a narrow export base, poor and unreliable infrastructure, low levels of education, and, in some countries, poor governance, corruption, and political instability. Even where preferential trade arrangements have attracted foreign direct investment, most foreign investors have relied on inputs from their home countries, thus limiting the potential for backward linkages. Moreover, some of the investors, particularly those in the textiles and apparel industry, are opportunistic and, therefore, nomadic in nature. They cannot necessarily be relied on for long-run projections.

Chapter 1 addresses questions related to the impact of trade on development in African countries. Needless to say, the ultimate objective in promoting trade is to bring about development, that is, to improve people's lives. Given that this book focuses on preferential trade arrangements, it is important first to discuss trade itself, to understand this link between trade and economic development. Trade models, from the simple, general equilibrium, Ricardian model, to what are called "new trade models," show that there are benefits to trade. This chapter examines some of these models. Careful attention is paid to some of the assumptions made and their relevance, specifically, to African economies. Trade is not a zero-sum game; that is, one nation does not gain only by another losing. Both trading partners can gain from trade. However, the distribution of those gains can be skewed. Which external and domestic factors determine the distribution of gains from trade to a country? Analysis of the market structures and the terms of trade can shed some light on this question. When realized, how are the gains from trade used to promote real development? What exactly are the linkages between trade and development? These questions call for a careful analysis of the structure of imports, exports, domestic economic structures and policies, and the international trading system.

Chapter 2 presents and analyzes the evolution of trade relations between European countries and the ACP countries, from the 1960s to the early 2000s. Needless to say, trade relations between these groups of countries arose from, and were informed by, their colonial history. In 1963, the European Economic Community and African countries signed the Yaoundé Convention, which allowed most dutiable imports from African countries to enter the European market duty-free. The Lomé Convention, signed in 1975, replaced the Yaoundé Convention and formalized all nonreciprocal preferential treatment of imports by the European countries from the ACP countries. Subsequently, in 2000, the Lomé Convention was replaced by the Cotonou Agreement between the EU and ACP countries with the understanding that the arrangement would evolve into Economic Partnership Agreements (EPAs), that is, reciprocal preferential trade agreements between the EU and ACP countries.

Chapter 3 presents a systematic analysis of EPA negotiations for each negotiating group in Africa by examining the specific features of countries in each group. It discusses why some countries have been quick to embrace EPAs while others have been ambivalent or outright against them. The chapter also presents results of empirical studies that have estimated the impact of EPAs on ACP countries. Manger and Shadlen (2014) describe how nonreciprocal preferential arrangements create "political trade dependence" for preference-receiving countries. Preference-receiving countries continually face uncertainty because the preferential treatment can be removed unilaterally at any time. Political trade dependence is determined by the uncertainty of the preferential treatment and the importance of the preference-giving country as a market. The greater the "political trade dependence," the more likely a developing country will be motivated to pursue predictable, reciprocal trade arrangements with developed countries. This phenomenon can be seen in the EPA negotiations. However, LDCs have more assurance of receiving nonreciprocal preferential treatment and, therefore, have generally not been ready for EPAs.

The nonreciprocal preferential trade arrangements that the EU had established with former colonies appear to have become a prototype for subsequent similar arrangements to support developing countries. Chapter 4 analyzes the key features of the GSP programs and other nonreciprocal preferential trade programs that favor African products. Special attention is given to such programs offered by China, the EU, and the U.S., as these are the most important trade partners of African countries. These preferential programs are generally similar to each other.

Chapter 5 examines the extent to which preferences are actually used by African countries. It provides information on actual preference utilization by a sample of exporting firms, and it considers the overall utilization of the EBA and AGOA programs. The chapter also discusses the potential benefits of these preferential trade arrangements to preference-receiving countries.

The conclusion provides a summary of the major findings and recommendations.

1 TRADE AND ECONOMIC DEVELOPMENT

TRADE CAN BE VERY IMPORTANT for economic development. This is the reason that nonreciprocal preferential market access is offered, selectively, to developing countries through various programs.

Highlighting the consensus among economists about international trade, Mankiw (2015) wrote that:

> Economists are famous for disagreeing with one another, and indeed, seminars in economics departments are known for their vociferous debate. But economists reach near unanimity on some topics, including [the desirability of freer] international trade.

Experience and trade models discussed below give economists confidence about the economic benefits of trade. Trade can be, has been, and will continue to be important and even critical for economic development. However, international trade is neither a panacea for poverty reduction nor an automatic guarantor of development. Trade takes advantage of differences between countries and economies of scale to bring mutual, albeit not necessarily equal, gains to trading partners. Those gains can be used to bring about human development.

Trade allows countries to consume combinations of products and services that are outside their production possibilities. It can be an important source of economic growth for a country. Economic growth is a prerequisite for human development, but economic growth in itself may not necessarily translate into human development. Real human development manifests itself in (a) improved access to basic needs (food, clean water, and shelter), social services (health care and education), and infrastructure (energy, roads, railways, airports, ports); (b) improved safety and security; and (c) reduced income inequality. It is improvement in the overall standard of living for a country's population.

Not surprisingly, these and other measures of development are not only indicators of, but also important factors for economic growth and human development. People with good health are more productive than people with poor health (Sharpe and Fard, 2022). People who are well educated are also more productive and can adapt to new technologies faster than those who are not well educated. Infrastructure is important in connecting communities, and it is fundamental for the production and trading of, and access to, goods and services. For example, Kenya has increasingly become an important producer and exporter of different varieties of cut flowers, in part because of the improvements it has made to the infrastructure needed to keep cut flowers fresh (Nippon Express, 2020; African Business Portal, 2022). Safety and security are also critical for investment and the overall economic vitality of a country.

AN OVERVIEW OF ECONOMIC DEVELOPMENT IN AFRICA

While it may not be possible to quantify all aspects of human development, the Human Development Index (HDI), published by the United Nations Development Program (UNDP), is a good indicator of human development. The HDI is calculated based on life expectancy, the average number of years of formal schooling, and the gross national income (GNI) per capita. The index is used to show countries' development trends and also to rank them according to their development. The HDI reveals significant differences in people's well-being between countries. For example, statistically, in 2021, a child born in Switzerland could be expected to have 16.5 years of schooling and to live for

84 years, while a child born in Chad could be expected to have only 8 years of schooling and live for 52.5 years (United Nations Development Program, 2022: 272–75).

As measured by the HDI, most African countries are among the poorest countries in the world. In the HDI ranking of 191 countries in 2021, 39 of the 50 lowest-ranked countries were African countries (United Nations Development Program, 2022: 277–80).

The World Bank likewise classifies countries based on gross national income (GNI) per capita. As measured by the GNI alone, as well, most African countries are among the poorest in the world. For 2022–23, these were the GNI per capita thresholds: low-income economies—$1,085 or less; lower middle-income economies—between $1,086 and $4,255; upper-middle-income economies—between $4,256 and $13,205; and high-income economies—more than $13,205 (Hamadeh et al., 2022). Most African countries are in the low-income or lower-middle-income range, as shown in Table 1.1. For context, according to the World Bank data, the GNI per capita in Sub-Saharan Africa and the world were, respectively, $1,562 and $12,026 in 2021.

Separately, the category of the least developed countries (LDCs), established by the United Nations in 1971, gives special attention to developing countries that have entrenched and widespread development challenges that impede their economic development. Three criteria are used to identify LDCs: (a) GNI per capita; (b) structural impediments related to a low level of human assets (measured by the Human Assets Index); and (c) a high vulnerability to economic and environmental shocks (measured by the Economic Vulnerability Index). The Human Assets Index is calculated based on education indicators (secondary school enrollment and adult literacy rate) and health indicators (percentage of population undernourished and under-five mortality rate). Economic vulnerability is calculated based on a number of factors, including population size, export concentration, and share of agriculture, forestry, and fishing in gross domestic product (United Nations, 2020). Countries whose sources of export revenues are not diversified, for example, tend to be more vulnerable to occurrences that are beyond their control, as is the case for countries that are highly

TABLE 1.1. Classification of African countries by income level, 2021–22

Low-income countries	Lower middle-income countries	Upper middle-income countries	High-income countries
Burkina Faso	Algeria	Botswana	Seychelles
Burundi	*Angola*	Equatorial	
Central African	**Benin**	Guinea	
Republic	Cabo Verde	Gabon	
Chad	Cameroon	Libya	
Congo, Dem. Rep.	**Comoros**	Mauritius	
Eritrea	Congo, Rep.	Namibia	
Ethiopia	Cote d'Ivoire	South	
Gambia, The	**Djibouti**	Africa	
Guinea	Egypt		
Guinea-Bissau	Eswatini		
Liberia	Ghana		
Madagascar	Kenya		
Malawi	**Lesotho**		
Mali	**Mauritania**		
Mozambique	Morocco		
Niger	Nigeria		
Rwanda	*São Tomé and Principe*		
Sierra Leone	**Senegal**		
Somalia	**Sudan**		
South Sudan	**Tanzania**		
Togo	Tunisia		
Uganda	Zimbabwe		
Zambia (demoted to low-income in 2022)	**(LDCs are listed in bold. However, Angola and São Tomé and Principe are scheduled to graduate from LDC status in 2024.)**		
[All of these are least-developed countries (LDCs).]			

Sources: UNDP Regional Bureau for Africa (2021) and World Bank reports on "World Bank country and lending groups."

dependent on oil exports or tourism. The criteria used to identify LDCs match very closely with the variables used to calculate the HDI.

Table 1.1 presents the classification of African countries according to GNI per capita. According to the United Nations, as of 2023, of the 46 LDCs in the world, 72 percent of them—33 countries—are in Africa. The inclusion in and graduation from the LDC category are the result of reviews and recommendations by the Committee for Development Policy (CDP), a subsidiary of the Economic and Social Council (ECOSOC) of the United Nations. The CDP carries out extensive reviews of LDCs every three years to determine their readiness for graduation. Only three Sub-Saharan African countries so far have graduated out of the LDC category—Botswana, Cabo Verde, and Equatorial Guinea, in 1994, 2007, and 2017, respectively. Angola and São Tomé and Príncipe are scheduled to graduate in 2024 (UNDP Regional Bureau for Africa, 2021). The difference between LDCs and non-LDC developing countries matters. Among other things, this difference plays out in the negotiations between the EU and the African, Caribbean, and Pacific (ACP) countries to establish Economic Partnership Agreements, as discussed in Chapter 3.

TRADE MODELS AND THE GAINS FROM TRADE

To the extent that trade is an important means for economic development and, therefore, a potential reason for economic disparity between countries, it is imperative to examine trade models. There are three key trade models: (i) the Ricardian model; (ii) the Heckscher-Ohlin model; and (iii) the economies of scale model.[1]

The Ricardian Model

Perhaps no trade model has been used to demonstrate the power of trade more than the Ricardian model, developed by David Ricardo in the early nineteenth century (Ricardo, 2001).[2] In the simple Ricardian model of trade, trading partners gain by taking advantage of their difference in relative production costs, that is, opportunity costs. A country has comparative advantage in a product if it can produce it at a lower opportunity cost than its trading partners.

Suppose, on average, a farmer in West Africa can produce 10 tons of cotton or 5 tons of corn, and, on average, a farmer in the U.S. can produce 20 tons of cotton or 30 tons of corn. In this example, the U.S. has absolute advantage in producing both products. However, the opportunity cost of producing a ton of cotton in West Africa is half a ton of corn, whereas the opportunity cost of producing a ton of cotton in the U.S. is 1.5 tons of corn. Therefore, West Africa has comparative advantage in producing cotton and the U.S. has comparative advantage in producing corn. In this simple model, the opportunity costs are constant. When trade occurs, the terms of trade—the price of exports relative to the price of imports—would be somewhere between 1 ton of cotton = 0.5 ton of corn to 1 ton of cotton = 1.5 tons of corn, depending on the demand for these goods and other factors, such as transportation costs. With trade, West Africa will be able to sell its export product, cotton, at a higher price, and buy its import product at a lower price. The reverse is true for the U.S., but both will gain from trade.

It is important to emphasize that the benefits of trade come from the specialization in the production and exchange of goods. Unless resources are totally immobile, trade causes a reallocation of resources. Trade reduces some jobs and increases others. But even when resources are totally immobile, trade can still be beneficial through the exchange of goods.

To illustrate this point about totally immobile resources, suppose West Africa has 6,000 units of labor and the U.S. has 5,000 units of labor. Both have full employment, but in the short run, labor, the only factor of production in the Ricardian model, is not mobile.[3] Suppose, under no trade, West Africa produces and consumes 30,000 tons of cotton and 15,000 tons of corn, while the U.S. produces and consumes 30,000 tons of cotton and 105,000 tons of corn. Suppose that West Africa and the U.S. start trading with each other with the terms of trade, 1 ton of cotton = 1 ton of corn, but that they cannot change their production combinations. Specifically, suppose West Africa exports 20,000 tons of cotton for 20,000 tons of corn from the U.S. With this pattern and the magnitude of trade, West Africa will consume 10,000 tons of cotton and 35,000 tons of corn. The U.S. will consume 50,000 of cotton and 85,000 tons of corn. In this hypothetical example, both trading partners gain from exchange as they consume combinations of cotton and corn that are above what they could produce on their own with the resources they have. West Africa and the U.S. would need, respectively, 8,000 and 5,333 units of labor to produce the combinations they can consume with trade.

Countries stand to benefit more from trade, though, if they are able to adjust production and allow for a more efficient allocation of resources. In this example, West Africa would increase its production of cotton and reduce its production of corn, and the U.S. would do the opposite.

The model assumes free trade, which, of course, is not the case in the real world. Nonreciprocal preferential trade arrangements themselves are meant to reduce trade barriers in the preference-giving countries for products originating from developing countries. In the example used here, suppose the U.S. gives subsidies to domestic cotton producers, therefore reducing their opportunity cost of producing cotton. Suppose, in effect, the subsidies reduce the opportunity cost of producing cotton in the U.S. to 1 ton of cotton = 1.2 tons of corn.[4] While both trading partners can still benefit from trade, other things being equal, the terms of trade will deteriorate for West Africa. The range within which the terms of trade could occur would decrease. The gains from trade for West Africa will be less than they would be in a situation with no subsidies.

Stepping away from the theoretical model and the hypothetical example for a moment, in reality, cotton subsidies by the U.S. alone, that is, not including those by the EU and China, lowered the world price of cotton by about 10 percent in the early 2000s, thereby hurting developing countries that produced cotton (ICAC, 2001; ICAC, 2002; Alston et al., 2007). Indeed, the role of cotton as a source of export revenues has decreased significantly since the early 2000s for some West African countries, in particular Burkina Faso, Chad, and Mali. However, for Benin, cotton continues to be the most important source of foreign currency, comprising about 40 percent of its export revenues (Food and Agriculture Organization, 2022).

In the Ricardian model, while the gains of trade may be different between trading partners, everyone in a given country gains equally because there is only one homogeneous factor of production. Since the opportunity cost is constant, the model also predicts complete specialization. However, the model accommodates the possibility of one country producing both products and the other one completely specializing in producing the product in which it has comparative advantage. This would be expected when trade is between a larger country and a small country. The small country may not be able to export enough of the product it produces to satisfy the larger country's demand for the product. So, the larger country would have to produce both products.

The Heckscher-Ohlin Model
The Heckscher-Ohlin model demonstrates that trade causes redistribution of income.

The Heckscher-Ohlin model was developed in the 1930s (Lloyd, 2011). It assumes two factors of production, two goods, and two countries. The underlying basis for trade in this model is the difference in factor endowments between the two countries and the difference in factor intensity between the two products. Assuming the two factors of production are labor and capital, a country is relatively labor abundant if its labor-to-capital ratio is greater than that of the other country. The trading partner would be relatively capital abundant. As trading partners, African countries are relatively labor abundant and European countries are relatively capital abundant. A product is relatively labor intensive if its production requires a higher labor-to-capital ratio compared to the other product. The other product will be capital intensive. In the textile industry, downstream processes, such as cutting and sewing, are relatively labor intensive, whereas upstream processes, such as yarn and fabric production, are relatively capital intensive. The Heckscher-Ohlin theorem states that a country has comparative advantage in producing the product that is intensive in the country's relatively abundant factor of production.⁵ African countries would, therefore, export apparel and, in exchange, import yarn and fabric. The Heckscher-Ohlin model does not produce complete specialization, because of increasing opportunity cost.

As a classic illustration of the Heckscher-Ohlin model, African countries have a comparative advantage in some minerals with which they have been endowed and in some crops, such as cashew nuts, cocoa, coffee, cotton, tea, tobacco, and sugar, because they are endowed with a tropical climate and soil suitable for producing these commodities. On average, African countries have a comparative *dis*advantage in pharmaceuticals, machines, and other manufactured products compared to developed countries, because technologies in developed countries are more advanced.

In the Heckscher-Ohlin model, before trade, the relative price of the labor-intensive product is lower in the relatively labor-abundant country. Therefore, opening up free trade increases the price of the labor-intensive product and lowers the price of the capital-intensive product in that country. The opposite happens in the relatively capital-abundant country. Corresponding to the changes in the prices of products brought about by trade, the price of the relatively abundant factor of production increases and the price of the relatively scarce factor of production decreases. Unlike the outcome in the Ricardian model, in the Heckscher-Ohlin model, trade creates clear winners and losers. This is because trade increases, indirectly, the demand for the respective abundant resource through exports (an expanded market), thereby increasing its price, and increases the supply of the respective scarce resource through imports (increased competition), thereby decreasing its price. That means, in the African and European countries example, in African countries wages will rise and the price of capital will fall. The opposite will happen in the European countries. It is important to note that the model shows that the gains of trade for the abundant factor will exceed the losses for the scarce factor. Therefore, while trade will cause redistribution of income between individuals, overall, national incomes will increase.

According to the Heckscher-Ohlin model, who gains and who loses from trade depends on the ownership of the factors of production and not necessarily the industries in which those factors are employed. This is because the model assumes that the two factors of production are perfectly mobile between industries. The model also assumes full employment. That means that workers, for example, who are displaced from certain industries by the increase of imports can easily be absorbed by the industries that are expanding due to the increase in production and exports.

In reality, resources are not perfectly mobile between industries, and certainly not so in the short run when displaced workers may need to acquire new skills and even move to different parts of the country. Displaced workers can find themselves structurally unemployed if their skills are not transferable and when it is hard or expensive for them to learn new marketable skills or move to places where new jobs are being created. Moreover, while job destruction may take place almost immediately in the less competitive industries, job creation in the competitive industries may take time to materialize. Studies by Muendler (2010) and Casacuberta and Gandelman (2010) on the impact of trade in Brazil and Uruguay, respectively, found that openness to trade caused less job creation than job destruction. A potential explanation is that workers' productivity in the industries that are expanding increases and, therefore, the need for labor does not increase by the same percentage that output increases. Another explanation is that firms may be hesitant to invest in physical capital until they have some confidence about the future demand for their products. But when demand is based in large part on nonreciprocal preferential trade arrangements over which the exporting country has no control, the future is unpredictable.

The U.S. and the European Union have, respectively, the Trade Adjustment Assistance (TAA) program and the Globalization Adjustment Fund (GAF) to help eligible workers displaced by freer trade. Trade-adjustment assistance in developed countries includes unemployment compensation, retraining, job-search support, a relocation allowance, tax credits on health insurance premium costs, subsidies to employers, and small business start-up assistance (Congressional Research Service, 2015; OECD, 2005). African countries and other developing countries do not have the fiscal means to provide such services to displaced workers. It is, in part, the reason that in the negotiations to establish the EPAs between the EU and ACP countries, the latter are given long transition periods.[6] It is also a reason developing countries ask for "aid for trade" from developed countries—to help them mitigate the adjustment costs of freer trade.

The rationale for "aid for trade" becomes even stronger when one considers a more realistic situation in which some factors of production are industry specific, and unemployment and the collapse of some industries can result from freer trade. Some resources are only productive in specific industries, so when they are displaced because their industries are shrinking, it is hard for them to find employment in other industries. This is the most likely situation in the short run. Of course, the "short run," even for labor, can be years, depending on the ability of and opportunities available for people to acquire new skills. Considering trade between African countries, on the one hand, and China and developed countries, on the other, the Heckscher-Ohlin model would suggest that manufacturing industries in African countries are vulnerable to free trade.

When factors of production are industry specific, who gains and who loses from trade, that is, the redistribution of income, depends on the industry in which resources are employed. This means an increase in the price of the labor-intensive product would increase real incomes for owners of both labor and capital in that industry. Likewise, a decrease in the price of the capital-intensive product would reduce real incomes for owners of both labor and capital in that industry.

The Economies of Scale Model

The economies of scale model and its many variations are what have come to be called "new trade models." The model is associated with Paul Krugman, who published several articles in the late 1970s and 1980s showing that similar countries traded with each other mostly to take advantage of economies of scale (Krugman, 1979; Krugman, 1980; Krugman, 1981; Krugman, 1989).[7]

Economies of scale refers to the reduction of a firm's long-run average cost of production as the firm expands and produces more (internal economies) or as more firms enter the industry (external economies). The Ricardian and Heckscher-Ohlin models assume constant returns to scale, that is, output increases by the same rate that inputs increase. Thus, if inputs are doubled, output will also double. Economies of scale models are characterized by increasing returns to scale that happens when, in production, output increases by a larger percentage than the increase in inputs. This causes the average cost of production to decrease as output increases. The long-run average total cost can also decrease as production increases due to a number of factors, including specialization within the company, having leverage on input prices (buying in bulk), taking advantage of better technology, the spread of fixed costs over large quantities of output, being able to obtain loans at lower interest rates, and experience that comes from many years of operation.

The basic theories of trade depicted by the Ricardian and Heckscher-Ohlin models explain inter-industry trade, in which a country exports some products and imports distinctly different products. For example, a country exports coffee and imports electronic equipment. The economies of scale model is important in explaining intra-industry trade in which a country exports and imports similar but differentiated products. For example, a country exports cars and, at the same time, imports cars. This model is useful in showing a very important benefit of trade—an increased variety of products.

The relative size of intra-industry trade for any product is given by this formula:

Intra-industry trade $= 1 - \dfrac{|\text{Exports} - \text{imports}|}{(\text{Exports} + \text{imports})}$. Intra-industry trade is expected to be high when products can be differentiated. Firms take advantage of economies of scale by specializing in a subset of products within a broader category. A horticulturist, for example, could specialize in producing roses and lilies, instead of producing many different types of flowers.

COMMENTS ON COMPARATIVE ADVANTAGE

While it can be shown that trade based on economies of scale can also bring gains to both trading partners due to improved productive efficiency, the model cannot predict which country will export which good. Firms that enter the industry first have an advantage of size and, therefore, lower average total cost. This is partly the challenge African countries have in gaining ground in the manufacturing sector, considering that developed countries and even China had a head start. Moreover, the integration of African countries into the world economy during the colonial era was characterized by a clear division of roles. African countries produced raw materials and imported processed and manufactured products (Rodney, 1989). The residual impact of the colonial economic system has been hard to reverse.

However, a key takeaway from the economies of scale model is that comparative advantage is not static; it is dynamic, changing over time. When an infant industry is given space to grow and mature, it can eventually take advantage of economies of scale and become competitive in the world market. One would be hard-pressed to find any developed country that had not, at one point or another, protected some of its once infant manufacturing industries to help them mature (Chang, 2002). At its core, the infant-industry argument for protection is not against trade. It is a means through which potential industries, mostly in developing countries, can grow and eventually be able to compete without protection. However, a word of caution is in order. It can be difficult, for economic and political reasons, to identify viable infant industries. Again, for the same reasons, trade barriers implemented to protect infant industries are usually difficult to remove, whether the industry remains an "infant" or it matures.

The product life cycle theory developed by Vernon (1966) shows explicitly the dynamic nature of comparative advantage, even in the context of the Heckscher-Ohlin model. A product can be: (i) a new product; (ii) a maturing product; or (iii) a product resulting from standardized production. In the first stage of the product life cycle, when a product is invented, development and production require high skilled labor, such as engineers and other scientists. While not exclusively, this initial stage is likely to happen in advanced economies. In the second stage, there is mass production, and the country in which the product was invented might still enjoy comparative advantage. Over time, there is factor-intensity reversal. The technology to produce the product becomes common knowledge and shifts from being high-skilled labor intensive to less-skilled labor intensive. Therefore, it becomes normal for production locations eventually to move from developed countries to developing countries. This can be seen with laptop computers, which were initially designed and produced in Japan, the UK, and the U.S. but are now mostly produced in China.

Under the Heckscher-Ohlin model, comparative advantage can still shift from one country to another, even without a reversal in factor-intensity. As the proportion of skilled labor and wages increases in countries that were initially abundant with unskilled labor, they lose their comparative advantage in producing labor-intensive products. That is, in part, the continual shift in comparative advantage in the textile and apparel industry. For example, in the early 1900s, Japan had a noticeable comparative advantage in the production of textiles (fabric) and apparel (clothing). However, as unskilled labor became relatively scarce and wages went up, it gradually lost the comparative advantage to other Asian countries (Park and Anderson, 1991; International Labor Organization, 1996). China is currently the world's largest exporter of textiles and apparel. In 2021, China's exports of textiles and apparel were 41 percent and 33 percent of the world total values, respectively (World Trade Organization, 2022). China will eventually lose its dominance in this sector as wages rise.

Production can move from one country to another for the reasons just described, but the actual producers may remain the same. Producers can relocate to, or open subsidiaries in, countries to which comparative advantage is moving. This is, for example, the case for the textile and clothing industry in Lesotho and other African countries. Since the 1980s, Lesotho has seen an influx of foreign producers of garments who want to take advantage of low wages and preferential trade arrangements (Tati, 2014; Calabrese and Balchin, 2022).

THE LINKS BETWEEN OPENNESS TO TRADE AND ECONOMIC GROWTH

While it is possible to find anomalies, a large body of empirical evidence overwhelmingly shows a positive relationship between open trade policies and economic growth (Sachs and Warner, 1995; Hallaert, 2006; Hendrik and Lewer, 2007; Tahir, 2014). Many studies simply assume causality to be in one direction, from openness to economic growth, but some studies suggest the causality between trade openness and economic growth runs in both directions. A study by Idris et al. (2016: 286) suggests "that growth in developing countries is caused by the openness and that a boost in economic performance is one of the causes of increased openness."

Because the quality of data and the measure of openness can always be questioned, empirical studies on the links between openness to trade and growth will never reach a point of irrelevance (Schor, 2016). Broadly speaking, the links between openness to trade and economic growth are similar among countries, but variations in domestic policies and institutional settings, differences in the level of factor mobility, and supply-side constraints can limit or enhance those linkages.

The links include: (a) increased incomes in expanding industries; (b) reduced prices for imports; (c) increased efficiency and innovation due to increased competition; (d) access to better technology; and (e) economies of scale. A benefit of trade is that it expands markets for products. It allows some industries to expand, thus creating more jobs and generating more incomes. This is precisely what happened when, for example, the U.S. African Growth and Opportunity Act (AGOA) made the U.S. market more open to clothing from African countries. It is estimated that in the first ten years of its existence, AGOA created 300,000 jobs, directly, and another 1.3 million jobs, indirectly (Schneidman and Lewis, 2012). The benefits of trade also come from having access to imports at lower prices than would otherwise be the case. The benefits of increased access to imports are evident in the imports of inputs used to augment domestic production. Openness to trade increases competition and, thus, fosters a better and more efficient allocation of resources. It also fosters knowledge spillovers and encourages innovation as firms strive to stay ahead of the curve. Openness also allows firms to take advantage of economies of scale as they sell to larger markets.

One can find many examples of how African countries have implemented policies that reduced the potential growth from trade. In the 1970s and 1980s, many countries in Sub-Saharan Africa implemented interest rate policies that inadvertently discouraged resource mobility by limiting private investment and the growth of industries that had the potential to expand through trade. Many countries set interest rate ceilings that resulted in negative real interest rates, leading to a shortage of loanable funds (Mshomba, 2000).[8] Supposedly, interest rates were set low to encourage borrowing for investment in an effort to speed up the industrialization process. However, the policy was not sustainable, since one cannot lend what one does not have.

To make things worse, until the early 1990s, many Sub-Saharan African countries had fixed exchange rate systems that overvalued the domestic currency. An argument for the overvaluation of the domestic currency was that it would subsidize imports of important inputs such as spare parts, fertilizers, and physical equipment. But, of course, the system was not sustainable. The end result was a shortage of foreign exchange. The central banks did not have enough foreign currency to fill the gap between the quantity of foreign currency demanded and the quantity supplied. The results were highly sophisticated parallel markets for foreign currency. The parallel market in foreign currency, inevitably, metastasized into full-blown black markets for goods and services because of shortages and price ceilings.

Perhaps even more damaging was that the overvaluation of domestic currency was a type of implicit tax on producers of export goods who were paid in local currencies. These were mostly small farmers, the backbone of African economies, who produced export crops such as cashew nuts, cocoa, coffee, cotton, tea, and tobacco. These crops could only be sold to marketing boards, which were government monopsonies.

Here is an illustration of how farmers were implicitly taxed by the system. Suppose the official exchange rate was 3 Ghanaian cedis per

U.S. dollar, the parallel market rate was 40 cedis per dollar, and the world price of cocoa was $2.20 per kilogram. This approximates reality in Ghana in the early 1980s.[9] The parallel market exchange rate premium, the percentage by which the parallel market exchange rate exceeded the official exchange rate, was 1,233 percent.[10] Suppose the Ghana Cocoa Board passed half of the world price to farmers, that is, 3.30 cedis (2.20 x 0.5 x 3) per kilogram. Dollars were converted using the official exchange rate and farmers were always paid in local currency. Since some of the imports were financed by foreign currency purchased in the parallel market, consumer prices generally reflected the parallel market exchange rate. Thus, in real terms, cocoa farmers were paid a much smaller fraction than what the official exchange rate suggested. This not only caused reductions in cocoa production, but also encouraged the smuggling of cocoa from Ghana into Cote d'Ivoire (May, 1985). This phenomenon was not unique to Ghana. For reasons similar to those explained here about Ghana, coffee was smuggled from Tanzania into Kenya (Mshomba, 1993).[11]

The structural adjustment programs (SAPs) implemented by Sub-Saharan African countries in the late 1980s and early 1990s created a better environment for trade to be an engine for growth. SAPs included liberalizing trade and the foreign exchange market, removing impediments to private investment, agricultural reforms that allowed the private sector to buy and export crops, removing price controls, and reforming the public sector (World Bank, 1994).

It is important to note that many studies have been critical of SAPs. For example, Mkandawire and Soludo (2003) discuss "failures of SAPs" as something obvious. It is true that policies implemented under SAPs imposed challenging austerity measures. Governments were required to reduce spending as a condition to qualify for loans. But SAPs were more far-reaching than that. They included privatization of public enterprises and liberalization of the agricultural, trade and investment, and financial sectors. According to World Bank data, on average, real GDP per capita in Sub-Saharan Africa declined annually by 1.54 and 0.62 in the 1980s and 1990s, respectively. In fact, a number of studies have described the 1980s as a lost decade for Africa and other developing countries (Easterly, 2001; Singer, 1989; United Nations Department of Economic and Social Affairs, 2017). Of all the possible suspects behind the economic decline of the 1980s, none has received more attention than the SAPs.

A critical analysis of SAPs is beyond the scope of this book. There are hundreds of studies and commentaries on SAPs, most of them blaming SAPs and their architects. It is easy to identify flaws in how the SAPs were implemented, such as the way that funds were reduced for education and health services. It is also easy to identify market imperfections and make a case for the direct and indirect role of government in the economy. However, blatant disregard for the power of market forces and a diminished role for the private sector, as was the case during the pre-SAPs era, is not sustainable. Although the SAPs came with many deficiencies and may have even increased macroeconomic instability in the beginning (for example, through increased debt due to reduced government revenues), they eventually created a measure of macroeconomic discipline and stability in many African countries. Countries that completely ignore the fundamental elements of the SAPs run the risk of placing great strain on their economies. While this is an extreme example, Zimbabwe reversed its structural adjustment program on foreign exchange and ended up with an astounding level of hyperinflation—230 million %—in 2008 (BBC, 2015).

While clearly the role of the private sector in many African countries has expanded significantly compared to before the 1990s, policies that hurt producers and limit the benefits of trade are still common. Most obvious are export taxes and export bans (Schulz, 2020). The rationale for these policies is that they increase government revenue and lower domestic prices of those products for domestic consumers and encourage local processing of raw materials; however, these policies can be shortsighted.

Tanzania has periodically banned exports of maize (corn) and other grains, even to its partners in the East African Community (EAC) (The Citizen, 2017). Export bans on grains redistribute income from peasants in the rural areas to urban residents. An empirical study on the impact of Tanzania's bans on exports of maize on household welfare concludes that:

> export bans can hurt the rural poor and in fact increase the number of people living in poverty in the rural areas, particularly in maize-exporting regions. While some urban poor households benefit, the increased number of poor in the rural areas is far greater than the number of those who benefit in the urban areas, resulting in an increase in the poverty rate for the country as a whole. (Diao et al., 2013)

Many countries have these export bans on grain, on and off. Ngo-Eyok (2013) explains how some countries in the Economic Community of West African States (ECOWAS) ban exports of grain even to other ECOWAS countries, blatantly disregarding their own agreement to allow the free movement of goods and persons within the region. Zambia has periodically banned exports of maize (Mail & Guardian, 2002; Lusaka News, 2016; Moss, 2020). Ghana and Uganda banned grain and food exports, denying farmers better prices for their crops, their only source of income, and pushing them into abject poverty (Mugabi, 2022). In 2023, Morocco banned exports of vegetables to West Africa, supposedly to stabilize domestic prices (Rahhou, 2023).

These bans invariably hurt small farmers, who end up having to accept lower prices, either because their products, such as vegetables, are not storable, or because their economic situation does not give them the luxury of storing their harvests to wait for better prices in the future. Overall, export taxes and export bans on grain have undesired income distribution effects, implicitly taxing subsistence farmers and subsidizing consumers, mostly in urban areas. The long-run effect of export bans on grain is a fall in production, to the extent that farmers switch to producing other products. Thus, eventually, consumers also lose.

Some countries impose export taxes or ban exports of raw materials altogether to encourage domestic processing and, therefore, create forward linkages. These measures are, in effect, subsidies for domestic processors of those materials. One can see the validity of this argument, given the discussion above that comparative advantage is dynamic. That is, African countries can gain comparative advantage in the processing of raw materials if their "infant industries" are given space to grow and mature. Moreover, export restrictions on raw materials would, potentially, lead to more exports of value-added products, more industrialization, and increased diversity of export goods. In other words, this is a way for African countries to get themselves out of a production structure that is not favorable for high economic growth rates.

In general, the argument for subsidies for domestic processors is stronger when developed countries have tariff escalation structures for their imports. A tariff escalation structure is one in which trade barriers are higher on processed and finished products than on raw materials. For those countries that produce raw materials, subsidizing the processing of those materials can be a way to counteract tariff escalation (Kim, 2010; Piermartini, 2004). Tariff escalation in developed countries has been a concern, though it is much less so now. As discussed in Chapter 4, Sub-Saharan African countries have duty-free market access for their products exported to China, the EU, and the U.S., due to preferential trade arrangements aimed at supporting African countries.

The caveat about export restrictions on raw materials is that they can hurt domestic producers of those materials by reducing their prices and could therefore end up reducing production. This is one of the concerns that miners in Uganda raised when a ban on exporting raw minerals was put into effect in 2015 (Kyatusiimire, 2015; John Odyek, 2019; The Independent, 2022). The Vice Chairperson of Uganda Chamber of Mines and Petroleum (UCMP) was quoted saying:

> "We support and encourage our members to embrace minerals value addition as a strategic policy. However, the omnibus ban on all minerals has created a credibility crisis for Uganda. We cannot be saying that we're attracting investment in the mining sector and at the same time we impose a ban on mineral exports." . . . "Currently many companies have obligations that they have failed to meet and some have closed shop while others have cut back on both operations and staff. Lifting the mineral exports ban will therefore go a long way in reinvigorating the young mining sector." (Kyatusiimire, 2015)

To be clear, African countries must make efforts to add value to their raw materials and diversify their exports. However, how they go about doing that matters. The end goal does not always justify the means. More importantly, the means may not produce the desired outcome. Export bans on raw materials could lead to diminished gains of trade and low investments. In 2015, Uganda instituted such an abrupt ban on exports of raw materials that operating miners who had contracts to supply raw minerals to foreign markets did not have time to fulfill their contractual obligations (The East African, 2015). This could discourage future investment in the mining sector. The limited capacity to process raw materials may also have been overlooked in Uganda.

Even when the government tries to protect farmers with price floors, when policies blatantly disregard market forces and realities, the economy will pay a hefty price by forcing the issue. In 2018, Tanzania banned exports of raw cashew nuts. To ensure that the producer price paid to the farmers did not fall, the government instituted a price floor that was almost 100 percent higher than the market price. The price floor was literally above the "choke price," that is, the minimum price that would result in the quantity demanded for a product to be zero. No traders or processors of cashew nuts were willing and able to pay the price that was set by the government. In response, the government deployed the military to buy cashew nuts from farmers, but the government did not have the capacity to process them. So it was left with thousands of tons of cashew nuts in storage and diminished export revenues (BBC, 2018; Reuters, 2018; The Citizen, 2019).[12]

Finally, two additional observations must be made regarding restrictions on exports of raw materials—first, about the harmonization of policies between neighboring countries, and second, about externalities. The logging industry provides a good illustration for both points. If neighboring countries that produce timber do not harmonize their policies, there is the potential for smuggling. Yet such harmonization is not easy to achieve. It has proven to be difficult even in a customs union, which is supposed to have uniform trade policies. Countries that are members of the Economic and Monetary Community of Central Africa (CEMAC) have had several target dates and postponements of their decision to ban exports of raw timber. This has been due, in part, to the differences in their reliance on timber revenues and export tax revenues (Ngounou, 2022). They also realize that they need to build local capacity for processing before they start limiting exports (Business in Cameroon, 2021). Notwithstanding the regional negotiations, each country seems to decide what to do on its own, based on specific economic and political interests (Voice of America, 2023).

Second, the possibility of reducing negative externalities brings another dimension to this discussion. Export bans on raw timber, with or without an explicit focus on the environment, can reduce negative externalities associated with deforestation. In some cases, for environmental reasons, countries explicitly limit or ban altogether the harvesting of raw materials. With that in mind, when developing local processing capacity for timber and other finite raw materials, businesses must take a long-term view regarding future supplies. They need to be careful not to build large capacities based on current supplies of raw materials, when there is a real possibility that the supply of those raw materials will decrease in the future.

WAYS TO PROMOTE ECONOMIC GROWTH, DEVELOPMENT, AND POVERTY REDUCTION

No matter how much credit is given to trade as an engine for growth, it is not a "magic bullet." In fact, in the extreme case, it could be used to exploit the most vulnerable. The power of trade to promote economic growth, development, and poverty reduction depends on external factors and domestic policies.

Until the early 1990s, it was possible to argue that African countries faced major external challenges: trade protection and subsidies in developed countries. When the General Agreement on Tariffs and Trade (GATT) was established in 1947, the U.S. and European countries kept the textile and apparel industry and the agricultural sector out of its jurisdiction. Domestic policy objectives took precedence over trade policy. The Uruguay Round of GATT and the establishment of the WTO in 1995 led to the Agreement on Textiles and Clothing and the Agreement on Agriculture. These have brought reductions in domestic protection of textiles and apparel in developed countries, as well as reductions in their agricultural subsidies.

The nonreciprocal preferential trade arrangements offered by the U.S., the EU, and other developed countries to African countries have actually eliminated barriers on textiles and apparel originating from most African countries, allowing the textile and apparel industry to grow in many African countries. A large percentage of workers in this industry are women. This is significant for economic development because, for a variety of reasons, women have fewer job opportunities.

External challenges notwithstanding, domestic factors are the most important in determining how trade can generate growth and reduce poverty in a given country. These include (a) property rights protection, (b) labor laws, (c) access to capital, (d) export diversification, and (e) good governance.

Property Rights Protection

Trade can open up opportunities for growth in some industries, but economic freedom is important if entrepreneurs are to be willing to take risks with those opportunities. Secure property rights (of land, intellectual property, and trademarks) are paramount in the broader picture of freedom of enterprise (Press and Murray, 2017). On average, African countries rank low in the International Property Rights Index (IPRI) (Property Rights Alliance, 2023). The problem is more acute with respect to land ownership, where in many countries women do not have the same rights as men. This means women are at a disadvantage in securing loans and owning businesses, thus limiting their potential to benefit from trade. In some cultures, a woman cannot even inherit her husband's properties (Kimani, 2012). In many cases, when the husband dies, the wife is subjected to intimidation by the husband's relatives and even forced to surrender property to those relatives. In most African countries, agriculture is still the main source of export commodities. As such, land rights protection and equal land rights for women and men will not only allow producers to respond better to trade opportunities, but will also close the income gender gap.

Labor Laws

Trade can create jobs, but labor laws are among the key determinants of the number and quality of jobs created. Governments must have laws and policies that protect employers and employees.

Even if developed countries continue to open their markets through preferential trade arrangements, employment in African countries may not increase if government policies create unnecessary obstacles. Businesses function better in places where policies are clear, stable, and predictable enough to allow them to take calculated risks. Thus, it is important to allow employers the flexibility to operate efficiently without unnecessary bottlenecks created by government bureaucracy and corruption. According to the World Bank's "Ease of Doing Business" index, in 2020, doing business was "very easy" or "easy" in only eight African countries.[13] In most African countries, the executive branch has excessive power that overshadows the legislative and judicial branches (Cranenburgh, 2009). As a result, oftentimes policies and decisions are made and changed, randomly, depending on the leader of the country. That was the predicament business owners faced during the reign of President John Magufuli in Tanzania (2015–21). It mattered little whether the official process for getting an export permit was streamlined or not. The process could be interfered with, arbitrarily, by a cabinet member, regional commissioner, district commissioner, or the Tanzania Revenue Authority, without recompense. Producers and other investors often dealt with frustration, fear, and confusion, as they were not even sure how much authority the local governments (their initial contact) actually had. When President Samia Hassan came to power after Magufuli's death, she made executive pronouncements that brought a sigh of relief to businesses. It was as if there was more oxygen in the air. Tanzania became friendly to entrepreneurs again. Moody's Investor Service gave Tanzania a B2 positive rating in 2023, up from B1 negative in 2019, commenting that

> [t]he current presidential administration under President Hassan has taken steps at dismantling regulatory impediments to investment, removing restrictions on media and opposition parties, and mending international relationships. (The Citizen, 2023)

When a country has a very high unemployment rate, as is the case in African countries, it is very easy for unscrupulous employers to take advantage of workers who are desperate to get and keep their jobs. African countries have established industrial parks or export processing zones and provide various incentives to attract investors, but they have not always been attentive to labor rights and conditions. A careful study by the Worker Rights Consortium (WRC) found that employees in Ethiopia in the textile and apparel industry worked in grim conditions and were paid "the lowest wages the WRC has documented in any garment exporting country in recent years: wages as low as US$0.12 per hour, less than US$25 per month" (Worker Rights Consortium, 2018:2). Ethiopia does not have a minimum wage policy for workers in the private sector. Ethiopia has promoted, with pride, its low wages as a way to attract investors. Gelan (2018) makes reference to remarks by Hailemariam Desalegn, a former prime minister of Ethiopia, that Ethiopia had outsmarted the rest of Africa by keeping its wages low. This apparent "race to the bottom" strategy is harmful to workers who are vulnerable because of limited job opportunities.

Chinese companies have created many jobs in African countries through their investment in natural resources that are key export commodities. However, labor abuses seem to be common. While the following example might be an extreme case, it highlights the reality that increasing jobs in itself is not sufficient to bring about human development. In 2005, an explosion at a Chinese-owned copper mining plant in Chambishi killed forty-six Zambian workers. Subsequently, there were protests in Chambishi over work conditions. Workers demanded improved safety measures and better working conditions. Instead of addressing their concerns, the Chinese managers, allegedly, shot the protesters (Human Rights Watch, 2011; Hsiang, 2023). Poor working conditions in Chinese copper mines, protests, and the crushing of protests became a sad feature of the copper industry in Zambia, with the government not doing enough to protect workers' rights (Okeowo, 2013).

The African Growth and Opportunity Act (AGOA) has contributed to the rapid growth of the textile industry in Lesotho and has had an overall strong positive impact on Lesotho's economy, both in terms of employment and GDP growth (Central Bank of Lesotho, 2011; Setipa, 2016). However, the lack of effective labor laws to protect workers and the lack of enforcement of existing laws has allowed for mistreatment of employees in the textile industry (Lesotho Times, 2009; Worker Rights Consortium, 2019). Oftentimes governments are overly zealous in inviting foreign investment, but turn a blind eye to the conditions of workers. These shortcomings limit what trade can do to improve people's livelihood.

Access to Capital

Trade causes a reallocation of resources to align with shifting domestic and foreign demand for goods and services. African countries often fail to take full advantage of trade because of the scarcity of capital. While there is great variation between countries, in general, small and medium-sized enterprises in Africa "are more likely to rate access to financing as the most important constraint on their operation and growth" (Beck and Cull, 2014:5). Financial capital is the path through which production in African countries can respond to open markets brought about by preferential trade arrangements. However, as a report by UNCTAD (2022: Chapter 3) shows, small and medium-sized enterprises have difficulties acquiring loans from commercial banks, which are the main source of capital. This has also been a challenge when it comes to export diversification. Runde et al. (2021) and UNCTAD (2022: Chapter 3) identify several factors that contribute to this constraint, including high capital requirements, high interest rates and transaction costs, the lack of a long credit history, the lack of adequate collateral, and overall leverage ratio requirements.

There is no quick fix to constraints on capital access. At the same time, without finding solutions, the benefits of trade will be limited and export diversification may not be achieved in the near future. A few ways to increase access to financial capital by small and medium-sized enterprises are the establishment of development banks as an explicit component of industrial and trade policy, government guaranteed loan programs, and simplified commercial lending processes. It is also possible for financial technology, such as crowdfunding and marketplace lending, to be important sources of capital. Crowdfunding is a way of raising funds from many individuals using an online platform. The funds can be a donation (donation crowdfunding) or an investment in a business (equity-based crowdfunding). "Marketplace lending is broadly defined to include any practice of pairing borrowers and lenders through the use of an online platform without a traditional bank intermediary" (Federal Deposit Insurance Corporation, 2015: 13). However, these frameworks are not yet well understood or adequately regulated, so they can be a big risk to both lenders and borrowers (International Monetary Fund and World Bank, 2018).

Export Diversification

Export diversification, and economic diversity in general, are important both for resilience of the economy and for adequate distribution of the benefits of trade. It could be argued that the structure of African exports reveals the dictates of comparative advantage. Nonetheless, dependence on just a few commodities leaves African countries highly vulnerable to a fall in prices of those commodities. Fluctuations in the price of oil are a good example. According to the International Monetary Fund's data on commodity prices, from 2011 to 2013, the price of oil was, on average, $110 a barrel. However, it subsequently fell to an average of $48 a barrel in 2015–16. Countries that are importers of oil saw an improvement in their terms of trade when the price of oil fell. However, countries that are highly dependent on oil exports saw a significant drop in their export revenues, as shown in Table 1.2.

Good Governance

It is possible to identify many other domestic factors that play a critical role in linking trade to economic growth and human development. Governance can be one way to pull all of them together, including even the four factors discussed above. A key element to

TABLE 1.2. Average annual export revenue

Country	Petroleum Exports as a Percent of Merchandise Exports—2015	Average Annual Export Revenue		
		2011–2013 ($ millions)	2015–2016 ($ millions)	Decrease (percentage)
Angola	95	68,883	30,244	56
Chad	90	4,467	2,100	53
Congo, Rep.	75	10,385	4,020	61
Equatorial Guinea	76	14,567	5,650	61
Gabon	72	9,766	5,079	48
Nigeria	80	111,033	42,100	62
Sudan	56	6,350	3,131	51

Sources: UNCTAD (2017) and IMF publications on primary commodity prices.

diversifying an economy is good governance (Usman and Landry, 2021). Governments need to create systems that are transparent, environments that are friendly to business, and capacity-building programs that encourage, for example, domestic forward and backward linkages in manufacturing.

Government revenues generated through trade and, clearly, proceeds from trade in natural resources can be used to improve people's lives, as they have in Botswana, and also to diversify the economy. However, many of the countries that are rich in natural resources have poor governance. In countries such as Angola, Chad, the Democratic Republic of the Congo, Equatorial Guinea, and Nigeria, revenues from natural resources have been the means by which to hold on to power rather than a means to finance economic diversification and increase social services to improve people's lives. Some African leaders have been able to amass great personal wealth as a result of resource deals, so they are not necessarily eager to change economic structures (Obiukwu, 2014; Kragelund and Carmody, 2015).

In the extreme, the impact of trade can be the exact opposite of human development. For example, the diamond trade (blood diamonds) fueled atrocities and human suffering in Angola, Central African Republic, Côte d'Ivoire, the Democratic Republic of the Congo, Liberia, the Republic of Congo, Sierra Leone, and Zimbabwe in the 1990s (Le Billon, 2008; Howard, 2015; Hoekstra, 2019). This example does not suggest that trade is the enemy. The enemies are the people who use natural resources and trade to fuel atrocities.

Economic models provide a strong argument for trade. However, economies are complex, and assumptions made by trade models do not always hold in the real world. For example, resources are not as mobile between industries as theoretical models assume. However, the mobility of resources is an important determinant of how the benefits of trade are distributed. Therefore, nations must have deliberate policies that aim at improving the conditions that enhance the gains from trade. They need appropriate labor and investment laws and regulations that ensure workers are paid fairly and that the proceeds from trade are channeled to enhance overall human development. Without them, it is possible for trade to generate profits that mostly go to foreign owners of companies who then transfer the proceeds to their home countries.

Human development requires the health of the economy as a whole. The economy, even of a small country, has many pieces, all of them linked to each other, directly or indirectly. Sustained human development is achieved through economic growth and good policies that keep human development as the ultimate goal. Because international trade can increase economic growth, it can be an engine and a catalyst for human development. That is why preferential trade arrangements that give African countries increased opportunities for trade can be so important for human development. Ironically, but understandably, as discussed in the following chapter, these arrangements started during the colonial era.

2 THE EUROPEAN ECONOMIC COMMUNITY AND FORMER COLONIES

TRADE RELATIONS BETWEEN EUROPEAN AND African countries are understandably tied to their colonial histories. Most African countries were under European colonial rule for eight decades before they achieved their independence in the 1960s. As such, the evolution of trade relations between Europe and Africa was born out of and informed by that colonial history. Those relations must also be understood in the context of the economic integration of European countries that has allowed them to negotiate as a bloc over the years, since 1957. Like other relationships between nations, trade relations between European and African countries continue to evolve. This chapter focuses on the evolution of these relationships from the 1960s to the early 2000s.

THE TREATY OF ROME: ESTABLISHING THE EUROPEAN ECONOMIC COMMUNITY

As of 1955, all African countries were still colonies of European countries, except Egypt, Ethiopia, Liberia, Libya, Namibia, and South Africa.[1] However, by then the demand for independence had intensified to the point where the colonizers were losing the upper hand. Between 1956 and 1963, thirty-four African countries gained their independence. At the same time that these momentous events were taking place, six European countries were diligently working toward advancing economic integration among themselves.

In 1957, Belgium, France, the Federal Republic of Germany (formerly West Germany), Italy, Luxembourg, and the Netherlands signed an agreement, commonly known as the *Treaty of Rome*, to establish the European Economic Community (EEC). The aim of the agreement was to integrate these economies to the level of a common market, in which member countries remove trade barriers between themselves, maintain common external barriers for goods imported from nonmembers, and allow free movement of labor, services, and capital within the bloc.

Given the distinctive relationship that Italy, the Netherlands, Belgium, and France had with their colonies, it was imperative that the Treaty of Rome include provisions regarding how the EEC would associate with their colonies. This was a sensitive issue, especially for West Germany, which at that point in its history did not want to be perceived as perpetuating colonialism. Of course, those colonies were not invited to join the EEC as equal members.

Thus, on the one hand, the colonies could not be given economic independence (certainly not without political independence), nor could they be invited to full membership into the EEC. They were economically too weak to have equal economic relations with the EEC member states. On the other hand, those overseas territories could not be shared as colonies of all EEC countries. Moreover, by the late 1950s, colonialism was nearing its end.

Nonetheless, an official relationship between the EEC and the colonies was imperative for France, which, apparently, had considerable leverage in the establishment of the EEC. France was vehemently opposed to any suggestion of excluding overseas territories altogether. France's intricate relationship with its colonies had to be accommodated somehow.[2] As Zartman (1971, 6) describes:

> For France, and to a lesser extent Belgium, the economies of their colonies
> were inseparably tied to the metropole by a system of preferential trade,
> budgetary and commercial subsidies, and/or expatriated personnel and

investment, and the economic needs of their colonies had grown beyond
the metropole's ability to handle them alone.

France wanted the special economic arrangements it had with its
colonies to be continued and shared by the EEC. Those arrangements included France providing aid to its colonies and offering them preferential access to its market. Aid from France to its colonies came in various
forms, including preferential tariff treatment, quotas on imports from
third parties, direct subsidies to cotton growers, and the *surprix* system
in which France bought raw materials from its colonies at guaranteed
prices (Lawrence, 1971). These prices were invariably higher than the
prevailing market prices—from 15 percent for cotton to 60 percent for
coffee, above market prices (van Benthem van den Bergh, 1963, 156).
French importers were required to import a given percentage of total
supplies from the French colonies. Thus, producers of certain products
(mostly agricultural products) in the colonies had a guaranteed market
in France. Oftentimes this led to an oversupply of commodities, and the
whole system became a heavy burden for France. It was in part for this
reason that France wanted a special relationship between the EEC countries and the colonies—to enlarge the market for the colonies' products.

It is important to note that France's commodity price support system
contributed to overspecialization in its colonies, a familiar feature of
colonization in Africa. Table 2.1 shows the percent of export revenue
generated by the major export commodities in some of the French colonies in 1957. Reinforcing the pattern of trade—the colonies as suppliers
of raw materials and France as a supplier of manufactured products to
colonies—was an accompanying requirement that the colonies buy manufactured goods from France, often at prices higher than world prices.
This was a feature of the French colonial trade system, known as the *surprix*. One of the outcomes, as Ravenhill (1985, 49) notes, was that "local
processing and manufacturing industries [were] being discouraged."

After successful lobbying by France, a compromise was reached in
which the colonies would become "associated" with the EEC. Part IV
of the Treaty of Rome, Articles 131–36, focused exclusively on the EEC's
association with overseas countries and territories. Table 2.2 shows

TABLE 2.1. Percent of total export revenue generated by major export commodities in 1957

Country/Countries	Commodity	Percent of Total Export Revenue
Mali, Mauritania, Niger, and Senegal	groundnut and groundnut oil	83
Chad	cotton	81
Ivory Coast (Cote d'Ivoire)	cocoa and coffee	79
Cameroon	cocoa	57
Madagascar	Coffee	40

Source: van Benthem van den Bergh (1963, 157).

the members of the EEC and the overseas countries and territories (associated states) to which the provisions of Part IV of the treaty applied. Article 131 of the Treaty of Rome states that:

> The Member States hereby agree to bring into association with the Community the non-European countries and territories which have special relations with Belgium, France, Italy and the Netherlands. . . . The purpose of this association shall be to promote the economic and social development of the countries and territories and to establish close economic relations between them and the Community as a whole.

Other key provisions with respect to external territories (associated states) stipulated that:

- EEC members shall provide financial aid to enhance development of the associated countries and territories;
- each associated country or territory shall apply the most-favored nation principle to all EEC members, in all areas of trade and investment opportunities;[3]
- the EEC members shall apply the same rules for products coming from associated countries and territories as they apply among themselves and, as such, those products will enter the EEC region duty-free; and

TABLE 2.2. Overseas countries and territories to which the provisions of Part IV of the Treaty of Rome applied

EEC Member	Associated Territories (Current Names in Parentheses)
Belgium	Congo (Democratic Republic of Congo) and Ruanda-Urundi (Rwanda and Burundi)
France	French West Africa: Senegal, French Sudan (Mali), French Guinea (Guinea), Ivory Coast (Côte d'Ivoire), Dahomey (Benin), Mauritania, Niger, and Upper Volta (Burkina Faso)
	French Equatorial Africa: Middle Congo (Republic of Congo), Ubangi-Shari (Central African Republic), Chad, and Gabon
	Saint Pierre and Miquelon, the Comoro Archipelago (The Comoros), Madagascar and dependencies (Madagascar), French Somaliland (Djibouti), New Caledonia and dependencies, French Settlements in Oceania (French Polynesia), Southern and Antarctic Territories
	The Autonomous Republic of Togoland (Togo)
	The trust territory of the Cameroons under French administration (most of what today is known as Cameroon)
Germany, Federal Republic of (former West Germany)	None
Italy	The trust territory of Somaliland under Italian administration (Somalia)
Luxembourg	None
The Netherlands	Netherlands New Guinea (Papua New Guinea)

Sources: Economic Community 1957; Luxembourg Centre for Contemporary and Digital History, 1957.

- associated countries and territories shall reduce and eventually eliminate duties on trade among themselves and also on goods originating from the EEC member states.

Supposedly, trade openness between the EEC and associated states was to be reciprocal, so trade with each other was to be conducted as if they were all members of a free trade area. Of course, in practice, given the huge economic disparity between the EEC members and their associates, such reciprocity was not realized. Keenly aware of that reality, the Treaty of Rome (Article 133) added a provision that allowed associated states to

> levy customs duties which correspond to the needs of their development and to the requirements of their industrialisation or which, being of a fiscal nature, have the object of contributing to their budgets.

All provisions were set to be implemented gradually. They were also temporary in nature and new negotiations were to follow. Tariffs and other forms of trade barriers were to be reduced and eliminated on a gradual basis. For example, a French colony that opted to reduce tariffs on products coming from other EEC members would do that progressively "to the level of those imposed on imports of products coming from the Member State with which each country or territory has special relations" (Article 133 of the Treaty of Rome). Nonetheless, what was really important was for the associated countries and territories to abide by the most-favored nation principle—no discrimination. Again, as an example, a French colony that levied zero duties on products from France could eliminate duties on products from all EEC countries or, instead, increase duties on goods coming from France to the level of duties levied on goods coming from the other EEC countries. The agreement with regard to associated states was for a period of five years. Germany was reluctant to agree on the provision of aid for a longer period than that. However, that provision and others were later extended and expanded, as discussed in the next section (on the Yaoundé Conventions).

The EEC agreed to establish a development fund—the European Development Fund (EDF)—to be used solely as a channel through which aid would be disbursed to associated states. The six members of the EEC committed to provide $581.25 million (equivalent to about $6 billion in 2022's value), mostly in the form of grants, to be disbursed in five years (Zartman, 1971). Because of the time required to prepare and approve of proposals, disbursement of aid did not start until 1960, with the final allocation given in 1965. The financial aid was used for social and economic development projects, as shown in Table 2.3.

Two facts deserve special attention. The first is that France and West Germany contributed the lion's share of the fund. The second is that only a tiny amount of the fund was allocated to industrialization.

West Germany did not have any associated state linked to it, yet it agreed to contribute as much as France. There are several reasons for this. The EEC members had agreed, in principle, to share the burden of establishing the fund, irrespective of whose colonies would be recipients. At the same time, West Germany had the largest economy. In addition, the number of votes allocated to each EEC member was roughly determined by each country's relative contribution to the EDF. Thus, the large contribution by West Germany gave it considerable leverage in the determination of how the funds would be distributed. The majority for the purpose of allocating funds was 67 out of 100 votes. If votes were allocated based purely on the percentages of contribution to the EDF, France and West Germany individually would have had veto power. The number of votes was deliberately allocated in a way that acknowledged the difference in contributions to the EDF, while at the same time preventing any single country from having veto power. West Germany also saw its contributions to the fund as a way to create opportunities for its companies to enter the French colonies. Still another reason why West Germany was a willing partner was that the EEC was not only established to form an economic bloc, but also to forge unity against threats from communist neighbors. West Germany was the only EEC member that shared borders with communist countries, those being East Germany and Czechoslovakia.[4]

Only one percent of the EDF was allocated directly to industrialization. This reflects the urgent need for social services at the time and also the emphasis on the production of cash crops to generate foreign

TABLE 2.3. Donors and recipients of the EEC European Development Fund

Donors	Contributions			Recipients			Distribution by Sector		% of total
	(millions of $)	% of the total	Votes		($ millions)	% of the total			
France	200.00	34.50	33	French Associates	511.25	87.80	Social services	Education	16
West Germany	200.00	34.50	33	Dutch Associates	35.00	6.02		Health	8
Belgium	70.00	12.04	11	Belgian Associates	30.00	5.16		Water	6
Netherlands	70.00	12.04	11	Italian Associates	5.00	1.02		Urban construction	3
Italy	40.00	6.90	11				Economic development	Transportation	40

(continued)

TABLE 2.3. (*continued*)

Donors	Contributions (millions of $)	% of the total	Votes	Recipients ($ millions)	% of the total	Distribution by Sector	% of total
Luxembourg	1.25	0.22	1			Agriculture production	17
						Telecommunications	2
						Industrial production	1
						Operating expenses	7
Total	581.25	100	100	581.25	100	Total	100

Source: Zartman (1971, 16–18).

revenue and supply industries in Europe with agricultural raw materials. Transportation projects were linked to agricultural production to facilitate the hauling of cash crops to the ports for export to Europe. African countries clearly had a comparative advantage in producing agricultural tropical crops. However, this pattern of trade between African and European countries was reinforced by complacency, the lack of an overall industrial base, policies in Europe that encouraged imports of raw products and discouraged imports of processed products, and the lack of intra-African trade.

The development of the agricultural sector in African countries was influenced in part by the Common Agricultural Policy (CAP) of the EEC. Articles 38–47 of the Treaty of Rome were devoted to commitments on agriculture. The CAP was intended to "increase agricultural productivity [of the Member States] by promoting technical progress" and ensuring "a fair standard of living for the agricultural community, in particular by increasing the individual earnings of persons engaged in agriculture" (Article 39). European farmers were to be subsidized using price floors. These were minimum prices that were typically set above equilibrium prices. At the time, the General Agreement on Tariffs and Trade (GATT) was only a decade old. More importantly, the agricultural sector was not under the jurisdiction of GATT. At the inception of GATT in 1947, developed countries kept the agricultural sector out of the multilateral negotiations. They decided that domestic policy objectives should take precedence over trade policy. The CAP created special and varied agricultural policies toward associated states, depending on the crops produced by those states, as discussed in the section below on "protocols on beef and veal, bananas, rum and sugar."

For various reasons, the prescribed linkages between the EEC and the associated countries and territories described in the Treaty of Rome faced pressure for change almost immediately. First, since the association arrangement was set for only five years, discussions on a new agreement had to start rather quickly. Second, there was almost immediate erosion in the margin of preference for products originating from French colonies, while at the same time the procedures for the distribution of the EDF seemed unwieldy. Third, the relationship between the EEC members and the associated countries had to be re-defined as colonies gained independence (Zartman, 1971).

The special relationship established between the EEC and the associated countries and territories was a work in progress. In many ways, it was an experiment from which to learn and respond with adjustments. The relationship was to evolve in phases, and as each phase expired, modifications were to be made to suit the changing circumstances. Article 136 of the Treaty of Rome committed that

> [b]efore the expiry of the Convention provided for in the preceding sub-paragraph, the Council, acting by means of a unanimous vote, shall, pro-ceeding from the results achieved and on the basis of the principles set out in this Treaty, determine the provisions to be made for a further period.

A decision on how and how much to support colonies required a lot of maneuvering by France. The agreed mechanism and amount of aid during the transition period were, thus, a compromise that was to be revisited periodically. The Treaty of Rome came into effect in 1958, and the provision on the EDF was to expire by the end of 1962. Thus, this timeline by itself meant the parties involved had to revisit, rather quickly, the terms of engagement, if not for anything else, then at least to renew the agreement. The agreement was transitory by design.

Another source of pressure for reexamination of the relationship between the EEC and the associated states was the side effect of the EEC's common external tariffs (CETs). Before the establishment of the EEC, France's imports were subjected to high tariff rates, except for those goods originating from its colonies, which entered duty-free. The CETs lowered France's tariff rates, thus shrinking the margin of preference its colonies enjoyed. According to Twitchett (1978), for France, CETs lowered 71.4 percent of its tariff lines, increased 14.1 percent of them, and did not change 14.5 percent of them. For West Germany, the percentages were, respectively, 9.2 percent, 79.5 percent, and 11.3 percent. Table 2.4 shows the reduction in tariff rates that France had to make for some of the major imports from its colonies.

While the reduction in the margin of preference for the French colonies can be seen as a loss by the colonies, the gain was having access to a larger market. A study by Lawrence (1971) suggests that

TABLE 2.4. Tariff rates in France before the establishment of the EEC and CET tariffs

Product	French Tariff (percent)	CET (percent)
Unroasted coffee	20	9.6
Shelled peanuts	10	0.0
Crude peanut oil	18	10.0
Refined peanut oil	18	15.0
Cocoa beans	25	5.4
Unprocessed wood	10	0.0
Processed wood	15	10.0
Fresh bananas	20	20.0
Palm nuts	20	0.0

Source: Lawrence (1971, 366).

there was no clear pattern of net gain or loss for the French associates. However, France was a clear winner, as the burden of maintaining favored markets for its colonies was now shared by all members of the EEC.

The French tariff rates and the common external tariffs shown in Table 2.4 reveal a cascading tariff structure with zero or lower tariff rates on unprocessed commodities, followed by tariff escalation. That is, the higher the degree of processing, the higher the tariff rate.

It is important to note that when the tariff rates were reduced to the CET levels, the rate of effective protection for processed commodities actually increased. In effect, it actually became harder for African countries to export processed products.

The rate of effective protection measures actual protection on the domestic value added. The formula for calculating the rate of effective protection is given by: $g = \dfrac{t - \Sigma a_i t_i}{1 - \Sigma a_i}$, where: g is the rate of effective protection of the final product; t is the nominal tariff rate on the final product; a_i is the ratio of the cost of input i to the price of the final product, at the free trade price; and t_i is the nominal tariff rate on input i.

Given the information in Table 2.4, this formula can be used to show that the rate of effective protection increased for refined peanut oil and processed wood, even though, in nominal terms, the tariff rates on those products actually went down. Consider the following illustration regarding peanuts and refined peanut oil.

According to Mundi's commodity indexes for peanuts and refined peanut oil for July 2017–January 2018, the price of peanuts is about 93 percent of the price of refined peanut oil.

The rate of effective protection of refined peanut oil under the French tariff, 124 percent, is calculated using the following numbers.

t is 18 percent—the nominal tariff rate on refined peanut oil;
a_i is 93 percent—the ratio of the cost of peanuts to the price of refined peanut oil; and
t_i is 10 percent—the nominal tariff rate on shelled peanuts.

$$g = \frac{.18 - (.93)(.1)}{1 - .93} = 124 \text{ percent.}$$

However, the rate of effective protection of refined peanut oil under the CET increased, as shown below, even though the nominal tariff rate went down from 18 to 15 percent.

t is 15 percent—the nominal tariff rate on refined peanut oil;
a_i is 93 percent—the ratio of the cost of peanuts to the price of refined peanut oil; and
t_i is 0 percent—the nominal tariff rate on shelled peanuts.

$$g = \frac{.15 - (.93)(0)}{1 - .93} = 214 \text{ percent.}$$

Thus, while the EEC countries made some effort to help associated states industrialize, some policy structures also undermined those efforts.

At the same time, the operation of the EDF was proving to be unwieldy. As it happened, the operation of the EDF added pressure to reexamine the process of delivering aid. The operation of the EDF was outlined in the "Implementation Convention," annexed to the Treaty of

Rome. The EDF was administered by a Commission that was supposedly an independent executive body of the EEC.

The Commission had a key role in project appraisal (Twitchett, 1978). It was responsible for considering requests for funds from the associated countries and territories and making allocation recommendations. The recommendations were guided by the need to have a mix of projects, such as schools, hospitals, roads, projects enhancing agricultural production, and technical research. In addition, the Commission had to be cognizant of the geographical balance in how the funds were allocated. It is not clear how much of that was accomplished, given that there was wide disparity in aid per capita received by associated countries and territories: Dutch colonies—$35, French colonies—$14, Italian colonies—$5, and Belgian colonies—$1.50 (Zartman, 1971, 17).

The Commission's proposals were submitted to the EEC Council for examination and final approval. The Commission also had the responsibility to ensure that approved funds were spent for the purpose for which they were intended. Any funds that were approved but not disbursed in a given fiscal year were forwarded to the following years.

The consolidation of funds through the EDF may have reduced administration costs borne by recipient countries. However, the procedures for the applications, allocation of funds, preparation of reports, and assessment of projects were cumbersome for the associated states, whose administrative capacities were very weak to begin with. For the first five years, $581.25 million was to be collected from the EEC countries and disbursed by the end of 1962. However, due to delays in acquiring the funds and the burdensome procedures for project approval, the final allocation and complete spending of the funds were delayed to 1965 and 1968, respectively (Zartman, 1971). For successful projects, it took an average of almost two years from the time of application to the actual receipt of funds (Twitchett, 1978, 43). Sometimes technical inadequacies in preparing project proposals required the assistance of the Commission that was also to review them. This was similar to a developing country asking World Bank officials to help it prepare proposals for applications for loans from the World Bank.

It should be noted that, even today, there is an intractable problem in providing aid to countries with weak administrative capacity. The donor countries and organizations feel compelled to impose an elaborate mechanism and conditions, including asking for frequent implementation reports, to ascertain that aid is allocated properly and used appropriately. Moreover, the donor or lending country or organization always has the upper hand.

In addition, the EDF was operating in a political environment in which paternalism was the rule of the game. Twitchett (1978, 30) underscores this point, as follows:

> It should be remembered that these procedures were designed to operate in the context of colonial administration. Thus, for the most part European civil servants would be the local officials acting as the Local Authorising Officers, in contact with European-based banks acting as the local paymasters, and in liaison with European consultancy enterprises acting as the Technical Control Officers.

But the challenge associated with the provision of funds had many dimensions, as discussed by Twitchett (1978). It took more than a year from the time the Treaty of Rome came into effect until the EEC Council could finalize financial regulations governing the operation of the EDF. Meanwhile, there was disagreement within the EEC regarding the communication protocol between the EEC Commission (responsible for project appraisal) and authorities in the associated countries and territories. France, having the most colonies and desiring to maintain close control, wanted all communication with its colonies to go through its Ministry of Overseas. However, the EEC Commission insisted on direct communication, and after two years of resistance, France acquiesced.

In the project implementation phase, the Commission had another daunting task—to monitor the issuance of tenders for projects financed by the EDF. Article 199 of the Treaty of Rome required that,

> [f]or investments financed by the Community, participation in tenders and supplies shall be open on equal terms to all natural and legal persons who are nationals of a Member State or of one of the countries and territories.

This stipulation for open competition and transparency in government procurement was specifically intended to ensure that there was an open competition for tenders and to avoid giving unfair advantage to firms from those EEC countries that had colonial control over the associated states. Notwithstanding this provision, over 75 percent of projects in the French colonies went to French companies, due to their familiarity with the circumstances in those countries (Twitchett, 1978).

While it is easy to identify a number of shortcomings in the administration of the EDF, this was an ambitious multilateral aid initiative that had no precedence from which to learn. In fact, many of the challenges observed in the operation of the EDF are common in (and even intrinsic to) all aid programs even at present, albeit to varying degrees. It is, therefore, not surprising that the basic procedures established for the EDF did not differ in any fundamental way from the subsequent agreements. Some of them, particularly those that tried to promote transparency and accountability, simply could not be different.

Even if the initial agreement of association between the EEC and the associated states had been set for a period longer than five years, the wave of independence in Africa dictated the need to reexamine the agreement. By the end of 1962, when the first phase of the agreement was to expire, all associated countries in Africa, except the Comoro Archipelago and Djibouti, had gained independence.

THE YAOUNDÉ CONVENTIONS

The provisions of the Treaty of Rome that advanced the relationship between the EEC Member States and associated countries and territories were succeeded in 1963 by those in the Yaoundé Convention I agreement. Negotiations that lead to Yaoundé Convention I had been launched officially in 1961.

The Treaty of Rome was forward-looking. It envisioned welcoming new members into the EEC. Article 238 opens with the following statement:

> The Community may conclude with a third country, a union of States or an international organization, agreements creating an association embodying reciprocal rights and obligations, joint actions and special procedures.

The former colonies were welcome and, in fact, encouraged to continue the special relationship with the EEC, as long as they adhered to the obligations set forth in the Treaty of Rome. But, of course, independence brought a measure of autonomy to African countries and an opportunity for them to unite and negotiate as a coalition.

While African countries had some concern that their relationship with the EEC countries was a form of neo-colonialism, they saw the benefit of preferential treatment and the financial aid they were receiving. These newly independent countries also saw this relationship with the EEC as a way to reduce their dependence on their respective metropoles. French colonies, especially Togo, welcomed the opportunity to avoid being overly dependent on France.

Negotiations for Yaoundé Convention I were more dynamic than those leading to the establishment of the EEC. There were negotiations among the six members of the EEC, among associated states that were now independent countries, and between the EEC members and associated states. Within the EEC, the main divisions were between France on the one hand and West Germany and the Netherlands on the other, regarding compensation for ending the *surprix*, the amount and duration of aid, the management of aid for the newly independent countries, and whether or not to extend benefits to Commonwealth African countries.

The disparity of associated states in terms of their major crops and economic size was obvious, but they were able to unite in their demands for: (1) negotiations with the EEC members on the basis of parity, (2) at least maintaining benefits contained in the Treaty of Rome, (3) compensation for the loss of *surprix* and the decrease in the margin of preference, (4) increased financial assistance, and (5) serving as co-managers of the EDF (Twitchett, 1978). However, since associated states participated in the negotiations primarily as recipients and seekers of financial aid and preferential treatment, they had little leverage apart from the moral argument that they had been subjected to exploitation by the Europeans. Their unity (which was precarious, to say the least) also gave them some leverage. Twelve of the former French colonies formed the Organisation Africaine et Malgache de Coopération Économique (OAMCE), also known as the Brazzaville Group, which negotiated as a group with the EEC members.[5]

However, when it was all said and done, Yaoundé Convention I represented, more or less, a compromise between the EEC members. The demands by associate members had no real weight, except when they matched the demands of a member of the EEC. Yaoundé Convention I extended the provisions in Part IV of the Treaty of Rome. Nonetheless, it contained some specific affirmations, some of which were welcomed by the associated states and some of which were not. Provisions in the agreement included an increase in financial aid, co-management of the EDF, compensation for the abolished *surprix*, a lower CET for the EEC, the creation of a free trade area between the EEC and associated states, and open association for other African countries with the EEC. Table 2.5 shows contributions to the EDF from the six EEC members.

Attempting to establish a free trade area, Yaoundé Convention I was aiming for reciprocity between the EEC countries and associated states with regard to the elimination of trade barriers. Thus, Article 3(2) of Yaoundé Convention I called for associated states to progressively remove customs duties on goods from the EEC. However, the obvious economic development disparity between the EEC and associated

TABLE 2.5. Contributions to EDF 1, 2, and 3 (millions of $)

Donor	EDF 1: 1959–64	EDF 2: 1964–70	EDF 3: 1970–75
France	200.00	246.50	298.50
West Germany	200.00	246.50	298.50
Belgium	70.00	69.00	80.00
Netherlands	70.00	66.00	80.00
Italy	40.00	100.00	140.60
Luxembourg	1.25	2.00	2.40
Total EDF	581.25	730.00	900.00
European Investment Bank	0.00	70.00	100.00
Overall Total	581.25	800.00	1,000.00

Source: Twitchett (1978, 118).

states made such a requirement unworkable. Bearing that in mind, Article 3(2) included the following provision:

> Provided always that each Associated State may retain or introduce customs duties and charges having an effect equivalent to such duties which correspond to its development needs or its industrialization requirements or which are intended to contribute to its budget.

In addition, even though quantitative limits generally restrict trade more than tariffs do, associated states were nonetheless allowed to retain quotas and even introduce new ones to meet their development needs, industrialization goals, and budget targets (Article 6). For all practical purposes, as far as the determination of trade policy was concerned, associated states were only minimally constrained by the EEC requirements.

What was most critical to the EEC was that the associated states not implement any policy that directly or indirectly discriminated between the EEC countries. This was also an important condition in the Treaty of Rome. The Treaty of Rome and Yaoundé Convention I aimed to diminish, to the extent possible, the special trade relationship that had been in place between colonies and their metropole.

The associated states never ran out of reasons to impose customs duties, so full reciprocity was never attained. This remained a contentious issue in GATT, as other developing countries felt discriminated against. Interestingly, Commonwealth African countries, Nigeria among them, were the most outspoken against this apparent violation of the *most favored nation* principle in GATT. However, GATT's dispute mechanism was not strong enough to enforce reciprocity. Moreover, the United Nations Conference on Trade and Development (UNCTAD) was advocating for these types of trade arrangements that gave nonreciprocal preferential treatment to developing countries. When GATT was replaced by the World Trade Organization (WTO) in 1995, enforcement of reciprocity received more attention and led to the process of establishing Economic Partnership Agreements (EPAs), as discussed in Chapter 3.

West Germany and the Netherlands were the two countries that pushed hard to allow other countries to have access to association. But this does not mean that the Commonwealth African countries were nec-essarily waiting at the door to be let in. Some, including Ghana, Nigeria, and Tanzania, were initially strongly opposed to the system of associa-tion. They saw it as a dangerous form of collective neo-colonialism that would lead to perpetual dependence, diminish Africa's efforts to indus-trialize, and limit intra-African trade. This view was just the opposite of how the UK perceived the situation. In fact, the UK found itself in an awk-ward position. It was negotiating for its entry into the EEC and also for its former African colonies to be accepted as associates. Yet the UK ended up being denied entry into the EEC, and key independent Commonwealth African countries were not even interested in being associates.

The rejection of associate status by Commonwealth African countries was short-lived. Their defiant tone softened rather quickly. Either they realized that their fears were exaggerated or they realized that they could actually take advantage of preferential treatment offered by the EEC. In 1966, the Lagos Agreement brought Nigeria, a former critic, in as an as-sociate of the EEC. However, this agreement was never ratified because of the outbreak of civil war in Nigeria—the Biafra War—that lasted for two and a half years, from July 1967 to January 1970. The negotiations be-tween the EEC members and the East African countries were protracted, and it was not until 1968 that they signed an agreement of association—the Arusha Agreement.[6] These Commonwealth African countries were, nonetheless, treated as second-class associates. They were not eligible for a share of the EDF, and in the EEC market their products received preferential treatment less favorable than that given to products from the Yaoundé associates. As described by Ravenhill (1985,77):

> As in the Lagos Agreement, East African imports would enjoy free access to the European market except for those products (unroasted coffee, cloves, and tinned pineapples) that threatened the production of the Yaoundé Associates where duty-free access was limited to specific quotas, at which point the Six [EEC members] had the option of reim-posing duties.

It always takes time for signed agreements to be ratified and im-plemented. Moreover, some agreements may require new institutions and a revamping of the old ones, and that can take time, too. Yaoundé Convention I expired in 1969 before the Arusha Agreement came into effect. However, it was renegotiated and Yaoundé Convention II was signed in July 1969. Due to delays in ratification, however, it did not come into force until January 1971.

The transition from the first to the second convention was seamless, as the provisions remained the same. The relationship between the EEC members and associated states was to be continued in the spirit of reciprocity, but still with ample policy space for the associated states to impose trade barriers on goods from the EEC countries.

The Yaoundé conventions also allowed associated states to maintain or establish customs unions or free-trade areas between themselves or with third parties (Articles 9 and 13 of Yaoundé Convention I and Yaoundé Convention II, respectively). It is interesting that both conventions required associated states to treat goods imported from the EEC countries no less favorably than goods imported from any other country (Articles 7 and 11 of Yaoundé Convention I and Yaoundé Convention II, respectively). Thus, if a group of associated states formed a free trade area and eliminated tariffs among themselves, they had to do the same for goods coming from EEC countries. In theory (that is, if this provision were to be adhered to by the associated states), those states could not have deeper economic integration with each other or with other countries than they had with EEC countries.

THE LOMÉ CONVENTIONS

The two Yaoundé agreements were followed by a total of four Lomé conventions. The first one, which replaced Yaoundé Convention II, was signed in February 1975 and came into effect in April 1976. Lomé Convention I was an agreement between an expanded EEC bloc and an enlarged number of developing countries. It came about as a result of the disillusionment with the EEC by the associated states and the enlargement of the EEC, especially the UK's entry into the EEC.

Yaoundé Convention II was to expire in 1975, so new negotiations had to be initiated. Ravenhill (1985) explains that disillusionment with the

Yaoundé conventions both by the EEC members and associated states made it easier to extend the benefits of association to more developing countries. The EEC members had not been able to help associated states compete on equal terms in the world market, and all along West Germany and the Netherlands were philosophically not comfortable with the idea of helping only a small group of developing countries. Even France was realizing the shortcomings of not having close economic ties with other African countries. The associated states had frustrations of their own. There had not been real compensation for the French *surprix* scheme, and the margin of preference was eroding further with the introduction of the Generalized System of Preferences (GSP) in the EEC in 1971. The GSP is a program under which developed countries provide nonreciprocal preferential reduction or removal of trade barriers for products from developing countries, as discussed in Chapter 4.

Meanwhile, the UK, which had applied to join the EEC twice before and been rejected both times, was accepted in 1973 on its third attempt. The first two times that the UK applied to join the EEC, the French president, Charles de Gaulle, used France's veto power to block the UK's entry. In 1970, when the UK applied for the third time, the president of France was Georges Pompidou, someone who was more open to an expanded EEC (Mourlon-Druol, 2015).

Denmark and Ireland also joined the EEC in 1973, thus increasing the EEC's membership by 50 percent, from six to nine countries. By then all British colonies in Africa, with the exception of Seychelles and Rhodesia, had gained independence. The Commonwealth preference scheme, of which the UK was an architect and a patron member, therefore had to be amalgamated with the EEC preferential system.

As a side note, and considering the decision by the UK to exit the European Union in 2016, it is worth mentioning that the decision by the UK to join the EEC was met by some domestic opposition. The heated internal debate on the issue brought about the UK's first referendum, held in 1975. The referendum question was:

> The Government [has] announced the results of the re-negotiation of the UK's terms of membership of the European Community. Do you think that

the UK should remain part of the European Community (the Common Market)? (Mourlon-Druol, 2015, 6)

The vote was in favor of continued membership in the EEC, with 67 percent voting yes.

Although rivalry remained among African countries, something that will likely never cease to exist, by the late 1960s and early 1970s, the Organization of African Unity (OAU) was inclined, more than ever before, to speak in unison on many issues. The "walls" between the Anglophone and Francophone African countries were falling or, at least, not as strong as they had been. In 1972, the leaders of Nigeria (an Anglophone country) and Togo (a Francophone country), General Gowon of Nigeria and General Eyadema, respectively (military men, no less), reintroduced the idea of forming a West African economic bloc. That idea was first raised in 1964 by President William Tubman of Liberia, but it did not gain traction at the time. West African countries ended up forming the Economic Community of West African States (ECOWAS) in 1975 with a total membership of 15 countries (8 Francophone, 5 Anglophone, 1 Arab, and 1 Lusophone.)[7]

With the entry of the UK into the EEC, Commonwealth countries became *associables*,[8] at least most of them.[9] Given the warm relations among African countries, the associated states and *associables* were able to negotiate with the EEC as a group. Of course, the Commonwealth countries were not only in Africa. The developing countries group actually consisted of what is commonly referred to as the African, Caribbean, and Pacific (ACP) countries. Altogether 46 ACP countries signed Lomé Convention I.

Lomé Convention I had several provisions, two of which stand out: nonreciprocal preferential treatment for exports from ACP countries to the EEC and a stabilization of the export earnings (STABEX) program.[10] Article 7 of Lomé Convention I states:

> In view of their present development needs, the ACP States shall not be required, for the duration of this Convention, to assume, in respect of imports of products originating in the Community, obligations corresponding to the

commitments entered into by the Community in respect of imports of the products originating in the ACP States, under this Chapter. (a) In their trade with the Community, the ACP States shall not discriminate among the Member States, and shall grant to the Community treatment no less favourable than the most-favoured-nation treatment. (b) The most-favoured-nation treatment referred to in subparagraph (a) shall not apply in respect of trade or economic relations between ACP States or between one or more ACP States and other developing countries.

There was now a clear departure from the idea of reciprocity that had been included in the Yaoundé conventions, even though it had never been realized or eagerly pursued. In fact, the call for reciprocity with African countries almost became a moot point in 1971 when the EEC created the GSP program. However, not all products (for which ACP countries received preferential treatment) were included in the EEC's GSP program.

An important distinction between the Yaoundé conventions and the Lomé conventions involves the requirement placed on the ACP countries, that they grant the EEC members the most-favored-nation status. In the Lomé conventions, this requirement did not apply to economic integration between ACP countries or between ACP countries and other developing countries. The ACP countries could, therefore, pursue regional economic integration without having to change their trade policy with the EEC countries.

The economies of ACP countries were (and many still are) dependent on just a few commodities for their export revenues. This made export revenues and incomes, in general, volatile, as commodity prices and output can fluctuate significantly. Thus, the Lomé conventions also used STABEX to stabilize export earnings of the major crops and iron ore of the ACP countries. Article 16 of Lomé Convention I included this provision:

With the aim of remedying the harmful effects of the instability of export earnings and of thereby enabling the ACP States to achieve the stability, profitability and sustained growth of their economies, the Community shall implement a system for guaranteeing the stabilisation of earnings from exports by the ACP States to the Community of certain products on which their economies are dependent and which are affected by fluctuations in price and/or quantity.

Table 2.6 shows products that were included in the STABEX scheme and the criteria for applying for stabilization assistance. Exceptions were made for some countries to include products that are not listed in the table. Note that the reference level (the third column) for each product was based on a given country's exports to the EEC. However, during implementation, for some countries the reference level was based on exports to all destinations. That was the case, for example, for Burundi, Cabo Verde, Comoros, Ethiopia, Guinea-Bissau, Lesotho, Rwanda, Solomon Islands, Swaziland, Tonga, Tuvalu, and Western Samoa (Aiello, 1999). The EEC had a lower threshold for the least developed, landlocked, or island ACP countries.

The following example will illustrate how the criteria worked. Niger was (and still is) a least developed country. One of its exports is groundnuts, one of the products in the list. Groundnuts contributed 15 percent of Niger's total export revenue, so the export revenue threshold (2.5 percent) was met (Ravenhill, 1985; Twitchett, 1978). Most of it was exported to Europe, so the reference level (2.5 percent) was also easily met. Now suppose, in the preceding four years, let us say 1971–74, Niger's exports of groundnuts to the EEC countries generated, on average, $50 million a year. During a calculating year (1975), suppose Niger's groundnuts export revenues from the EEC fell by 4 percent to $48 million. This then allowed Niger to apply for a transfer of funds from the STABEX scheme to cover the difference or at least to reduce the gap. It should be emphasized that the assistance was a transfer and not a loan. Loans must be paid back.

The recipient country was not required to pay back the transfer. However, it was expected that in the five years following each transfer, the recipient ACP country would contribute to the STABEX fund. This contribution was expected in any of the five years only if the following

TABLE 2.6. Eligibility for STABEX under Lomé Convention I

Criteria for Eligibility

Product	Export revenue threshold	Entitled to Request
Groundnuts	The product being	Export earnings of the
Cocoa	considered must	product are at least
Coffee	have contributed at	7.5 percent below the
Cotton	least 7.5 percent of	reference level. For
Coconut	total merchandise	the least developed,
Palm	export revenue in	landlocked, or island
Hides, skins, and	the preceding year.	ACP countries, the
leather	The threshold was 5	percentage was 2.5.
Wood	percent for sisal.	The reference level for
Fresh bananas	The threshold for	each product is the
Tea	least developed,	annual average export
Raw sisal	landlocked,	revenue generated by
Iron ore	or island ACP	that product in the
	countries was 2.5	preceding 4 years for
	percent.	exports only to the
		EEC.

Source: Summarized from Articles 17 and 19 of Lomé Convention I, ACP-EEC (1975).

two conditions applied: (a) the price of the product was higher than the reference price,[11] and (b) the volume of that product exported to the EEC was at least equal to the reference volume (Article 21 of Lomé Convention I). The formula for contribution was the following:

Contribution = (current price—reference price) multiplied by the reference volume.

To continue with the example of Niger and groundnuts, suppose the reference price of groundnuts was $400 per ton and the reference volume of exports of peanuts from Niger to the EEC countries was 125,000 tons. In any of the five years following receipt of a transfer (say, 1976–80), Niger would contribute to the STABEX fund only if the price of groundnuts was higher than $400 per ton and its volume of exports of groundnuts to the EEC was at least 125,000 tons. Therefore, suppose in 1976, the price of groundnuts was $410 per ton and Niger exported 130,000 tons of groundnuts to the EEC. Niger would then be expected to contribute $1,250,000, that is, ($410-$400) multiplied by 125,000. However, Niger would never contribute more than the amount of the transfer it received. This arrangement was good in principle. It acknowledged that sometimes there could be export revenue windfalls. In practice, however, the needs of LDCs were so immense and urgent that those countries could not be pressured successfully to replenish the fund.

There were four Lomé conventions altogether. Lomé Convention IV was for a ten-year period, 1991–2000. In 1993, under the Maastricht Treaty, the EEC was succeeded by the European Union (EU). When Lomé Convention IV was under review in 1995, there were actually 15 EU countries and 70 ACP countries (ACP-EU, 1996).

The main provisions of Lomé Convention I were maintained throughout. Each subsequent convention expanded areas of cooperation and monitoring. The criteria for qualifying for transfers became less demanding, even though conditions for receiving transfers were expanded to include the promotion of human rights, good governance, and strengthening the position of women. Lomé Convention II included a system for the promotion of mineral production and exports (SYSMIN), similar to STABEX, for countries that were dependent on the mining industry. Lomé Convention III removed the obligation for LDCs to contribute to the STABEX fund and Lomé Convention IV removed that obligation altogether. This was not a dramatic decision, since ACP countries rarely replenished the fund. The total amount of resources for the STABEX program between 1975 and 1988 was about 2.3 million European Currency Units (ECU). Only about 9.5 percent came from replenishment from the ACPs (European Commission, 1997, 9).

ANALYSIS OF STABEX

The relationship between the EU and African countries has many facets, but one that has persisted is the aid giver–aid recipient relationship. It is not a relationship between equals, even though the reliance by the EU on commodities from African countries has given African countries some leverage. STABEX was a program only for export commodities—on the basis of each individual commodity—and primarily for unprocessed products. STABEX was confined to exporters.

The main objective of STABEX was to help aid-recipient countries stabilize their export revenues. Instability or, more precisely, a fall in export revenue is a major problem for African countries. It limits their ability to import and to make long-term development plans. Making a strong case for STABEX and inviting the international community to join in stabilizing export earnings of developing countries, the Commission of the EEC (1984, 7) made the following observation:

> More than a quarter of a century after decolonization, the record is far from satisfactory. The Third World as a whole is still largely under-industrialized, it has a considerable external debt, it has been unable to ward off famine properly and its share of world trade in manufactures is still small. It is still, in fact, largely dependent on its raw material exports. These provide most of the developing countries' foreign exchange and much of the national budgets as well, via the taxes levied on export products. This means that any major drop in earnings may have dramatic consequences on their economy.

Empirical studies on the effectiveness of STABEX in stabilizing export earnings produce mixed results, as the following two studies illustrate. Herrmann (1982) concludes that instead of stabilizing export earnings, STABEX actually contributed to the instability of export revenues. The destabilizing effects of STABEX had to do with the timing of the issuance of funds. They were not distributed in advance for the anticipation of a downfall in export revenues, but rather in reaction to a downfall that had already happened. Because of the time lag, STABEX assistance often came when export revenues had already rebounded.

According to the study, the few times that STABEX had stabilizing effects, it was purely coincidental.

An empirical study by Aiello (1999) showed that even though the effectiveness of STABEX was sensitive to the time lag in funding, overall STABEX was successful in stabilizing export earnings of ACP countries and, as such, achieved its primary objective. But even if this positive outcome is more acceptable, any type of aid program, no matter how well-intentioned it may be, has side effects. This is a theme of this book. It is not to condemn aid per se, but rather to warn that one must be extremely cautious when it comes to aid. It is important to examine the impact of various types of aid and preferential treatment offered to African countries, on African countries. Let's consider the following questions: What is harmful about export earnings instability? And what are the potential negative side effects of a program like STABEX?

First, it is not a surprise that export revenues generated by agricultural products fluctuate considerably. This is due to instability in output and prices. The fluctuations in output stem from fluctuations in the weather and attacks by crop pests and diseases. This is especially the case in African countries, where irrigation and treatment for crop pests and diseases are limited, at best. Perennial trees, such as coffee trees, are also characterized by a botanical cycle. Mature coffee trees tend to bear less fruit in the year immediately following a large output (Wickizer, 1943). Prices fluctuate due, in part, to fluctuations in output, expectations, and changes in demand. It is important to note that while African countries are highly dependent on exports of agricultural products, they are, nonetheless, price takers, except for cocoa. West Africa supplies 70 percent of world cocoa (Wessel and Quist-Wessel, 2015). Fluctuations in aggregate export revenues in African countries are mostly due to dependence on commodities and, even more so, on just one or a few of them.

But is instability in prices or income necessarily harmful? No, it is not, if countries can build their savings as a precaution when their export revenues increase (Ghosh and Ostry, 1994). Moreover, instability can convey signals that should be considered in deciding how to allocate resources. Is it possible that STABEX fostered narrow specialization and thus perpetuated instability in export earnings, instead of encouraging diversification? In other words, did STABEX reinforce a vicious cycle of dependence on a few cash crops?

Following independence, many African countries adopted marketing boards established during the colonial era, or they formed new ones, using the colonial prototype. A marketing board had both monopoly power (the sole provider of key inputs for a given crop) and monopsony power (the only legal buyer of the crop). Thus, even if farmers wanted to switch from producing one crop to another, they could not necessarily get the inputs and agricultural extension services required to do so. In fact, laws in some countries prevented the uprooting of perennial plants for crops that benefited from STABEX. It is one reason Tanzania was a latecomer (compared to Kenya) to the cut-flower industry. Owners of coffee plantations had to wait to get permission to uproot coffee trees and use the land to plant flowers (Mshomba, 2000, 52–53). While lack of diversification cannot be attributed to a single factor, clearly the specificity of STABEX—to fund only select products—did not help.

The availability of STABEX funds, generous as they might have been, may also have fostered African leaders' apparent culture of complacency and reliance on external assistance. Moreover, they did not put in place any mechanisms to assist producers of agricultural products that were not traded in the world market (nontradables) whose incomes were also volatile.

If the marketing boards had been established to truly assist farmers, mechanisms that would have stabilized farmers' income could have been put in place without aid from STABEX. For example, in the years when export revenues were high, some percentage of them could have been saved, in anticipation of revenues falling in the future. Governments could have done the same regarding the revenues they collected from exports—save some when revenues go up.

Of course, stabilizing income is not necessarily good in itself. In the 1970s and 1980s, through marketing boards, many African countries consistently paid farmers very low producer prices, compared to world prices. Any farmer would prefer volatility in producer prices rather than stable low prices if, on average, the former provides more income. Moreover, left on their own, even subsistence farmers can and do try to stabilize their spending by buying livestock, building materials, and other items that can be resold in the future. An empirical study by Deaton (1992) on saving patterns in Cote d'Ivoire supports the assertion that farmers save in anticipation of a decline in income.

It is important to mention that international commodity agreements also trapped African countries into narrowly specializing in a few commodities. These agreements, such as the International Coffee Agreement and International Cocoa Agreement, were strong in the 1970s and 1980s. The primary objective of these agreements was to stabilize and support prices of primary products. The more successful the agreements were in keeping prices high, the more entrenched the specialization became, even though some of the proceeds from the agreements were supposed to finance diversification.[12]

Unlike the Organization of the Petroleum Exporting Countries (OPEC), commodity agreements had a mix of producing countries (developing countries) and consuming countries (developed countries). Developed countries participated as a way to demonstrate their support for developing countries and also to ensure a steady supply of primary products. Moreover, during the Cold War era, the West wanted to maintain a close relationship with as many developing countries as possible. When the Cold War ended, so did the support from developed countries to stabilize and support prices. Commodity agreements are now just a shadow of what they used to be. As organizations, they are still in place partly because once established, it is difficult to do away with them completely. They also play a very minor role in consultations, gathering statistics, and sponsoring research on production and consumption (UNCTAD, 2016).

PROTOCOLS ON BANANAS, BEEF AND VEAL, RUM, AND SUGAR

In addition to supporting specific products through STABEX, the EEC/ EU had special protocols for bananas, beef and veal, rum, and sugar under its Common Agricultural Policy (CAP). CAP policies, which set import quotas for these products, kept the prices of these products considerably higher in the EU, compared to world prices. At the same time, the EU allowed specific quantities of imports of these products from ACP countries and, for some, at domestic prices in the EU that were higher than the world price. These protocols benefited 21 ACP countries, some more than others.

Table 2.7 shows the EU's commitments as they stood in the mid-1990s. Given that commitments were negotiated and renegotiated every few years, they did not remain constant. However, throughout this period, the EU offered preferential access and prices that were above market prices for products from ACP countries. For most of the 1990s and early 2000s, the price of bananas in the EU stabilized at a level that was at least 100 percent higher than the price of bananas in the U.S. (Borrell and Yang, 1992; Vanzetti et al., 2005). In Africa, the largest exporters were Côte d'Ivoire and Cameroon. From 1990 to 2004, the import price of beef in the EU was, on average, more than 500 percent higher than the import price of beef in the U.S. (Iimi, 2007). Botswana was the biggest beneficiary, contributing 30–50 percent of the quota (Davenport et al., 1995). As for sugar, except in 1980 when the world price of sugar soared, the sugar price in the EU throughout the period of the Lomé Conventions was, on average, 250 percent higher than the world price of sugar (Laaksonen et al., 2007). The purchase and resale commitment for sugar meant that the EEC bought sugar at a high price from the ACP countries and re-exported it at a lower price. This was a feature of the export subsidy program in the EU. Mauritius benefited the most, as it contributed 40 percent of the sugar imports by the EU from the ACP countries (Davenport et al., 1995). The protocol on rum mostly benefited countries in the Caribbean.

While these protocols were clearly lucrative for ACP countries, just like the STABEX program, they also had the similar side effect of making countries too dependent on a single product. A clear anomaly is Mauritius, which used its sugar windfalls and deliberate trade and investment policies to industrialize and to grow its service sector (Zafar, 2011). Many ACP countries also relied too much on the EU market because of the preferential access and lack of competitiveness

TABLE 2.7. EU commitments from protocols on bananas, beef and veal, rum, and sugar—1996

	Bananas	Beef/Veal	Rum	Sugar
Tariff preferences	x	x	x	x
Duty free	x		x	x
Tariff quota	x	x	x	x
Country specific allocations		x		x
Purchase and resale commitments				x
Guaranteed prices		x		
Trade development assistance	x		x	
Beneficiary African countries	Cameroon	Botswana	Madagascar	Congo
	Cape Verde	Kenya	Mauritius	Côte d'Ivoire
	Côte d'Ivoire	Madagascar		Kenya
	Madagascar	Namibia		Madagascar
	Somalia	Swaziland		Malawi
		Zimbabwe		Mauritius
				Swaziland
				Tanzania
				Uganda
				Zambia
				Zimbabwe

in other markets (LMC International and Overseas Development Institute, 2012).

As could be expected, the EU's nonreciprocal preferential treatment for ACP countries did not sit well with other developing countries, as they felt discriminated against and disadvantaged. Clearly the discrimination was more conspicuous with the four products listed in Table 2.7. The dispute settlement under GATT was not strong enough to address complaints from countries that felt they were adversely affected by the EU's trade policies that were favorable for ACP countries. That changed when the WTO replaced GATT, as discussed in Chapter 3.

———

This chapter has described, with respect to international trade, the complex relationship between African countries and the EU from the late 1950s to the 2000s. It provides historical context with which to understand, at least partially, the persistent economic challenges of some African countries, such as the lack of diverse exports, the dependence, and the dynamics of trade negotiations between African countries and their major trading partners.

The nonreciprocal trade arrangements that European countries established with the ACP countries provided a model for the GSP programs and similar programs that followed. These programs have become both alternatives and complements to direct aid. By their very nature, they illustrate a relationship between two unequal sides: the preference givers, on the one hand, and the preference recipients, on the other. Because of the seeming "benevolence" of these programs, it can be easy for the preference-receiving countries to focus on the short-run benefits of receiving preference and overlook the need to develop ways to avoid being trapped into long-term dependency on just a few markets and products. The fact that certain things have been done the same way for decades does not necessarily make them right. Complacency can be the enemy of progress. Some African countries are too tied up with internal instability to have the time to pay attention to what may seem to be mundane issues about preferential trade arrangements. This challenge is magnified in countries where manufacturer and business associations are weak.

One clear lesson from the long relationship between the EU and ACP countries is that relationships between countries are dynamic; they change. For example, the nonreciprocal preferential treatment that the EU had accorded to ACP countries for decades was found to be inconsistent with the WTO rules. That spurred the move toward establishing EPAs. In addition, global perspectives about the effectiveness of different forms of aid change over time. The relationship between the EU and ACP countries will surely continue to evolve. ACP countries cannot afford to be passive in this evolution. They should always do their homework to be clear about their objectives. They must refrain from being enticed by some small short-term gains (such as direct aid) at the expense of policy space and long-term growth. The discussion in the following chapter on Economic Partnership Agreements (EPAs) suggests that some African countries have learned that lesson.

Thus, Chapter 3 is an extension of the discussion in this chapter on the special and evolving relationships between the EU and the African countries in the ACP group. Chapter 4 will then pick up on the nonreciprocal preferential trade arrangements that are still allowed by the WTO.

3 THE ECONOMICS AND POLITICS OF ECONOMIC PARTNERSHIP AGREEMENTS

THE SPECIAL RELATIONSHIP BETWEEN THE EU and the African, Caribbean, and Pacific (ACP) countries was put to the test when the World Trade Organization (WTO) was established in 1995.[1] The EU had had a system of nonreciprocal preferential trade arrangements with its colonies that was continued even after those colonies had gained their independence. As could be expected, the EU's special treatment for the ACP countries did not sit well with other developing countries. Yet the dispute settlement mechanism under the WTO's predecessor, the General Agreement on Tariffs and Trade (GATT), was not strong enough to address complaints from developing countries that felt adversely affected by the EU's trade policies that favored the ACP countries.

A major accomplishment of the Uruguay Round of GATT was the establishment of the Dispute Settlement Understanding (DSU), which gave the WTO a coherent and predictable mechanism with which to enforce trade rules. No sooner was the WTO established than the U.S., joined by Guatemala and Mexico, filed complaints alleging that the EU's banana trade deal with the ACP countries violated the WTO rules. The WTO found the EU's banana trade regime to be inconsistent with its obligation.

The ruling by the WTO against the EU was an important reason why the Lomé Convention between the EU and the ACP countries was replaced by the Cotonou Agreement. The Cotonou Agreement, signed in 2000, was designed to convert the nonreciprocal trade arrangements into reciprocal agreements—Economic Partnership Agreements (EPAs) between the EU and the ACP countries (ACP Secretariat, 2000).

Negotiations between the EU and the ACP countries started in 2002 and were expected to be completed by 2007. A few EPAs have been concluded, but many are still under negotiation. The ACP countries negotiate with the EU as regional groups in order to streamline the process. The 79 ACP countries divided themselves into seven regions—the Caribbean (15), Central Africa (8), the East African Community (6), Eastern and Southern Africa (12), the Pacific (15), the Southern African Development Community (7), and West Africa (16). (The numbers in parentheses are the number of countries in the negotiating region.) This chapter examines the opportunities, challenges, and progress and dynamics of negotiations, as well as the economic impact of EPAs on African countries.

OPPORTUNITIES

EPAs provide the opportunity to (i) reduce uncertainty in trade relations, (ii) increase robust competition, (iii) increase development aid from the EU, and (iv) enhance intraregional trade among African countries.

Reducing Uncertainty

For all practical purposes, the nonreciprocal preferential trade arrangements that the EU has had with the ACP countries have always been controlled by one side, the EU. As the preference-giving side, the EU has dictated the magnitude and duration of preferences for various products. Therefore, there has always been an element of uncertainty for ACP exporters of products to the EU. Such uncertainty may have limited investment that relies on long-term access to the EU market. EPAs will significantly reduce such uncertainty, since market access on both sides will be maintained through the principle of reciprocity, and decisions by either side will be less arbitrary. Essentially, this will enable businesses to make long-term plans for investment and production with an increased sense of certainty.

Increasing Competition

In fact, this is both an opportunity and a challenge at the same time. Overall, EPAs have the potential to open up the ACP countries to strategically managed, increased competition that will lead to a more efficient allocation of resources. It is important to note that with or without EPAs, competition is unavoidable unless countries want to hold back innovation and economic growth. The key is for competition to be strategically managed and linked to the overall national development goals.

One inherent concern is that EPAs will strangle the manufacturing sector in African countries because of their relative competitive disadvantage, compared to the EU producers. This legitimate concern is addressed, albeit not necessarily convincingly, by allowing the ACP countries to have long transitional periods and ample space to apply safeguard measures for sensitive products. Article XXIV, paragraph 5(c), of the General Agreement on Tariffs and Trade (GATT) allowed contracting members of a free trade area to set a reasonable transitional period for implementation. "The reasonable length of time referred to in paragraph 5(c) of Article XXIV should exceed 10 years only in exceptional cases" (GATT, 1994: 34). These provisions were adopted by the WTO. Considering the economic disparity between the EU countries and the ACP countries, EPAs will, undoubtedly, qualify as exceptional cases. So it will likely be the norm to give transitional periods of more than ten years to African countries. The Cameroon EPA agreement with the EU provided a fifteen-year transition period, and for certain products deemed to be very sensitive, Cameroon will not be obliged to reduce import duties at all. Cameroon was even able to suspend liberalization that was already under way, due to unforeseen economic challenges (Mbodiam and Andzongo, 2020). A remark by Curran et al. (2008: 535) that "the European Commission has not been subject to any significant lobbying by EU industry for either tariff pro-tection or market access in the ACP region" continues to be true. This makes it politically easy for the EU to accommodate requests from ACP countries for long transitional periods. ACP countries are, therefore, able to preempt disruptions that can be caused by a sudden increase in competition from the outside.

Increasing Development Aid from the EU

It is always the case that when developed countries reach agreements of any nature with developing countries, aid becomes a central issue. Aid is usually needed to enable developing countries to fulfill their obligations. It is also used as an incentive to get developing countries to sign on to those agreements. The EU promised increased devel-opment funds to assist with implementation costs, supply-side con-straints, and adjustment costs (ACP Secretariat, 2000; South Centre, 2007). Negotiations for EPAs can, therefore, be a unique opportunity for African countries to conduct a thorough analysis of their pro-duction competitiveness and identify priority sectors, supply-side constraints, and adjustment costs that might be addressed by "aid for trade" assistance from the EU. However, the ACP countries must avoid the temptation to initiate policy or program changes simply because they have been promised assistance. Those changes must be made on their own merits.

The European Development Fund (EDF), established in 1957, is the main channel through which the EU provides development aid to the ACP countries, as discussed in Chapter 2. The EDFs are multi-annual financial commitments. Each EDF is usually scheduled to be implemented within a period of at least five years, as shown in Table 3.1. Until 2020, EDFs were financed by direct contributions from EU member states and were not formally part of the EU budget. The main reason for the separation from the overall budget was that when the EDF was initially established, key EU countries wanted to maintain different types and levels of relationships with the ACP countries, based on their historical ties (Pouwels, 2021). However, over time,

TABLE 3.1. European Development Fund

	Years	Legal basis
1st EDF	1959–1964	Convention on Overseas Countries and Territories (OCTs) annexed to the Treaty of Rome
2nd EDF	1964–1970	1st Yaoundé Convention
3rd EDF	1970–1975	2nd Yaoundé Convention
4th EDF	1975–1980	1st Lomé Convention
5th EDF	1980–1985	2nd Lomé Convention
6th EDF	1985–1990	3rd Lomé Convention
7th EDF	1990–1995	4th Lomé Convention
8th EDF	1995–2000	4th Lomé Convention (revised)
9th EDF	2000–2007	Cotonou Agreement
10th EDF	2008–2013	Cotonou Agreement (revised)
11th EDF	2014–2020	Cotonou Agreement (revised)
12th EDF	2021–2027	Post-Cotonou

Sources: D'Alfonso (2014) and European Parliament (2021).

shares of contributions came to be based on each country's relative economic size, measured by the gross national income. For example, Germany contributed 21 percent of the 11th EDF because its gross national income was 21 percent of the EU's aggregate gross national income in 2013. The total contributions for the 11th EDF were €29 billion (D'Alfonso, 2014).

In 2021, the EDF and other EU development funds were made part of the EU general budget, thus placing them under close parliamentary scrutiny. While EU taxpayers may welcome this change as a way to bring more transparency to the allocation of these funds, it has the potential to constrain negotiations between the EU and the ACP countries. The EDF may be caught up in disagreements over the EU budget in general and could lose the flexibility it had when it operated outside the EU budget. The EDF provided multiannual funding, allowing funds not spent in one year to be carried over to the next and giving it "more space to act on unforeseen events as not all the funding [was] allocated at once" (Pouwels, 2021:4).

However, even if there was additional assistance to African countries through the EDF, it is not clear how that would help in the establishment of EPAs in any direct way. A key criterion for EDF funding has been a country's level of poverty. About 85 percent of the 11th EDF that was allocated to 49 African ACP countries went to the 33 LDCs in the region (Herrero et al., 2015). Yet these are the countries that do not need EPAs to have free access to the EU market; they already have that access through the EU's EBA program.

Enhancing Intraregional Trade among African Countries

EPAs will make permanent the cumulation provisions for the rules regarding country of origin for trade between the EU and ACP countries. An input produced and imported either from the EU, a regional economic bloc to which an EPA member country belongs, or from any ACP member country will be counted as a domestic input. These flexible rules of origin have the potential to increase intraregional trade and especially trade among ACP countries, thus promoting South-South trade and, in turn, diversifying exports and markets. If and when a genuine African Continental Free Trade Area (AfCFTA) is established, these flexible rules regarding country of origin will further support trade complementarity (supply chains) among African countries (UNCTAD, 2022). Nonetheless, other aspects of EPAs create disunity in African regional economic blocs, as discussed below.

CHALLENGES

EPA negotiations face at least seven challenges: (i) a mismatch between EPA negotiating regions and regional economic blocs; (ii) privileged access for LDCs and certain products to the EU market; (iii) ACP countries' access to the Generalized System of Preferences (GSP); (iv) reduced tariff revenues; (v) the inability of the WTO to exert pressure to speed up the process; (vi) the exit of the UK from the EU; and

(vii) the fact that the EU is not an important market for some African ACP countries.

A Mismatch between EPA Regions and Regional Economic Blocs

There are seventeen African regional economic blocs, as shown in Table 3.2. Except for Algeria and Mozambique, which only belong to the Union of Arab Maghreb (UMA) and the Southern African Development Community (SADC), respectively, all other African countries belong to two or more African regional blocs. As such, it is impossible to match precisely the ACP negotiating regions with the African regional economic blocs. Moreover, membership in regional economic blocs has continued to change since the initiation of EPAs. For example, Burundi and Rwanda joined the East African Community (EAC) in 2009, South Sudan joined the EAC in 2016, Comoros joined SADC in 2018, and the Democratic Republic of the Congo (DRC) joined the EAC in 2022. Even Somalia has taken preliminary steps to join the EAC (EAC Secretariat, 2023).[2]

Countries must choose one of their regional economic blocs from which to negotiate an EPA with the EU, and apparently they can switch their alliance in the middle of negotiations. This points to how half-hearted and confusing these negotiations are. The SADC-EU EPA applies to only seven of the sixteen SADC countries. The other nine SADC members are negotiating an EPA with the EU through other regional blocs. When negotiations started in 2002, the EAC states negotiated together with other countries in Eastern and Southern Africa (ESA). However, in 2007, following the establishment of a customs union, the EAC states decided to separate from ESA and negotiate as their own group. The DRC joined the EAC in 2022. That meant it had to switch from the Central Africa negotiating group to the EAC one. These nomadic tendencies will continue for as long as the negotiations do and membership in regional blocs continues to change.

Table 3.3 shows some of the mismatches. The EAC is congruent with an ACP negotiating region. The same could also be said about ECOWAS as an economic bloc, and West Africa as an ACP region, if it were not for Mauritania being included in the latter. However, even

TABLE 3.2. Regional economic blocs in Africa

Regional Economic Bloc	Members
Economic and Monetary Community of Central Africa (CEMAC)	Cameroon, Central African Republic, Chad, Congo (Republic), Equatorial Guinea, and Gabon
Community of Sahel-Saharan States (CEN-SAD)	Benin, Burkina Faso, Cabo Verde, Central African Republic, Chad, Comoros, Côte d'Ivoire, Djibouti, Egypt, Eritrea, Gambia, Ghana, Guinea, Guinea-Bissau, Kenya, Liberia, Libya, Mali, Mauritania, Morocco, Niger, Nigeria, São Tomé and Principe, Senegal, Sierra Leone, Somalia, Sudan, Togo, and Tunisia
Common Monetary Agreement (CMA)	Eswatini, Lesotho, Namibia, and South Africa
Common Market for Eastern and Southern Africa (COMESA)	Burundi, Comoros, Djibouti, DRC, Egypt, Eritrea, Ethiopia, Kenya, Libya, Madagascar, Malawi, Mauritius, Rwanda, Seychelles, Sudan, Swaziland, Uganda, Zambia, and Zimbabwe
East African Community (EAC)	Burundi, DRC, Kenya, Rwanda, South Sudan, Tanzania, and Uganda
Economic Community of Central African States (ECCAS)	Angola, Burundi, Cameroon, Central African Republic, Chad, DRC, Congo (Republic), Equatorial Guinea, Gabon, Rwanda, and São Tomé and Principe
Economic Community of Great Lakes Countries (ECGLC)	Burundi, Congo (Republic), and Rwanda

Regional Economic Bloc	Members
Economic Community of West African States (ECOWAS)	Benin, Burkina Faso, Cabo Verde, Côte d'Ivoire, Gambia, Ghana, Guinea, Guinea-Bissau, Liberia, Mali, Niger, Nigeria, Senegal, Sierra Leone, and Togo
International Conference on the Great Lakes Region (ICGLR)	Angola, Burundi, Central African Republic, DRC, Congo (Republic), Kenya, Rwanda, South Sudan, Sudan, Tanzania, Uganda, and Zambia
Intergovernmental Authority on Development (IGAD)	Djibouti, Eritrea, Ethiopia, Kenya, Somalia, South Sudan, Sudan, and Uganda
Indian Ocean Commission (IOC)	Comoros, France/Réunion[3], Madagascar, Mauritius, and Seychelles
Mano River Union (MRU)	Côte d'Ivoire, Guinea, Liberia, and Sierra Leone
Southern African Customs Union (SACU)	Botswana, Eswatini, Lesotho, Namibia, and South Africa
Southern African Development Community (SADC)	Angola, Botswana, Comoros, DRC, Eswatini, Lesotho, Madagascar, Malawi, Mauritius, Mozambique, Namibia, Seychelles, South Africa, Tanzania, Zambia, and Zimbabwe
West African Customs and Economic Union (UEMOA)	Benin, Burkina Faso, Côte d'Ivoire, Guinea, Mali, Niger, Senegal, and Togo
Union of Arab Maghreb (UMA)	Algeria, Libya, Mauritania, Morocco, and Tunisia
West African Monetary Zone (WAMZ)	Gambia, Ghana, Guinea, Liberia, Nigeria, and Sierra Leone

Sources: The websites of the regional blocs listed.

TABLE 3.3. African ACP Negotiating Groups

ACP Negotiating Groups	Countries	Commentary
Central Africa	Cameroon, Central African Republic, Chad, Congo (Republic), Equatorial Guinea, Gabon, and São Tomé and Principe[4]	All of these countries, except São Tomé and Principe, are members of CEMAC. CEMAC is a subset of ECCAS. All of these countries are also members of ECCAS. However, ECCAS has four additional members—Angola, Burundi, Democratic Republic of the Congo, and Rwanda.
East African Community (EAC)	Burundi, Democratic Republic of Congo, Kenya, Rwanda, South Sudan, Tanzania, and Uganda	Comprised of all members of the EAC.
Eastern and Southern Africa (ESA)	Comoros, Djibouti, Eritrea, Ethiopia, Madagascar, Malawi, Mauritius, Seychelles, Somalia, Sudan, Zambia, and Zimbabwe	Comprised of the 5 members of the Intergovernmental Authority on Development (IGAD) that are not members of the EAC and 7 of the 16 members of SADC.
Southern African Development Community (SADC)	Angola, Botswana, Eswatini, Lesotho, Mozambique, Namibia, and South Africa	Comprised of 7 of the 16 members of SADC.

ACP Negotiating Groups	Countries	Commentary
West Africa	Benin, Burkina Faso, Cabo Verde, Côte d'Ivoire, Gambia, Ghana, Guinea, Guinea-Bissau, Liberia, Mali, Mauritania, Niger, Nigeria, Senegal, Sierra Leone, and Togo	Comprised of all 15 members of the Economic Community of West African States (ECOWAS) and Mauritania.

Source: South Centre, 2007a.

with these matches, all EAC and ECOWAS members belong to other economic blocs. Therefore, any agreement between the EAC and the EU, for example, still has the potential to disturb the relationship between the EAC members and countries in other economic blocs to which they belong. This is also happening while an agreement is under negotiation to establish a COMESA-EAC-SADC Tripartite Free Trade Area. At the same time, African countries are trying to establish a genuine continental free trade area. The inconsistencies between EPA regions and regional economic blocs and Africa's ongoing efforts to combine regional economic blocs add to the complexity of the negotiations.

Privileged Access for LDCs and Certain Products to the EU Market[5]
Every ACP negotiating group in Africa has a mix of LDCs and non-LDCs. All LDCs have nonreciprocal preferential access to the EU market, with zero duties, through the Everything But Arms (EBA) program, so they do not need an EPA. Likewise, not all products imported by the EU are subject to import duties. Raw materials and minerals

enjoy an MFN duty of zero or close to zero tariff rates (World Trade Organization, 2022a).

It is not in the self-interest of the LDCs to subject their relatively infant manufacturing industries to increased competition from producers in the EU and increased competition for the EU market from the non-LDC countries. Unlike the EBA program, EPAs would require African countries to reciprocate the reduction of trade barriers. At the same time, EPAs would extend access to the EU market to the non-LDCs, access that was previously available only to LDCs.

Economic theory shows that freer trade increases the economic welfare of countries, as discussed in Chapter 1. However, the short-run displacement of labor and other resources can be devastating if trade barriers are removed abruptly. A former president of Tanzania, Benjamin Mkapa, was strongly opposed to the EPA proposition (Mkapa, 2016). Among his remarks: "I don't understand how such a powerful trade bloc can have a free trade agreement with the developing economies of Africa. There is no way that our small economies can have a free trade agreement with Europe" (The New Times, 2016).

Although EPAs would include provisions for long transitional periods and safeguard measures to protect sensitive products, LDCs may still be reluctant to engage in negotiations, given what the EBA program already offers them (Luke and Suominen, 2019). Moreover, within all negotiating groups, countries have various lists of sensitive products. For example, the following four countries in the ESA have different sensitive products that they want excluded from trade liberalization:

Madagascar: meat, milk and cheese, fisheries, vegetables, cereals, oils and fats, edible preparations, sugar, cocoa, beverages, tobacco, chemicals, plastic and paper articles, textiles, metal articles, furniture.

Mauritius: live animals and meat, edible products of animal origin, fats, edible preparations and beverages, chemicals, plastics and rubber articles of leather and fur skins, iron and steel, consumer electronic goods.

Seychelles: meat, fisheries, beverages, tobacco, leather articles, glass and ceramics products, vehicles.

Zimbabwe: products of animal origin, cereals, beverages, paper, plastics and rubber, textiles and clothing, footwear, glass and ceramics, consumer electronics, vehicles.

(London School of Economics, 2021: 23)

This is a complication particularly for those countries belonging to custom unions, which are supposed to have uniform external trade barriers. LDCs maintain that partnership agreements would adversely reduce their policy space and the flexibility needed to determine their own development path.

In October 2014, the EAC and the EU concluded what appeared to be successful negotiations on an EPA. However, in July 2016, Tanzania (followed by Uganda) decided that it would not sign the EPA. The reasons given were that the EPA would hurt domestic industries. One can understand Tanzania's decision. Why subject your country to reciprocity demanded by the EPA, when it can still benefit from the EBA, which is nonreciprocal? This is not a reason that LDCs would publicly state, but they do not have to—it is obvious. The EU has pledged "aid for trade" to ACP countries, to assist them in mitigating the short-run costs of increased trade liberalization. However, this would be a nonbinding, nonspecific promise that no LDC can reasonably count on in making policy decisions for the future. Moreover, "aid for trade" may not necessarily increase development assistance but simply redistribute current levels of aid to allocate more of it to trade-related activities. In fact, they can simply be relabeled as "aid for trade" because, literally, any activity or program on which aid funds are actually spent can be linked to trade, directly or indirectly.

Some ACP countries have privileged access to the EU market by virtue of the products they export. Crude oil and raw minerals enter the EU duty-free. Countries such as Equatorial Guinea and Nigeria and other countries whose exports are dominated by raw materials and natural resources may see little value in negotiating an EPA. Most economies of the natural resource-rich African countries are not diversified. Note that some African ACP countries are doubly "privileged"—being in the LDC category and exporting products that are not subject to tariffs. These include Chad, the DRC, Liberia, Niger, and Zambia.

ACP Countries' Access to the Generalized System of Preferences Program

Developing countries that are not LDCs can use the EU's GSP or GSP+ to access the EU market at tariff rates more favorable than the *most favored nation* (MFN) tariff rates.[6] While EPAs would provide more favorable access and more certainty than the GSP or GSP+, these nonreciprocal preferential arrangements reduce the urgency for EPAs.

Reduced Tariff Revenues

Import tariffs are an important source of government revenue for developing countries. Developing countries, and LDCs in particular, have limited sources of government revenue. For this reason, import duties may not be used primarily as a trade barrier, as they are in developed countries, but rather to generate revenue. For most Sub-Saharan African countries for which data is available, taxes on international trade and transactions contribute 10–20 percent of total tax revenues.[7]

Inability of the WTO to Exert Pressure to Speed Up the Process

The old relationship in which the EU gave nonreciprocal preferential trade treatment to a subset of developing countries was not compatible with the WTO's *most favored nation* (MFN) principle. Nonetheless, the WTO is limited in its ability to speed up negotiations and formation of the EPAs because this is not simply a legal issue. It is also an issue involving diplomacy and development.

As an international organization, the WTO must try to manage relationships between countries and be especially sensitive to trade-related challenges experienced by developing countries. Moreover, the unsuccessful Doha Round of negotiations launched at the WTO Ministerial Conference in 2001 had attempted to bring rules into greater harmony with the development objectives of developing countries. The Doha Round was even declared proudly to be a development round. However, the round died silently, leaving developing countries frustrated (Financial Times, 2015).

The WTO walks a fine line between upholding principles and enforcing rules, on the one hand, and being an advocate for developing countries, on the other. As such, the WTO is not in a strong position to give an ultimatum as to when EPA negotiations must be completed or to ask the EU to immediately start applying MFN tariffs on goods imported from non-LDCs countries in the ACP group.

The provisional extension of nonreciprocal trade arrangements under the Cotonou Agreement was supposed to end in 2007. Article 37(1) of the agreement states:

> Economic partnership agreements shall be negotiated during the preparatory period which shall end by 31 December 2007 at the latest. Formal negotiations of the new trading arrangements shall start in September 2002 and the new trading arrangements shall enter into force by 1 January 2008, unless earlier dates are agreed between the Parties. (ACP Secretariat, 2000)

The road map was overly ambitious, if not outright wishful thinking. The deadlines could not be met and there was no desire to penalize protraction. The Cotonou Agreement itself, which covers many areas of development and cooperation between the EU and ACP countries, was supposed to end in 2020 but has since been extended one year at a time (European Parliament, 2021; Jacobsen, 2022).

Exit of the UK from the EU (Brexit)

When the United Kingdom left the EU on December 31, 2020 (The New York Times, 2020), it ended a formal relationship that had existed for forty-seven years. The UK joined the European Economic Community (EEC) in 1973 (Mourlon-Druol, 2015). In 1993, the Maastricht Treaty transformed the EEC into the EU. With the UK leaving the EU, agreements between the EU and ACP countries would not apply to the UK. ACP countries would need to have separate negotiations with the UK.

Tanzania used the exit of the UK from the EU (Brexit) as a reason to back out of the EAC-EU deal. Tanzania's argument was that "with the exit of its core market from the EU, it had little to gain from the partnership negotiations" (Otondi, 2016). In fact, the UK is not a "core market" for Tanzania. According to data from the IMF Direction of Trade Statistics, Tanzania's total exports, from 2014 to 2020, were $34.7 billion. Exports to the UK in that period were $158.3 million, only 0.45 percent of the total exports. Nonetheless, there is no denying that the UK was a significant member of the EU. It was the EU's second-largest economy, after Germany, accounting for 20 percent of the EU's GDP in 2020. Brexit also complicated EPA negotiations in part because it put into question development assistance that had been promised to ACP countries, to which the U.K was contributing 14 percent (Gustafsson et al., 2017).

The EU—Not an Important Market for Some African ACP Countries

The dependence of African countries on the EU market has gradually diminished since those countries got their independence. China is increasingly becoming an important trade partner for African countries, especially for those that are rich in natural resources. In the period 2014–20, aggregate exports from the DRC, Djibouti, Eritrea, Gambia, Mali, Somalia, South Sudan, Sudan, Zambia, and Zimbabwe to the EU were less than 3 percent of their total exports.[8] These countries and a few more that do not rely on the EU market may not see any practical benefits in establishing an EPA with the EU.

THE PROGRESS AND DYNAMICS OF NEGOTIATIONS[9]

The progress and dynamics of EPA negotiations are different for each group because of the salient features of each group's members. The EU provides periodic updates on the status of its negotiations with all ACP groups. While the process was designed for ACP countries to negotiate with the EU as regional groups, the challenges experienced in negotiations necessitated applying the principle of "variable geometry." This principle allows negotiations that could lead to agreements that are not binding on all members of a group. It allows for different speeds of integration of countries in a group. Therefore, while on the one hand the EPAs might enhance regional economic integration, on the other hand they may divide members that belong to a regional bloc.

Before proceeding to consider the status of the EU's negotiations with each group, it may be helpful to note the typical provisions sought in EPAs:

i.   All products from the ACP countries must have duty-free and quota-free access to the EU market;

ii. ACP countries must gradually eliminate import duties on most of their products in order to establish reciprocity;

iii. ACP countries must be allowed to maintain import duties on sensitive products so as to avoid disrupting and creating an excessive burden on the economies of those countries;

iv. ACP countries must not introduce new export taxes (to allow the EU to maintain easy access to raw materials); and

v.   The EU must accord treatment to ACP countries not less favorable than the treatment it gives to third parties. Likewise, ACP countries must agree to a "most-favored-nation" clause to prevent ACP countries from granting to developed and major trading economies more favorable access to their markets (CUTS International, 2009; Pichon, 2022).

In addition, it is important to highlight a controversy surrounding the EPA negotiations. The EU is pushing for negotiations beyond what is required by the WTO (South Centre, 2014). Regarding the *most favored nation* clause, the EU is demanding that "a major economy" be defined not only as any developed country, but also any country whose share of world trade is above one percent (CUTS International, 2009; South Centre, 2014; Chimanikire, 2019). That includes emerging economies such as Brazil and India. That means that if an ACP country entered a free trade area agreement with Brazil and eliminated tariffs, for example, it must also eliminate tariffs with the EU. Yet under the WTO rules, preferential trade arrangements among developing countries are protected by the 1979 Enabling Clause. This clause allows for the formation of free trade areas among all developing countries (GATT, 1979). It was adopted under GATT and has been continued by the WTO. If ACP countries yield to the EU's pressure, it will limit the expansion of South-South trade.

While the EU wants to ignore the WTO provision in the matter of the enabling clause, it wants to hide behind the WTO's curtain on other issues that are politically sensitive at home. For example, the EU wants the issue of agricultural subsidies to be discussed within the WTO and not within EPA negotiations (South Centre, 2014). Between 2021 and 2027, the EU will have given its farmers subsidies of at least $72 billion a year (Reuters, 2021). These subsidies, which were formally introduced under the EU Common Agricultural Program (CAP) in 1962, give European farmers an unfair advantage and lead to export dumping (Oxfam, 2002). These subsidies are a huge challenge to African farmers. Agriculture is the most important economic sector in many African countries. It is, therefore, hypocritical of the EU to want to exclude agricultural subsidies from the EPA discussions, and it would be imprudent for African countries to accept the EU's position.

What follows is a close look at the dynamics of the EU's EPA negotiations with each of the negotiating groups in Africa.

Central Africa

Table 3.4 provides a summary of the Central African countries' magnitude of exports to and imports from the EU. Negotiations between the EU and Central African countries to form an EPA began in 2003, but only Cameroon has reached an agreement with the EU. The EU–Central Africa (Cameroon) EPA took effect in 2014. The EU removed all duties on products imported from Cameroon. For its part, Cameroon agreed to gradually phase out import duties on 80 percent of the products it imported from the EU, to be completed over a period of fifteen years, thus, in 2029 (Economic Commission, 2019). The products for which duties would be removed were divided into three groups, as shown in Table 3.5. The first two groups included most industrial inputs and

TABLE 3.4. Exports and imports of Central African countries to and from the EU

Country	Income Group	Percent of Exports to EU (2014–2020)	Percent of Imports from EU (2014–2020)
Cameroon	Lower-middle	46	27
Central African Rep.	Low-income/LDC	45	38
Chad	Low-income/LDC	13	30
Congo, Republic of	Lower-middle	19	25
Equatorial Guinea	Upper-middle	25	40
Gabon	Upper-middle	27	51
São Tomé and Principe	Lower-middle/LDC	70	62
Group		26	32

Source: IMF's database for Direction of Trade Statistics.

consumer goods that were not produced domestically (European Commission, 2019). Import duties on these products were primarily used to generate tariff revenues and not necessarily to limit imports. While the specifics of EPAs between the EU and ACP negotiating groups are likely to be different, they all have general characteristics similar to those found in Cameroon's EPA with the EU, displayed in Table 3.5 (United Nations Economic Commission for Africa, 2018).

Cameroon excluded from liberalization, indefinitely, products that are deemed to be sensitive for domestic employment and/or critical for generating tariff revenues. They comprise about 20 percent of all Cameroon's exports to the EU. They include: "most meat products (20%), wines and spirits (30%), malt (10%), milk products (5%), flour (30%), certain vegetables (30%), wood and wood products (30%), used clothes and textiles (30%), and paintings (30%)" (European Commission, 2020: 2). The numbers in parentheses are tariff rates.

TABLE 3.5. Cameroon's trade liberalization schedule on imports from the EU

Product Group	Example of products	Liberalization (percent of the original tariff reduced per year)	Implementation Period
1	medicines, medical tools, fertilizers, gas, and seeds	25%	4 years—started in 2016, completed in 2019
2	inputs for the food industry, generators, trucks, vans, and plotters	15%	7 years—started in 2017, suspended in 2020, and resumed in 2021
3	fuels, cement, passenger vehicles, and motorcycles	10%	10 years—supposed to start in 2020, but pushed back to 2021

Sources: Akuo, 2021; Economic Commission, 2019; European Commission, 2020; and Mbodiam and Andzongo, 2020.

Cameroon signed on to the EPA because it had a lot to lose (and a lot to gain), compared to all the other Central African countries without (or with) some trade arrangement with the EU. At least 45 percent of Cameroon's exports go to the EU. About 40 percent of those exports are raw minerals that face zero MFN tariffs (Economic Commission, 2019). However, the remaining products, including bananas, pro-cessed cocoa, and timber, benefit from the EPA. Cameroon is not an LDC and, therefore, it cannot benefit from the EBA, and the EU's GSP was not good enough, given its main export products. Cameroon has negotiated a separate agreement with the UK that has been applied provisionally since January 1, 2021 (UK Secretary of State for Foreign, Commonwealth and Development Affairs, 2021; UK Department of

Trade, 2021). On average, Cameroon's exports to the UK from 2014 to 2020 were 2 percent of its total exports.

The other countries in the Central African group have little to gain from an EU–Central Africa EPA. Chad, the Central African Republic, and São Tomé and Principe are LDCs with access to the EBA program. São Tomé and Principe will be removed from the EBA program in 2024 when it graduates from the LDC category (European Commission, 2020). However, merchandise exports contribute only 3–4 percent of São Tomé and Principe's GDP. While 70 percent of those exports are destined to the EU, only about 30 percent of those are eligible for the EBA. The rest take advantage of the zero MFN rate, that is, the duty-free rate for everyone. It is unlikely São Tomé and Principe would sign on to an EPA just so that exports that contribute only one percent of its GDP would have duty-free access. Moreover, São Tomé and Principe is an insignificant market for the EU.

The Republic of Congo qualifies for the EU GSP program. Gabon and Equatorial Guinea do not qualify for the EU GSP because they are in the upper-middle-income category (European Commission, 2022; European Commission, 2022a). For all three of these countries, more than 97 percent of their exports are raw minerals and other products that face zero MFN duties. In 2020, the last year that Equatorial Guinea could have taken advantage of being an LDC, it was not even able (or did not bother) to take advantage of its one percent of exports to the EU that was eligible for the EBA. Unless the EU is willing to give substantial financial aid to these others members of the Central Africa Group as an incentive to join, what is now referred to as the "EU–Central Africa (Cameroon) Economic Partnership Agreement" will, in effect, remain just the EU-Cameroon Economic Partnership Agreement for a long time.

Notwithstanding that Cameroon is a gateway for its two landlocked neighbors, the Central African Republic and Chad, it has no political or economic leverage, or perhaps even interest, in convincing other Central African countries to join the agreement. Political instability in many of the countries in the region makes it hard for them to forge some sense of long-term unity. Cameroon itself is too embroiled in internal conflicts to be able to play a leadership role in bringing its neighbors together (Ndofor and Ray, 2022). Like its neighbors, Cameroon is also a very corrupt country, ranking 142nd out of 180 in 2022 in the Corruption Perception Index (CPI) (Transparency International, 2023).[10] Its autocratic leader, Paul Biya, has clung to power since 1982, winning elections under questionable circumstances (Morse, 2019; O'Donnell and Gramer, 2018). On the economic side, Cameroon is not an important market for any of the Central African countries. Less than 0.5 percent of exports from those countries are destined to Cameroon. The overall intraregional trade in the Central African region is less than 3 percent.

Not only is Cameroon unable to influence other Central African countries to join the agreement, it has also outright annoyed the other members of CEMAC (Sixtus, 2016). CEMAC is both a customs union and a monetary union. How Cameroon was able to negotiate with the EU bilaterally when it belongs to a customs union speaks volumes about the obvious disconnect between what some African regional economic blocs claim to be on paper and the reality on the ground. It is also a demonstration that the EU-ACP EPAs can destabilize regional economic blocs rather than strengthen them.

East Africa (EAC)

Table 3.6 shows the magnitude of exports and imports of the EAC countries to and from the EU. As of June 2022, the EAC group had seven countries, after South Sudan and the DRC joined the EAC economic bloc in 2016 and 2022, respectively. The DRC initially negotiated with the EU as a member of the Central Africa group. Somalia is waiting in the wings, hoping to be the newest member of the EAC soon (EAC Secretariat, 2023).

In 2014, all five EAC members at the time successfully concluded negotiations with the EU to form an EPA. The signing ceremony was to take place in 2016. However, it did not happen. Tanzania, followed by Burundi and Uganda, pulled out claiming the deal would be bad for their countries. Kenya and Rwanda signed the EAC-EU EPA in 2016, but only Kenya has ratified it (Pichon, 2022).

TABLE 3.6. Exports and imports of East African Community countries to and from the EU

Country	Income Group	Percent of Exports to EU (2014–2020)	Percent of Imports from EU (2014–2020)
Burundi	Low-income/LDC	12	15
DRC	Low-income/LDC	3	12
Kenya	Lower-middle	15	11
Rwanda	Low-income/LDC	6	11
South Sudan	Low-income/LDC	0	8
Tanzania	Lower-middle/LDC	11	9
Uganda	Low-income/LDC	17	8
Group		8	11

Source: IMF's database for Direction of Trade Statistics.

All EAC countries, except Kenya, are LDCs with duty-free-quota-free access to the EU market through the EBA. It is not clear why Tanzania agreed to the EPA deal in the first place and then changed its mind. However, it is important to note that Tanzania got a new president in 2015 whose policies were noticeably inward-looking, compared to his predecessor's (Anami, 2020). Needless to say, the decision by Tanzania was not well received by Kenya, which does not qualify for the EBA.

The EU is an important market for Kenya. From 2014 to 2020, 15 percent of Kenya's exports went to the EU, as shown in Table 3.6. Even more important is that Kenya's main exports to the EU are agricultural and horticultural products that, without special trade arrangements, would be subject to high import duties. Production of these products has become an important source of foreign currency and employment, especially for women, in Kenya. In 2020, the horticulture subsector (of the agricultural sector) in Kenya employed 6.5 million people directly and indirectly, about 25 percent of the labor force. In 2020, horticulture generated $1.4 billion in export revenues, 27 percent of total export revenues. About 45 percent of Kenya's horticultural exports go to the EU, making it the most important market for its horticultural exports (Kilimo News, 2021). Kenya pushed to be allowed to pursue an EPA with the EU on its own. At a virtual meeting of the EAC's presidents in 2021, it was acknowledged that

> not all Partner States are in a position to sign, ratify and implement the agreement. The Summit recognized the importance of some Partner States to move forward and concluded that Partner States who wish to do so should be able to commence engagements with the EU with a view to starting the EU-EAC-EPA implementation under the principle of variable geometry. (EAC Secretariat, 2021)

In 2022, the EU and Kenya started negotiations on an interim EPA with binding provisions that will be subject to a dispute settlement mechanism. The interim EPA will be open to other EAC countries to join, if and when they decide to do so (Pichon, 2022). Kenya also reached a bilateral EPA agreement with the UK that took effect in 2021 after being ratified by both sides (British High Commission, Nairobi, 2021).

An EPA between all members of the EAC and the EU is highly unlikely in the near future. None of the other countries in the EAC will be in any rush to join Kenya in its EPA with the EU. Even Rwanda, which was quick to sign the agreement in 2016, has made no apparent effort to ratify it. Tanzania stands as the main opponent of the EPA, arguing that it would slow down its industrialization initiatives. Tanzania is concerned that the phasing out of import duties, even if it would take a period of more than twenty-five years to complete, would bring about unfair competition. In addition, Tanzania holds that a ban on new export taxes would limit the government's ability to increase revenues and limit domestic processing of raw materials.

Export taxes on raw materials (or any other product) reduce the domestic price of those products (by reducing exports and increasing the amount sold locally), thus reducing production costs for domestic processors who use those raw materials as inputs. That is, export taxes can be used to promote domestic processing of raw materials and, therefore, add value to them. The caveat is that export taxes on raw materials can hurt domestic producers by reducing their prices and could, therefore, reduce production of those raw materials. In effect, an export tax on raw materials is an indirect tax on producers and an indirect subsidy for domestic buyers of those materials. Export taxes caused production of agricultural export commodities like coffee, tea, and cotton to fall in Tanzania in the 1970s and 1980s.

It is not an exaggeration to say that, given the history of the EAC, the economic and political powers, and the geographical location Kenya and Tanzania enjoy in the EAC, these two countries are the leaders in the bloc.[11] The other countries are, by and large, followers. Currently, on the issue of an EAC-EU EPA, the other countries have sided with Tanzania mostly because, as LDCs, they have nothing to lose from not joining an EPA. Moreover, exports from Burundi, the DRC, and South Sudan that are subject to import duties in the EU are less than 2 percent each. These countries would not experience a meaningful increase in access to the EU market by joining an EPA, even if the EBA program did not exist.

Although the EAC leadership has given Kenya the green light to proceed with an EPA on its own, two major problems, related to each other, must be addressed. First, the EAC is a customs union and, second, by African standards, the EAC has a high level of intraregional trade. It is the highest among regional economic blocs in Africa, at 19.6 percent in 2021, according to the UNCTAD database. Kenya's exports to the EAC bloc in 2021 were 17 percent of its total exports, which is more than its exports to the EU. Conflicts among the EAC members are common. Kenya and Tanzania, in particular, always seem to be able to find something to quarrel about.[12] Since the EAC has no functioning dispute settlement mechanism, the conflicts often escalate to the point of requiring the presidents of the two countries to intervene.

In a fully fledged customs union, member countries maintain common external trade barriers and, thus, eliminate the possibility of illegal transshipment. Transshipment occurs when a product exported from country A to country B is, in turn, exported to country C as if it were produced in country B. Consider a product for which trade among EAC countries is duty-free. Assume that the same product imported by Kenya from the EU is not subject to import duties because of the

EU-Kenya EPA deal. However, this product, imported from the EU, would be charged a tariff in any other EAC country. Transshipment happens if, for example, the EU exports that product to Kenya duty-free and then the product is repackaged in Kenya and exported to Tanzania, as if it were produced in Kenya. Notwithstanding the rules-of-origin provisions that are supposed to prevent such transshipment, the bilateral agreements between Kenya and the EU and the UK would, undoubtedly, be a source of tension among the EAC states. Moreover, the EAC countries are planning to form a monetary union and eventually become a political federation. The "do it alone" agreements, even when done in the spirit of the principle of variable geometry, will only make the path to these deeper levels of integration more difficult to achieve and sustain.

Kenya and other countries in similar predicaments will, undoubtedly, find themselves in situations where they cannot satisfy countries in their regional economic blocs and the UK/EU countries at the same time, as the following case illustrates. The EAC divides products into four broad groups with a typical tariff escalation scheme on imports, something that is common in many countries (East African Community, 2004). That is, no tariffs or very low tariffs are imposed for raw materials and inputs (first group) that cannot be produced domestically, and the highest tariffs are imposed for finished and sensitive products (fourth group). Until 2022, the minimum tariff for products in the fourth group had been 25 percent. However, that minimum was raised to 35 percent in 2022. The products affected included dairy and meat products, cereals, cotton, iron and steel, edible oils, beverages and spirits, furniture, leather products, fresh-cut flowers, fruits and nuts, sugar and confectionery, coffee, tea and spices, textiles and garments, headgear, ceramic products, and paints. The EAC raising the common external tariffs created problems for Kenya with respect to its EPA with the UK. The UK asked Kenya to respect the provisions of their EPA agreement and exempt its exports to Kenya from the new tariff rates (The East African, 2022), thus creating tensions, which were anticipated, in the EAC (Lanktree, 2020). These types of dilemmas will be common to African countries that belong to custom unions and yet have special trade arrangements with countries that are outside their unions.

Eastern and Southern African Countries (ESA)

This is a very diverse group with four island states in the Indian Ocean (Comoros, Madagascar, Mauritius, and Seychelles), five countries in the Horn of Africa (Djibouti, Eritrea, Ethiopia, Somalia, and Sudan), and three countries in Southern Africa (Malawi, Zambia, and Zimbabwe). The island states are all highly dependent on the EU market, as shown in Table 3.7. The EU market is also important for exports from Malawi and Ethiopia.

TABLE 3.7. Exports and imports of Eastern and Southern African countries to and from the EU

Country	Income Group	Percent of Exports to EU (2014–2020)	Percent of Imports from EU (2014–2020)
Comoros	Lower-middle/LDC	42	23
Djibouti	Lower-middle/LDC	3	27
Eritrea	Low-income/LDC	1	22
Ethiopia	Low-income/LDC	12	14
Madagascar	Low-income/LDC	41	16
Malawi	Low-income/LDC	32	7
Mauritius	Upper-middle	35	20
Seychelles	High-income	34	26
Somalia	Low-income/LDC	2	5
Sudan	Low-income/LDC	4	9
Zambia	Low-income/LDC	1	7
Zimbabwe	Lower-middle	2	3
Group		11	12

Source: IMF's database for Direction of Trade Statistics.

Although Comoros and Madagascar could have used their LDC status card to refrain from signing an EPA with the EU, the four Indian Ocean islands are a tightly knit group in the Indian Ocean Commission (IOC) bloc. This bloc is closely linked to the EU, through France.

Another member of the IOC is Réunion, which is a region of France (Kolodzejski, 2018). As such, France is actually a member of the IOC. In fact, France held the presidency of the IOC in 1992–93 and 2021–22. France provides 40 percent of the IOC's operating budget and, therefore, has significant influence on the IOC countries (French Ministry for Europe and Foreign Affairs, 2022).

In 2009, all IOC states signed on to an interim EPA with the EU. Zimbabwe is the only other ESA country that joined them (European Union, 2012a). The implementation of the agreement started in 2012, except for Comoros, which started implementing it in 2019. Zimbabwe's exports to the EU are a small percentage of its total exports. However, Zimbabwe may have wanted to thaw its relationship with the EU, which had been sour since 2002 when the EU imposed sanctions on Zimbabwe due to "escalation of violence and intimidation of political opponents and the harassment of the independent press" (European Union, 2002: 1). The other seven ESA countries are not anywhere near ready to join the agreement. All of them are LDCs and, except for Ethiopia and Malawi, the EU is not an important market for their exports. Therefore, an EPA between the EU and all ESA countries is not likely to happen.

Southern African Development Community (SADC)

As Table 3.8 shows, the EU is an important market for Southern African countries (SADC 7)[13] in this group. These countries certainly have an incentive to nurture a good relationship with the EU. In 2016, the EU-SADC EPA was signed by the EU and all members of the SADC 7, except Angola. Angola subsequently requested accession to the agreement in 2020 and formal negotiations started the following year, with near certainty that it would be accepted. It appears that this will be one ACP group where all members will be included in an EPA with the EU.

TABLE 3.8. Exports and imports of Southern African Development Community countries to and from the EU

Country	Income Group	Percent of Exports to EU (2014–2020)	Percent of Imports from EU (2014–2020)
Angola	Lower-middle/LDC	14	32
Botswana	Upper-middle	22	6
Eswatini	Lower-middle	6	4
Lesotho	Lower-middle/LDC	30	1
Mozambique	Low-income/LDC	30	17
Namibia	Upper-middle	18	9
South Africa	Upper-middle	18	26
Group		18	24

Source: IMF's database for Direction of Trade Statistics.

This is not happening by chance. In addition to the importance of the EU market to the group, South Africa has great influence on its fellow member states. South Africa's economy is at least three times the size of the other six countries combined and at least seven times bigger, when Angola is excluded. Again, excluding Angola, whose most important export commodity is oil, South Africa is the most important market to its neighbors, importing, on average, as much as 37 and 65 percent of all exports from Lesotho and Eswatini, respectively, between 2014 and 2020. The Southern African countries also have strong ties through the Common Monetary Area (CMA), comprised of Eswatini, Lesotho, Namibia, and South Africa, as well as the Southern African Customs Union (SACU), the oldest customs union in the world, comprised of all CMA members plus Botswana. Angola and Mozambique are also not strangers to the group, given that they are neighboring states and share membership in the broader SADC comprised of sixteen member states.

The EPA between the EU and the seven SADC countries was a solution to a complication that was caused by the EU and South Africa when they established a free trade area in 1999. It was called the Trade, Development, and Cooperation Agreement (TDCA). The complication was that South Africa belonged to a customs union, SACU. The TDCA was replaced by the EU-SADC EPA. An enduring problem, but not unique to SADC 7, is the fragmentation of well-established African regional economic blocs, caused by the subgrouping of ACP countries.

West Africa

The West Africa group includes all fifteen ECOWAS members plus Mauritania. Twelve countries in this group are LDCs, as shown in Table 3.9. As to be expected in such a large and diverse group, the application of the principle of variable geometry has been the norm.

The four countries that do not have EBA benefits are Cabo Verde, Côte d'Ivoire, Ghana, and Nigeria. Cabo Verde stands out in its reliance on the EU market, with almost 90 percent of its exports destined to the EU. Fishery products (mostly processed fish) are its main exports, contributing 75 percent of all its exports. Cabo Verde graduated from LDC status in 2007, but had a three-year transition period before it lost its EBA benefits. In addition, in 2008, the EU granted Cabo Verde an exemption from the rules of origin, allowing certain processed fishery products to be considered as originating from Cabo Verde, even though the fish were caught elsewhere (European Union, 2011). In 2011, the EU granted GSP+ status to Cabo Verde, which is more generous than the regular GSP (African Development Bank, 2012). Cabo Verde's preference utilization of preferential GSP+ duties averaged 95 percent from 2011 to 2020.[14] Given the access to the EU market it already enjoyed, Cabo Verde was not in any rush to establish an EPA with the EU.

The situation was different for Côte d'Ivoire and Ghana. They are also dependent on the EU market. However, the EU's regular GSP program, which is open to them, does not cover their main exports to the EU. Their main exports include processed cocoa, bananas, vegetables,

TABLE 3.9. Exports and imports of West African countries to and from the EU

Country	Income Group	Percent of Exports to EU 2014–2020	Percent of Imports from EU 2014–2020
Benin	Lower-middle/LDC	8	25
Burkina Faso	Low-income/LDC	5	26
Cabo Verde[15]	Lower-middle	86	77
Côte d'Ivoire	Lower-middle	36	28
Gambia	Low-income/LDC	3	18
Ghana	Lower-middle	19	20
Guinea	Low-income/LDC	22	33
Guinea-Bissau	Low-income/LDC	4	55
Liberia	Low-income/LDC	18	15
Mali	Low-income/LDC	2	20
Mauritania	Lower-middle/LDC	24	32
Niger	Low-income/LDC	26	30
Nigeria	Lower-middle	24	18
Senegal	Lower-middle/LDC	13	39
Sierra Leone	Low-income/LDC	22	17
Togo	Low-income/LDC	9	29
Group		22	23

Source: IMF's database for Direction of Trade Statistics.

fruits, and preserved tuna. Côte d'Ivoire and Ghana wanted to avoid the trade disruption with the EU that would have followed the end of special preferences that were sustained by the Cotonou Agreement (Bilal, 2021). Each country, independently, established an EPA with the EU, that has been applied provisionally since 2016.

Nigeria is a unique case. It is, by far, the largest economy in the group, contributing 60 percent of the group's GDP. While the EU market is also important for Nigeria, 95 percent of its exports are oil and other mineral fuels that are not subject to tariffs (European Commission, 2022b).

As Krapohl and Van Huut (2020; 574) conclude, "Nigeria thus enjoys a privileged position compared to Ghana and [Côte d'Ivoire]." If Nigeria were at all interested in being party to the West Africa–EU EPA, it would hold a leadership role, the way South Africa does in SADC. Instead, it has remained on the outside. As of 2018, all countries in the West Africa group, except the Gambia and Nigeria, had signed the EPA with the EU. Still, as of 2022, the agreement had not yet come into effect because it had not yet been ratified.

From 1963 to 2000, the economic and development relations between the EU and ACP countries featured nonreciprocal market access granted by the EU in the two Yaoundé conventions (1963–75) and four Lomé conventions (1975–2000), as discussed in Chapter 2. The renewal of those conventions happened, by and large, by default. There were clear potential gains to be realized by ACP countries, without obvious direct losses, if any. At the same time, the EU secured a stable supply of raw materials and more favorable diplomatic relations with ACP countries than would have been possible otherwise.

The switch from the Lomé Convention to the Cotonou Agreement, designed to have the nonreciprocal trade arrangements evolve into reciprocal agreements, was, in effect, a "reset button" for ACP countries. Some of them had just gone with the flow of the Yaoundé and Lomé conventions, without taking the time to fully examine the value of the trade arrangements they had with the EU. However, as they were asked to do something in return, that is, to reciprocate market access, they had to pause and weigh more carefully the benefits and costs of EPAs and become more strategic and deliberate.

ECONOMIC IMPACT OF EPAs

A number of empirical studies attempt to assess the impact of EPAs on ACP countries, including Vollmer et al., 2009; Troster et al., 2020; Fontagne et al., 2010; and Frederik et al., 2021. The results of these and other studies can inform policy makers, but must always be used with great caution. Large margins of errors are inevitable. It is impossible to control for all key variables, such as policy changes by other trading partners and nontrade factors that determine production, not to mention the shortcomings related to the availability of reliable data and the application of unrealistic, simplifying assumptions that are often necessary to make empirical studies possible. So results can vary because of the different assumptions made, among other reasons. Moreover, even where agreements have been reached, EPAs are at the provisional stage, and if there is anything to be said about the path to full implementation, it is that it is characterized by unpredictable pacing and changes.

EPAs require that ACP countries reduce, and eventually eliminate, tariffs on imports from the EU to bring about reciprocity in market access. The trade liberalization will be asymmetrical in the sense that the EU has relatively less to liberalize to bring its market access to conform with EPAs. This is because the EU was already giving preferential market access to goods originating from the ACP countries. As such, EPAs will increase EU exports to the ACP countries, more than EU imports from the ACP countries. However, since EPAs bring an element of certainty of market access, it is possible that exports from the ACP countries to the EU will increase in the long run.

Removal of tariffs by the ACP countries on goods coming from the EU will decrease tariff revenues in the ACP countries. At the same time, an increase in imports from the EU will displace domestic production in, and imports from other countries into, the ACP countries (Troster et al., 2020). A study by Fontagne et al. (2010) suggests that the EPAs would increase EU exports to ACP countries by 17.7 percent and ACP exports to the EU by 13.7 percent. The estimated increase of ACP exports to the EU must be an exaggeration. To make their partial equilibrium model workable, the authors assume that the supply of products by ACP countries is perfectly elastic. That is, an increase in demand for ACP goods will be met fully, without even the need for the price to increase. In reality, many ACP countries are unable to respond fully to open market opportunities, due to supply-side constraints. These include poor infrastructure, limited access to financial capital, lack of skilled labor, and low levels of technological capabilities. These constraints are part of the reason many African countries have a narrow range of export products. Supply-side constraints run through the whole supply chain—production, product sorting and grading, storage, health and labeling requirements, packaging, and customs procedures. It is in consideration of these supply-side constraints that ACP countries plead for aid for trade, which, of course, is never enough to address all constraints.

One of the concerns of the ACP countries is that EPAs would reduce the tariff revenues that they need to provide critical services. Tariff revenues contribute more than 10 percent of the total government revenue in at least 20 ACP countries in Africa.[16] Fontagne et al. (2010) estimate that EPAs would reduce tariff revenues by the following percentages: 38 for ECOWAS, 41 for CEMAC, 21 for COMESA, and 22 for SADC. The potential decrease in tariff revenues is probably overstated. The study assumed complete implementation of EPAs by 2022, something that has not been achieved and will not be achieved in the near future. Nonetheless, even small decreases in tariff revenues can be a real concern if there are no new sources of revenues. In 2020, Cameroon suspended (temporarily) tariff reductions in the implementation of its EPA with the EU, citing a government revenue shortfall at the height of the Covid-19 pandemic, no less (Mbodiam and Andzongo, 2020). Cameroon used the situation also to push for more development aid from the EU.

Of course, the fear of losing tariff revenue must be weighed against the potential improvement of production efficiency and the increase in consumer surplus due to the lower prices of imports. A study by Vollmer et al. (2009) estimates the potential welfare effect of EPAs for Botswana, Cameroon, Côte d'Ivoire, Ghana, Kenya, Mozambique, Namibia, Tanzania, and Uganda. The study considers imports of products that are not produced domestically. Before the establishment of EPAs, these countries imported products from a partner country in a trading bloc and also from the "rest of the world." The rest of the world did not include the EU. Imports from a partner state were duty-free, but imports from the rest of the world were subject to tariffs. When the EU and ACP countries form EPAs, the EU would completely displace imports from "the rest of the world" and partially displace imports from partner states. The study finds the net welfare impact of EPAs—gain in consumer surplus minus government tariff revenues—to be positive for Botswana, Cameroon, and Namibia and zero or negligible for the other countries in the study.[17] They develop their analysis by emphasizing the need to protect infant industries that have the potential to grow and mature and become less dependent on protection.

This policy recommendation, which is not new by any means, is supported by the results of an ex-post empirical study (which examines the actual resultant impact of EPAs) by Frederik et al. (2021). The study shows that the provisional EPAs have caused imports of agricultural products from the EU to increase by 41 percent for the ESA and 134 percent for SADC. In the manufacturing sector, the EPA did not have a noticeable impact on the ESA. However, in SADC, manufacturing imports from the EU increased by 28 percent. The infant industry argument is valid even without the benefit of empirical evidence. It is borne out of a compelling argument that developing countries can gain comparative advantage in some products, given protection and the time to mature. Of course, the caveat is that it can be hard to identify viable infant industries, and removing protection in the future can be difficult. Nonetheless, it is the easiest argument to make, particularly when an EPA is between a group of developed countries and a group of developing countries.

At the same time, it should have been anticipated that the nonreciprocal market access that the EU provided discriminately to its former colonies was going to end, sooner or later. Undoubtedly, the WTO rules and the adoption of the Dispute Settlement Understanding (Annex 2 of the WTO Agreement) were the forces behind the end of the EU discriminatory, favorable trade policy toward the ACP countries. However, even way back in 1957, when the Treaty of Rome was signed to establish the European Economic Community (EEC), the EEC's territories and associates were expected to progressively eliminate duties on trade among themselves and also on goods originating from the EEC Member States (European Economic Community, 1957: Articles 131–133). For various reasons—economic, political, and strategic—the EU did not push hard for reciprocity, until it was backed by strong WTO rules.

Notwithstanding some progress that has been made in establishing EPAs, overall they have put trade relations between ACP countries and the EU in a state of confusion and of "wait and see." It was assumed erroneously that all ACP countries would sign up for EPAs, rather than first determining which countries actually wanted to be part of this new relationship. Promises of development assistance, nostalgic historical trade relations, and the eagerness to complete EPA negotiations by the end of 2007 jump-started the process without careful consideration of its potential impact.

The grouping of African ACP countries was not congruent with regional economic blocs in Africa, as discussed above in the section about "Challenges." Yet it is hard to conceive of any grouping that would have matched regional economic blocs, given that African countries belong to multiple regional blocs. In other words, regional economic integration in Africa is in a state of flux, even without these new relationships with the EU and the UK (Mshomba, 2017). Although the EPAs were supposed to enhance regional integration, they have, inadvertently, become another source of friction within and between African regional blocs, as each country focuses on its own interests.

For informed decisions, African countries must always start first with clear economic goals, independent of what the challenges and actual means might be to achieve them. Among those goals should be increased export diversity, expanded backward and forward linkages in production, and increased productivity. These and many other goals would inform countries regarding comprehensive and coherent economic strategies, domestic policies, and trade partnerships to be pursued, and they would avoid the compartmentalization of economic policies. Instead, oftentimes, African countries act the other way around. An agreement is sought first and then they try to figure out how it would support economic development.

The fundamental problem with EPAs is that negotiations are not between equal partners. Negotiations are driven mostly by the EU. If the ACP countries are the ones who stand to lose the most (for example, by forfeiting market access) if EPAs are not established, they should be the ones driving the negotiations. Instead, many have become reactive and opportunists for development aid. That is not a secure path to sustainable economic development.

CONCLUDING REMARKS ON EPA NEGOTIATIONS

The negotiations between the EU and African, Caribbean, and Pacific (ACP) countries to establish Economic Partnership Agreements (EPAs) brought or at least revealed divisions, rather than unity, in African regional blocs. Notwithstanding that most African countries belong to multiple regional economic blocs, in many instances there is a mismatch between those blocs and negotiating groups. The diversity of countries in each bloc makes negotiations very difficult, if not next to impossible. In trying to deal with those differences, in some customs unions, such as the East African Community (EAC) and the Economic and Monetary Community of Central Africa (CEMAC), individual countries have negotiated with the EU separately. Needless to say, that approach is bound to create constant tension in those blocs. A key feature of a customs union is its common external tariffs, something that will not be possible if individual countries are establishing trade agreements separately.

The African Continental Free Trade Area (AfCFTA) that was established in 2018 came into force in 2021 (Ighobor, 2022). An overly optimistic view would hold that as AfCFTA matures, African countries will be able to negotiate as a group and use their unity as leverage. While the establishment of AfCFTA is an important achievement, a more realistic view is that it will not be able to negotiate an EPA as a coalition anytime soon. If even small groups of countries, custom unions, no less, are not able to negotiate as coalitions, how can fifty-four countries negotiate a free trade area with the EU? Negotiating an EPA is complex and, invariably, there will be many instances where countries will have divergent interests. Add to the challenge the fact that some countries are too fragile to be able to participate in negotiations effectively. Needless to say, the element of "divide and conquer," which is what produced these divisions to begin with, is still alive today, though in subtle ways (Chimanikire, 2019).

Part of the problem with economic blocs in Africa, and AfCFTA itself, is that they are not what they claim to be. Clearly, if AfCFTA were a genuine free trade area, many regional economic blocs would be redundant.[18] Note that even in the WTO, the African group has not always been able to speak with one voice, except through some very general statements. Negotiating an EPA is a long, complex, and arduous process. A weak coalition will always split up along the way.

The way by which EPAs were to be established was misguided from the very beginning, at least with regard to African countries in the ACP group. It gave the EU the role of convincing ACP countries to enter into these agreements, rather than having ACP countries seek these partnerships on their own volition. The EU even promised financial assistance to countries or groups willing to form EPAs, in effect, as a way to twist their arms.

After agreeing on the duration of the Cotonou Agreement, a better approach would have been for the EU to simply declare its openness to EPAs, but to leave the ACP countries to initiate negotiations, based on their own interests. This would have given ACP countries the freedom and responsibility to determine the kind of economic relationship they wanted to maintain or pursue with the EU, if any. Most likely, African countries would have still worked through their economic blocs.

It is not too late for the EU simply to be an active participant, while letting African countries take the leadership role in pursuing negotiations, if they desire to form EPAs with the EU. African countries knew, or at least should have known, that the nonreciprocal preferential trade arrangements that they were privileged to have under the Yaoundé and Lomé conventions had to come to an end at some point. They should now figure out what they want on their own. This would not be a matter of Europe neglecting Africa. Rather, it would be an acknowledgment that African countries can and should make their own decisions, even if they end up making mistakes in doing so.

The situation is different with respect to the nonreciprocal preferential trade arrangements (like the GSP programs, the EU's Everything But Arms program, and the U.S. African Growth and Opportunity Act) that continue to exist, in which African countries are among the beneficiary countries. These arrangements are controlled by the preference-giving countries and, therefore, African countries have very limited negotiating power, as discussed in the following two chapters.

4 THE GENERALIZED SYSTEM OF PREFERENCES AND OTHER PREFERENTIAL PROGRAMS

THE NONRECIPROCAL PREFERENTIAL TRADE ARRANGEMENT between the European Union and the African, Caribbean, and Pacific (ACP) countries had a certain uniqueness to it because of the colonial legacy. This arrangement was not consistent with the *most favored nation* (MFN) principle under the General Agreement on Tariffs and Trade (GATT). Nonetheless, it served as a prototype for the Generalized System of Preferences (GSP) programs and similar, nonreciprocal preferential trade arrangements. Some, including the EU Everything But Arms (EBA) program and the U.S. African Growth and Opportunity Act (AGOA), are of special interest to many Sub-Saharan African countries. The continuation of these programs is not guaranteed, but so far, they have always been renewed, sometimes after a lingering period of uncertainty.

THE GSP PROGRAMS

The GSP, broadly speaking, are programs under which developed countries provide preferential market access to products originating in developing countries. The GSP was established in 1971 under the auspices of GATT, and it continues to operate under the World Trade

Organization (WTO). The WTO replaced GATT in 1995. As of 2023, the WTO had 164 member countries, representing 98 percent of global trade, and 25 countries with observer status.[1]

As early as the 1950s, a decade before most African countries got their independence, there had been loud and persistent complaints from developing countries that the multilateral trading system under GATT was not friendly to developing countries, at best, and exploitative and fashioned only to extract natural resources, at worst. When GATT was established in 1947, African countries were only appendages to their European colonizers. The challenges of developing countries were discussed as if they were incidental, with no clear, demonstrated long-term commitment to the advancement of the economies of those countries.

Two sectors—agriculture and textiles—that had the potential to be catalysts for economic development for developing countries were kept out of the jurisdiction of GATT. Developed countries treated those sectors as sensitive and exceptional and, therefore, demanded that domestic policy take precedence over multilateral trade policy.[2] They protected the agricultural sector with tariffs, quotas, and production and export subsidies. The textile industry was insulated by the Multi-Fiber Arrangement (MFA) under which developed countries set tariffs and quotas for textiles and apparel imported from developing countries. It should be pointed out, however, that it is not clear that the MFA quotas actually hurt Sub-Saharan African countries. These countries had very low capacity to produce textile and apparel at the time and most of them could not even meet the quotas set for them. Nonetheless, overall, the MFA held back the economic development of developing countries that were looking to expand their textile industry as a stepping-stone to industrialization. The United Nations Conference on Trade and Development (UNCTAD) characterized the MFA as "a major contradiction of the basic principle of GATT" (UNCTAD, 1994: 129).

In the late 1950s, GATT formed committees to examine the complaints from developing countries and the trade barriers in developed countries (Wells, 1969). Among the findings was that developed countries had:

high tariffs and tariffs which differentiated disproportionately in favour of imports of raw materials, as compared to processed goods as constituting serious barriers to exports of less-developed countries, particularly with respect to vegetable oils, coffee, tea, cocoa products, manufactures of jute, of cotton and of coir, and certain other manufactured consumer goods. The Committee was convinced that a reduction of these barriers would be of considerable assistance to less-developed countries. (GATT, 1962: 2)

In addition:

the Committee identified quantitative restrictions as one of the most serious barriers confronting the exports of less-developed countries. The report noted that exports from less-developed countries of such important products as vegetable seeds and oils, coffee, raw cotton, tobacco, tropical timber, manufactures of jute, of cotton and of coir, and sewing machines, were often adversely affected by quantitative import restrictions which were sometimes applied in a discriminatory manner. (GATT, 1962: 3)

Among those who argued forcefully for the restructuring of the global trading system was an Argentine economist, Raul Prebisch. He was the first secretary general of UNCTAD, established in 1964 primarily to represent and advocate for the interests of developing countries. In his first report to UNCTAD, Prebisch made a formal proposal for the institution of preferential trade arrangements (United Nations, 1964). The case for these arrangements was made using, in part, the infant-industry argument. This is an argument often used by developing countries to justify protection of industries that have the potential to grow and compete at the global level. It is not an argument against trade; rather, it is an argument that acknowledges that comparative advantage is dynamic. The rational extension of that argument as UNCTAD presented it was that, "if infant industries [in developing countries] need protection in the domestic market because of high costs, they obviously need even more protection in foreign markets, whether developed or developing, in the form of preferential treatment" (United Nations, 1964: 66). The argument is particularly strong considering economies of scale, which can only be taken advantage of in a large market. In their infancy, when firms are small, their average costs are very high. To grow and be able to survive competition, they must produce more to spread their fixed costs, and that may need protection and foreign markets.[3]

UNCTAD's persistent advocacy for developing countries led GATT to make a fundamental exception to the *most favored nation* (MFN) principle with a temporary waiver, in 1971, and to officially establish the GSP program (U.S. International Trade Commission, 1979: 228). The waiver to the MFN principle was made permanent in 1979 at the conclusion of the Tokyo Round of GATT, by an enabling clause titled "Differential and More Favourable Treatment, Reciprocity and Fuller Participation of Developing Countries," which states that, "Notwithstanding the provisions of Article I of the General Agreement, contracting parties may accord differential and more favourable treatment to developing countries, without according such treatment to other contracting parties" (GATT, 1979: 1). The GSP program has since remained a main feature of the multilateral trading system in the WTO.

It is important to understand that the GSP "program" is not a collective program in which preference-giving countries join together to give uniform preferential treatment. There are actually several GSP programs, as shown in Table 4.1.[4] In addition to the GSP programs, there are other special trade arrangements that give nonreciprocal, preferential trade treatment to African countries. These include AGOA, between the U.S. and Sub-Saharan African countries, and a number of preferential tariff schemes that are specific for least developed countries (LDCs), notably, the EBA program. To the extent that these LDC-specific schemes are beneficial, the African continent is the main potential beneficiary. According to the United Nations reports, as of 2023, there were 46 LDCs, 72 percent of them—33 countries—in Africa.

What is common about these preferential trade arrangements is that they are nonreciprocal in nature and that they are not entitlements. Countries, particularly developed countries, are encouraged and expected to establish them, but they are not required to do so. Therefore, it is not surprising that each GSP program has its own depth and breadth of preference and its own set of requirements. Most GSP

TABLE 4.1. Preferential trade programs

Preference Provider	Type of Preferential Program	Starting Date
Armenia	GSP	April 6, 2016
Australia	GSP	January 1, 1974
Belarus	GSP	January 1, 2010
Canada	GSP	July 1, 1974
European Union	GSP	July 1, 1971
	GSP Plus	January 1, 2006
	Everything But Arms (LDC-specific)	March 5, 2001
Iceland	GSP	January 22, 2002
Japan	GSP	August 1, 1971
Kazakhstan	GSP	January 1, 2010
Kyrgyz Republic	GSP	April 6, 2016
	LDC-specific	March 29, 2006
New Zealand	GSP	January 1, 1972
Norway	GSP	October 1, 1971
Russia	GSP	January 1, 2010
Switzerland	GSP	March 1, 1972
Turkey	GSP	January 1, 2002
United Kingdom	GSP	July 1, 1971
	GSP Plus	January 1, 2006
	Everything But Arms (LDC-specific)	March 5, 2001
United States	GSP	January 1, 1976
	AGOA (Sub-Saharan African-specific)	May 18, 2000
Chile	LDC-specific	February 28, 2014
China	LDC-specific	July 1, 2010
Chinese Taipei (Taiwan)	LDC-specific	December 17, 2003
India	LDC-specific	August 13, 2008
Korea, Republic of	LDC-specific	January 1, 2000
Montenegro	LDC-specific	January 1, 2017
Morocco	African LDC-specific	January 1, 2001
Tajikistan	LDC-specific	October 25, 2003
Thailand	LDC-specific	April 9, 2015

Sources: WTO database on preferential trade arrangements and reports by individual programs.

programs provide more generous preference to products originating in LDCs than from other developing countries.

AN OVERVIEW OF THE PREFERENTIAL TRADE PROGRAMS
OF CHINA, THE EU, AND THE U.S.

There are several reasons for focusing on the programs of China, the EU, and the U.S. Since the late 1970s, when China started to reform its economy and move away from the command system toward managed capitalism, China has increasingly become an important trade partner for many African countries. This is especially the case for African countries endowed with natural resources, such as oil and copper. The value of China-Africa trade grew from $10 billion in 2002 to an annual average of $175 billion from 2015 to 2018.[5] When China joined the WTO in 2001, it immediately started to offer preferential trade arrangements to LDCs with which it had diplomatic relations. China is the world's second largest economy, after the U.S., so its trade policies are consequential.

The EU and the U.S. are important markets for African products and, of course, there is a long history between the EU and Africa, as discussed in Chapter 2. The EU and the U.S. have unique preferential trade programs that are of special relevance to African countries. In addition, much more information is available on the EU and U.S. programs than other programs. Moreover, most of what can be learned with respect to these three programs is applicable to other similar programs.

Table 4.2 provides a summary of key elements of a few other selected preferential trade arrangements that are most relevant to African countries. It is important to note that the table only provides a general overview. Within each element and each country, some specific details and caveats make these programs more different than they might appear in general. For example, in Japan's scheme, LDCs are only those countries that are classified as such by the United Nations (UN). Australia's scheme treats some developing countries that are not LDCs as if they were. Every program has specific rules of origin for textile and apparel that can be very complicated, as illustrated by this convoluted excerpt about the Canadian rule of origin regarding textile and apparel from LDCs.

Apparel products are deemed originating in an LDC if they are assembled in an LDC from fabric cut in that country or in Canada, or from parts knit to shape, provided the fabric, or the parts knit to shape, are produced in any of the following countries:

a. Any LDC or Canada from yarns originating in an LDC, a [General Preferential Tariff] GPT beneficiary country or Canada, provided the yarns or fabric do not undergo further processing outside an LDC or Canada; or

b. A GPT beneficiary country from yarns originating in an LDC, a GPT beneficiary country or Canada, provided (i) The yarns and fabric do not undergo further processing outside an LDC, a GPT beneficiary country or Canada; (ii) the value of any materials, including packing, that are used in the manufacture of the goods and that originate outside the LDC in which the goods are assembled is no more than 75 per cent of the ex-factory price of the goods as packed for shipment to Canada. For the purpose of this subparagraph, any materials used in the manufacture or production of the goods referred to in that subparagraph that originate from Canada are deemed to have originated in the LDC. (UNCTAD, 2013: xvi)

All preferential trade arrangements include the following fundamental elements:

i.   criteria for country eligibility;
ii.   criteria for product coverage;
iii. duration of the program;
iv.   domestic content rule-of-origin requirements; and
v.   documentation requirements.

All of these elements are set independently by each individual preference-giving country or customs union. Some preference-giving

TABLE 4.2. Summary of key elements of selected preferential trade programs

Preference Provider	Preferential Trade Arrangement	Country eligibility	Product Coverage	Domestic content rule-of-origin requirement for products that are wholly produced in the beneficiary country	Expiration of the current program (typical duration)
Australia	GSP	Low-income to upper-middle income economies	• duty-and-quota-free access for all products originating in the LDCs • 98.2% of the tariff lines are duty-free	• final stage of manufacturing process conducted in the beneficiary country • 50% (25% for LDCs) of the value added must come from the beneficiary country • bilateral and developed-countries cumulation	not specified
Canada	GSP	Low-income to middle-income economies	• duty-free for all products originating in LDCs except for dairy, poultry, and egg products	• 60% (40% for LDCs) of the value added must come from the beneficiary country • bilateral and developed-countries cumulation	December 2024 (10 years)

(continued)

Preference Provider	Preferential Trade Arrangement	Country eligibility	Product Coverage	Domestic content rule-of-origin requirement for products that are wholly produced in the beneficiary country	Expiration of the current program (typical duration)
Japan	GSP	Low-income to upper-middle income economies	• duty-free for most products originating in LDCs	• imported inputs must be transformed enough to result in a different tariff heading at the four-digit level • specific requirements for some products	March 2031 (10 years)
Korea, Republic of	LDC-specific		• duty-free for 93% of tariff lines	• 40% of the value added must come from the beneficiary country • bilateral cumulation	not specified

Sources: Canada Gazette, 2013; UNCTAD, 2013; UNCTAD, 2017a; UNCTAD, 2018a; and UNCTAD, 2020.

countries also establish conditions for the beneficiaries, for example, regarding labor laws or intellectual property rights protection.

i. Criteria for Country Eligibility

The most important criterion for a country to be eligible for preferential trade policy under a GSP program is that it must be a developing country. For the most part, this excludes countries that are classified as upper-middle-income or above.

There are some slight variations on how preference-giving countries decide which countries are to be considered "developing" countries. Different GSP programs apply different levels of economic development to determine when preference-receiving countries graduate and, thus, are removed from the program. Some GSP programs have requirements for partial graduation. Partial graduation involves excluding certain products from the list of GSP-eligible countries when a country reaches a certain economic development threshold.

a. China

China is a middle-income country, and its GSP program is only for LDCs with which it has diplomatic relations. As of 2015, there were three LDCs in Africa, Burkina Faso, Gambia, and São Tomé and Principe, that did not have diplomatic relations with China because of their ties to Taiwan. However, in 2016, Gambia and São Tomé and Principe severed ties with Taiwan and established diplomatic relations with China. In 2019, Burkina Faso did likewise. China's program extends duty-free, quota-free access to eligible products from eligible countries.

b. EU

All low-income and lower-middle-income economies are eligible for GSP benefits. However, the EU has different types of preferential trade arrangements. In 2001, the EU restructured its GSP program to introduce five different programs, each with its own criteria for country eligibility: (i) the general GSP scheme; (ii) two GSP schemes linked to labor rights and environmental standards for additional preferences; (iii) a GSP scheme linked to combating drug production and trafficking; and (iv) Everything But Arms, a special scheme for LDCs.

A country graduates if it is classified as high-income or upper-middle-income for three consecutive years (UNCTAD, 2015: 6). The graduation requirements are revised occasionally. The last major revision was done in 2014. That revision led the number of beneficiary countries to fall from 177 to 88 (UNCTAD, 2015: 6).

Because of the subjective nature of some of the criteria and discretion in enforcing them, there exists real potential for the preference-giving countries to provide preference in a discriminatory fashion, thus violating the spirit of the MFN principle. In 2002, India brought a case against the EU, challenging its GSP scheme that was linked to combating drug production and trafficking (DS246).[6]

India argued that the tariff preference offered by this special arrangement discriminately benefited Pakistan, India's major competitor in textiles and apparel. India further argued that the scheme was inconsistent with the enabling clause that established the legality of GSP programs. While the ruling of the WTO was only partially in favor of India, it was enough to make the EU revise its GSP schemes to conform to the WTO rules.[7] Specifically, the EU replaced the schemes that were linked to labor rights, environmental standards, and combating drug production and trafficking with the GSP+ (European Commission, 2005).

The GSP+ is EU's special incentive arrangement under which beneficiary countries can receive additional preferential treatment if they have ratified twenty-seven international conventions—seven on human rights, eight on labor rights, eight on the environment and climate, and four on good governance—and are making a genuine effort to implement them (European Union, 2012: Annex VIII). Notwithstanding the reports required from the beneficiary countries and the monitoring system applied by the EU, the determination for eligibility can be highly subjective. As it is, the beneficiary countries have very different standings on human freedom, as the Human Freedom Index

(HFI) suggests (Vásquez et al., 2021). As of 2022, there were only eight GSP+ beneficiaries—Bolivia, Cabo Verde, Kyrgyzstan, Mongolia, Pakistan, the Philippines, Sri Lanka, and Uzbekistan (European Commission, 2019; Liuima, 2022). Armenia and Paraguay were removed from the GSP+ program in 2018 and 2022, respectively, after being classified as upper-middle-income countries.

It is not surprising that only a few countries are beneficiaries of the GSP+ program. Potential beneficiary countries must initiate the process by applying to the EU for consideration. It is likely that because of the conditionalities, some countries simply do not want to be in the spotlight and face scrutiny for human rights violations and a wide range of other violations. Sri Lanka was removed from the EU's GSP+ in 2010 for violating human rights. It was allowed back in 2017 when it was determined that Sri Lanka was making effective efforts to improve governance and respect for human rights (European Commission, 2017).

With respect to Africa, thirty-three countries are LDCs and, thus, benefit from the EBA program, which is even more generous than the GSP+ and has fewer conditionalities. The EBA program removes quotas and tariffs on all products, except for weapons and ammunitions. As discussed in Chapters 2 and 3, during the GATT era, the EU had a special preferential trade arrangement for African, Caribbean, and Pacific (ACP) countries. However, in 1997, the WTO ruled that this arrangement was inconsistent with the MFN principle, since the EU did not extend the preferential treatment to all developing countries, but only to the EU's former colonies. In order to comply with the WTO rules, the EU sought to establish Economic Partnership Agreements (EPAs) with the ACP countries, as discussed in Chapter 3. But the EU was also aware that the process to establish EPAs with all 79 ACP countries would be long and arduous. To be sure that its preferential trade treatment, at least for the LDCs, was not interrupted, in 2001 it created the EBA. In 2001, 49 countries were LDCs, of which 39 were ACP countries.

As McQueen (2002) points out, even before the EBA was established, LDCs already had duty-free, quota-free access to the EU market for all manufactured and agricultural products, except for fresh bananas, rice, and sugar. The EBA paved the way for the gradual removal of all duties and quota limits on those products, a process that was completed in 2008.

A country that graduates from the LDC classification has a transitional period of at least three years before it loses its EBA eligibility. Cabo Verde was removed from the EBA program in 2010, but it is a beneficiary in the GSP+ program. Equatorial Guinea was removed from the EBA in 2021 and São Tomé and Principe will be removed in 2024. Angola was initially scheduled to graduate from the LDC classification in 2021, but it was given an extension of three years for that status (United Nations, 2020: 9; United Nations Economic and Social Council, 2021). Given the EBA program, the GSP+, and the free trade arrangements the EU has with a number of African countries, only three African countries—Kenya, Nigeria, and the Republic of Congo—are in the EU's general GSP program, as shown in Table 1.

Except for Cote d'Ivoire, Equatorial Guinea, Gabon, and Libya, all African countries are beneficiaries of either the EU's general GSP program, GSP+, or EBA, or have special trade agreements with the EU.

c. U.S.

All developing countries, that is, all low-income and middle-income countries, are eligible for U.S. GSP benefits. There is mandatory graduation once a country advances into the "high-income" classification (Office of the U.S. Trade Representative, Executive Office of the President, 2018). Seychelles was eliminated from the U.S. GSP in 2017 when it became a high-income country (The White House, 2015).

In addition to using GNI per capita as a criterion, the U.S. uses other criteria to determine country eligibility. The U.S. GSP program prohibits the president from extending eligibility to countries that (i) are communist; (ii) collude with other countries to limit the supply of resources into the world market; (iii) provide preferential trade treatment to another developed country to the disadvantage of the U.S.; (iv) violate intellectual property rights of U.S. companies; (v) have nullified existing agreements of U.S. companies; (vi) provide sanctuary to international terrorists; (vii) violate worker rights; or (viii) use child labor (Congressional Research Service, 2019: 10–11). In general, the U.S. president has the discretion to terminate GSP benefits to a country based on just about anything with which the U.S. may not be satisfied. But this is not unique to the U.S. All preference-giving countries have great latitude because offering preferential trade treatment is optional, not an obligation.

Apart from the GSP program, the U.S. has a special program for Sub-Saharan African countries, AGOA. Through AGOA, products from those countries can enter the U.S. market duty-free. AGOA was introduced in the U.S. House of Representatives just three years after the WTO had replaced GATT. This is notable because the establishment of the WTO promised adherence to the MFN principle and close monitoring and enforcement of multilateral trade rules. Yet, in principle, what was being proposed by the U.S. was a nongeneralized system of preferences that was to benefit specific countries based on geography (Moss, 2006). While Sub-Saharan African countries met the distinction of being "developing countries" and, in fact, most are "least developed countries," AGOA targeted countries in a specific region rather than those with specific economic conditions. It is also interesting that AGOA was being proposed precisely at a time when the EU was under pressure to end its discriminatory relationships with the ACP countries. The pressure was coming, no less, from the U.S. and Central American countries who, together, were complainants in the infamous banana case in the WTO. Yet, the debate over the AGOA proposal remained pretty much a domestic affair, without any serious opposition from the WTO. Perhaps this was because Europe, which was often quick to point out trade violations committed by the U.S., did not have the "moral" authority to criticize the U.S., given its own history with the ACP countries. In addition, AGOA was presented as a development program for a region that at the time was being ravaged by the HIV/AIDS epidemic. Europe would have appeared uncaring to criticize such a program at the time.

AGOA became operational in 2000 (as AGOA I) before the U.S. even bothered to apply for a waiver from the WTO. It was not until 2015 that the U.S. submitted a request for a waiver to the WTO (World Trade Organization, 2015). The waiver was granted. While AGOA aims to promote investment in Sub-Saharan Africa and more openness in trade, fundamentally, it is a more favorable extension of the GSP program to Sub-Saharan Africa.

The minimum criterion for eligibility is that a country must be in the Sub-Saharan African region. Eligibility for the GSP program is a prerequisite, but not a sufficient condition. Eligibility criteria for AGOA build on those for the GSP program and call for poverty reduction policies. For example, AGOA countries are required to have made or to be making continual progress toward establishing "economic policies to reduce poverty, increase the availability of health care and educational opportunities, expand physical infrastructure, promote the development of private enterprise, and encourage the formation of capital markets through micro-credit or other programs" (U.S. Congress, 2000: 4).

Only 34 of 48 Sub-Saharan African countries were designated as AGOA beneficiaries in 2000. Because of the subjective nature of many of the eligibility criteria and the fact that the U.S. has full discretion to determine adherence, the number of AGOA beneficiaries changes almost every year. At no point have all Sub-Saharan African countries been designated as beneficiaries.

It is worth noting that the EU's program that was linked to combating drug production and trafficking was actually modeled on the U.S. program called the Andean Trade Preference Act (ATPA). The ATPA was established in 1991 to provide duty-free access for certain products originating in Bolivia, Colombia, Ecuador, and Peru as a strategy to have producers of illicit drugs in those countries shift to producing other crops, such as cut flowers. In 2002, this initiative took a more determined approach to combating the production of drugs through trade, and ATPA was rebranded to become the Andean Trade Promotion and Drug Eradication Act (ATPDEA) (U.S. International Trade Commission, 2013).

Neither the ATPA nor the ATPDEA was challenged by any member of the WTO. India, which brought a case against the EU for establishing a similar program, did so only because that particular program benefited India's neighbor and trade rival, Pakistan. In the WTO, a country does not file a complaint simply because a member country has violated the MFN principle or breached an obligation; the complainant must also demonstrate that the infringement causes an adverse effect on its economy. India could make that argument with respect to the EU's program, but not the U.S.'s program. Nonetheless, even without a case against it, the ATPDEA ended in 2013 after the U.S. established free trade area agreements with Peru and Colombia that went into effect in 2009 and 2012, respectively.

ii. Criteria for Product Coverage

Preference-giving countries have complete discretion with respect to products eligible for their GSP programs. In all GSP programs, the tariff preference on different products varies, depending on the sensitivity of the products to the preference-giving country.

a. China

China has gradually increased the number of products that are eligible to the point where it reached 97 percent of all tariff lines in 2015. "Excluded tariff lines mostly concern automobile, paper and timber products." Also excluded are "chemical fertilizers, corn, raw cotton, rice, sugar, wheat, wool and wool fiber" (UNCTAD, 2016a: 4).

b. EU

The general EU GSP program has duty reductions for two-thirds of the product lines. Those products face zero duties if they originate from the beneficiaries of the GSP+ program. Of course, what matters to any specific preference-receiving country are the products that are actually produced by that country. All imports, except arms, from EBA beneficiary countries enter the EU duty-free and quota-free.

The EU product graduation is applied to a *combined nomenclature* (CN), that is, groups of similar products based on product classification codes.[8]

Products classified in one CN face the same external tariff and graduate together. A group of products from a beneficiary country graduates from the EU GSP program if imports of those goods exceed 17.5 percent (14.5 percent for textile and apparel) of the total imports of the same products from all GSP beneficiary countries for three consecutive years. Prior to the GSP review in 2014, the thresholds were 15 percent, in general, and 12.5 percent for textile and apparel (European Commission, 2015: 11). GSP+ and EBA beneficiaries are exempted from product graduation.

c. U.S.

The U.S. GSP excludes the following: textile and apparel articles; watches; import-sensitive electronic articles; import-sensitive steel articles; footwear, handbags, luggage, flat goods, work gloves and leather wearing apparel; import-sensitive semimanufactured and manufactured glass products; any agricultural product that is subject to a tariff-rate quota, if entered in a quantity in excess of the in-quota quantity for such product; and any other articles which the president determines to be import-sensitive in the context of the GSP (U.S. International Trade Commission, 2020: 13). LDCs enjoy a broader range of products that are GSP-eligible.

AGOA beneficiaries are spared from the exclusions just mentioned above. However, to be eligible for apparel benefits, they must have "visa systems" and verification procedures that can effectively prevent illegal transshipment—trade deflection (U.S. Congress, 2000: 13–16; U.S. Trade Representative, 2016). This requirement stemmed from legitimate concerns that apparel could be deflected from Asia to the U.S. through African countries. In 2023, 24 of the 36 AGOA beneficiaries were also eligible for apparel benefits (Congressional Research Service, 2023).

The U.S. GSP program imposes ceilings called Competitive Need Limitations (CNLs) on all GSP eligible products, except for those originating in LDCs or AGOA countries. The ceilings are measured in percentage terms and in absolute terms. Whichever ceiling is reached first is the one applied. A beneficiary country loses its GSP eligibility on a given product if U.S. imports of that product from that country "(1) account for 50 percent or more of the value of total U.S. imports of that product; or (2) exceed a certain dollar value. In accordance with the GSP statute, the dollar-value limit is increased by $5 million annually; the 2019 limit is $190 million" (U.S. Trade Representative, 2019: 9).

The rationale behind CNLs is that if a beneficiary country has reached those ceilings, then it is competitive enough and should not continue to rely on preferential treatment. The U.S. also wants to avoid being too dependent on a single supplier for any given product. A country whose product is subject to a CNL can request a waiver. While granting a waiver is a discretionary decision, the following factors support a waiver: the country is reasonably open to U.S. products, the country is committed to protecting U.S. intellectual property rights, and the total value of U.S. imports of a product are *de minimis*, that is, very small. The *de minimis* level in 2019 was $24.5 million and is adjusted every year in increments of $500,000 (U.S. Trade Representative, 2019: 10). African countries have not been impacted by the U.S. GSP ceilings.

iii. Duration of GSP Programs

There is no single GSP program that has been terminated altogether. While they are all temporary by their nature or design, they are renewable.

a. China

China's scheme does not specify any duration. It can be considered "temporary" only due to the fact that it is voluntary and can be suspended at will.

b. EU

The EU GSP program was established in 1971 and was good for ten years. In 1981, it was renewed for another ten-year period. In 1991, when it was up for renewal for another period, the Uruguay Round of negotiations under GATT were under way. Many agreements were under negotiation and, therefore, to be sure that the GSP program would align with the final agreements, the GSP program was extended only up to 1994 (European Commission, 2015).[9] From then on, while still subject to frequent reviews and amendments, the EU GSP program has been renewed for ten-year periods. The current GSP scheme expires December 31, 2023 (European Union, 2012). There is no set time for expiration of the EBA, so unless there is a major shift in the thinking about preferential trade, it may remain for decades.

c. U.S.

When the U.S. GSP program was established in 1974, it was authorized for ten years. It was renewed in 1984 for another nine years, but since then, renewals have been for shorter periods, with the longest one being for four years (2002–6). From 1993 to 2020, the U.S. GSP has been renewed thirteen times, sometimes for just a year. The most recent reauthorization came into effect in April 2018 and expired December 31, 2020 (Congressional Research Service, 2019: 32–33; 2022: 1). It is often the case that reauthorization of the U.S. GSP program does not happen on time, although each time it has expired, reauthorization has been retroactive.

To understand these apparently reluctant renewals, it is important to note that in 1990, the U.S. adopted a "pay-as-you-go" budget rule. In this attempt to have a balanced budget, any legislation that increases spending on entitlements, or decreases revenue, has to be offset by another measure (UNCTAD, 2016b: 28). Each time the GSP program comes up for reauthorization, the Congress must identify other programs through which it can increase revenue or decrease spending, no matter how small the forgone tariff revenues might be.

In relative terms, the forgone tariff revenues have been less than one percent of the total customs duties. For example, it was estimated that for three years, 2018–20, the US GSP program would decrease tariff revenues by an annual average of $438 million (Congressional Budget Office, 2018). Total customs duties for the 2018–19 fiscal year were $72.7 billion. Customs duties themselves were only 2 percent of the total government revenues (Department of the Treasury, 2019, 55). Nonetheless, the GSP program is not immune from the complexity that comes with the pay-as-you-go budgetary rule. Just like many other programs, it gets caught up in the politics that are inevitable when you have this type of budgetary rule. This budgetary constraint is the main reason discussions for reauthorization of the GSP scheme are protracted and why renewals are only for a short period. It did not help that international trade came under sharp attack by President Donald Trump (Bown and Kolb, 2020). In short, the U.S. GSP program is less predictable than the EU's program.

AGOA, phase I, was initially set to expire in 2008, but it was renewed in 2004 to 2015 and again in 2015 to 2025, as AGOA V. In between were AGOA II-IV, all targeted at expanding eligibility for textiles and apparel (U.S. International Trade Commission AGOA, 2014: 34–36). After four years of negotiations, in 2009, the U.S. was granted a waiver by the WTO for AGOA. That waiver was renewed in 2015 and extended to 2025.

iv. Domestic Content Rule-of-Origin Requirements

Preferential trade arrangements have the potential to be abused through trade deflection, similar to what can happen in free trade areas. A product can be exported from a non-GSP beneficiary country to a GSP beneficiary country and then re-exported to the preference-giving country, as if it originated from the GSP beneficiary country. Thus, all GSP programs include "rules of origin." A general rule is that preference-giving countries require products to be exported directly from the preference-receiving country. Beyond that, since each GSP program is independent, the rules of origin for different programs vary. A producer in a developing country wanting to export to different GSP markets must abide by different rules of origin, except for the EU, Norway, Switzerland, and Turkey, who have the same rules. These GSP programs operate as if they were one.[10]

a. China

To be eligible, products must be wholly obtained or "substantially transformed" in the preference-receiving country. Wholly obtained products include live animals born and raised in the beneficiary country, products obtained from those live animals, agricultural products harvested in the beneficiary country, fish caught in the country's territorial waters, fish caught outside the country's territorial waters but using its vessels, and all goods produced exclusively using these products, "used and waste goods generated in the course of consumption in the beneficiary country and collected for recycling purposes, and waste scraps for recycling purposes generated in the manufacturing process in the beneficiary country" (UNCTAD, 2016a: 6).

Different sets of rules are used to determine the country of origin for products that are not wholly produced in the beneficiary country. For a few products, specific rules are used to determine their originating status. For the majority of products, "substantially transformed" is accomplished when (a) the transformation of inputs acquired from nonbeneficiary countries leads to final products with different tariff headings at the four-digit level and (b) at least 40 percent of the value added has taken place in the beneficiary country.

In 2017, in line with many other preferential trade arrangements, China added a cumulation provision (KPMG, 2017). There are two types of cumulation—bilateral, also known as "donor country content," and regional. Inputs imported directly from China and regional economic blocs in which a beneficiary country is a member are counted as originating in the beneficiary country.

b. EU

The EU's rules of origin have three criteria for products that are not "wholly obtained" from the originating country—change in harmonized tariff code, value added, and "specific process." The description for wholly obtained products includes that local seeds must have been used for agricultural and forestry products. "Even the smallest addition or input from any other country disqualifies a product from being 'wholly obtained'" (Economic Commission, 2019: 10).

Clearly, most manufactured products would not qualify as "wholly obtained." Globalization and specialization have created long and intricate supply chains where raw materials, parts, intermediate goods, and final products are crisscrossing national borders. The harmonized tariff code criterion requires that imported inputs be transformed enough for the final product to have a different harmonized tariff code. For example, a straw hat exported using imported straw material would meet this criterion because the harmonized tariff code for straw material is 1401, while the tariff code for a straw hat is 4602.

The value-added criterion requires that the value of imported materials does not exceed a certain percentage of the "ex-works" price of the product, that is, the price of a product before including shipping costs. The thresholds are different for different products, and for some products they are set in terms of value and weight. These thresholds are reviewed and adjusted periodically.

The "specific process" criterion requires that certain processes be conducted in the beneficiary country, for a product to receive the GSP tariff reduction. For example, for garments, the latest manufacturing process that a beneficiary country must conduct could be weaving, followed by subsequent processes.

The rules of origin under the EU GSP and EBA operate with cumulation provisions. There are four types of cumulation—bilateral, regional, cross-regional, and extended. Under bilateral cumulation, inputs produced in and imported from the EU, Norway, Switzerland, or Turkey count as originating in the preference-receiving country. Regional cumulation allows inputs produced and acquired from a free trade area to which a beneficiary country belongs to be counted as originating in the preference-receiving country. Bilateral and regional cumulation can be used in combination. Cross-regional cumulation is an extension of regional cumulation, treating neighboring free trade areas as if they were one. Extended cumulation allows inputs produced and imported from a country with which the EU has a free trade area to be counted as produced in the preference-receiving country. While these cumulation provisions make it easier for preference-receiving countries to meet the country-of-origin requirement, taking advantage of them is not simple. There are many variations in the domestic content requirement for different products, and documentation requirements can be cumbersome.

c. U.S.

For products that are not wholly produced in the beneficiary country, at least 35 percent of the value added must have taken place in the beneficiary country. Imported materials can be counted toward the 35 percent if they have been "substantially transformed" to acquire different names, character, and use (U.S. Trade Representative, 2019, 13). Similar to other GSP programs, the rules of origin in the U.S. GSP contain cumulation provisions. Regional associations are treated as one country. Inputs originating within the association can be counted toward the 35 percent. There are currently six regional associations to which the cumulation provision can be applied. Two of them are in Africa—the Southern African Development Community and the West African Economic and Monetary Union (UNCTAD, 2016b: 14).[11] An LDC in a recognized regional association is allowed to take advantage of the cumulation provision for products reserved for LDCs (for GSP eligibility), even if inputs originate from a non-LDC country.

The rules of origin applied to AGOA beneficiaries are more accommodating than those applied to GSP beneficiaries. The ones that apply to "general goods" (all products except textiles and apparel) include all cumulation of inputs from all Sub-Saharan African beneficiaries and a donor country content provision. Of the 35 percent minimum value added that is required, 15 percent of it may be inputs imported from the U.S. Textile and apparel that qualify for duty-free benefits under AGOA include apparel made using U.S. and third-country yarns and fabrics, that is, yarns and fabric "originating from anywhere in the world."[12] The provision for the third-country yarns and fabrics does not apply to South Africa.

v. Documentation Requirements

All international trade requires documentation for determination of custom duties and other practical purposes. Custom duties are applied to products depending on their identification (harmonized tariff codes), volume, originating countries, and importing countries. Documentation becomes even more critical since different products, and similar products imported from different countries, face different custom duties and other forms of taxes and trade barriers.

Every preference-receiving country must designate a competent authority to certify proof of country of origin. The certification process starts with the exporter applying for a certificate of origin and providing proof of origin and other specifications to the certifying authority. If certified by the designated authority, the documents are sent to the importer who has the ultimate responsibility to apply for preference benefits and provide the necessary documents to the customs authorities in their country (World Customs Organization, 2014). The amount of documentation and evidence varies among preference-giving countries. The EU and the U.S. require that supporting documents and all other records be kept for a period of at least three and five years, respectively (European Commission, 2016: 28; U.S. Trade Representative, 2019: 8).

PREFERENTIAL TRADE ARRANGEMENTS AND CONDITIONALITY

The nonreciprocal nature of the GSP and similar programs does not mean preference-giving countries offer them free of conditions. There are differences in conditionalities and safeguard measures, which, combined with all other features of preferential trade arrangements, show that it is the domestic conditions of and politics in the preference-giving countries that determine the parameters of these arrangements, not necessarily the conditions of the developing countries. Notwithstanding the benefits of freer trade, domestic producers who must compete with producers in developing countries are not enthusiastic about arrangements that reduce trade barriers, even when the competition is going to come only from small LDCs.

One of the shortcomings in how international economics is often taught is that international trade is presented as if it were an activity between nations, on a macro level, rather than between companies of different countries, on a micro level. Small countries are presented as price takers whose actions are inconsequential to the rest of the world. However, in reality, while an increase of imports of shirts by Walmart in the U.S. from a producer in Lesotho (a small country), for example, may not change the price of shirts in the world, it may have adverse effects on a small local supplier of shirts in the U.S. But then, one may ask, how much political influence do one or two small producers in the U.S. have? Not much, individually. However, in most countries, and certainly in advanced economies, producers in a given industry have associations that allow them to speak and lobby in unison and, therefore, with strength. In the late 1990s, when the establishment of AGOA was being hotly debated in the U.S., the projection at the time was that AGOA would reduce employment in the textiles and apparel industry in the U.S. by a minuscule amount—0.045 percent, 676 out of 1.5 million jobs (U.S. International Trade Commission, 1997). Yet the U.S. textile and apparel manufacturers were strongly opposed to AGOA, and it was only after assurance that the textile industry in Sub-Saharan Africa was not expected to grow much in the near future that the opposition mellowed.

Some conditions, therefore, are placed to appease domestic constituencies or as means to address a particular concern or interest. Kennedy (2011: 529) notes that

> [t]he overarching focus of some of the U.S. and EU GSP conditions appears to be more on the welfare of U.S. and EU nationals than it is on the economic welfare of persons living in the developing world.

The current system also gives preference-giving countries a great deal of leverage, even on matters that are only remotely related to trade. Undoubtedly, the greatest leverage these countries have is the fact that their favor to developing countries is voluntary.

The EU's offer of preferential trade arrangements for specific countries that are burdened by drug production and trafficking is an interesting case. It is not clear what makes this particular challenge more unique than others to justify some countries being singled out for preferential trade. If GSP programs were established to support countries based on very specific problems, there could be many more unique GSP programs, each for a single trade partner, since it is possible to find many countries with unique economic problems. That

pattern would have completely undermined the WTO's basic principle of nondiscrimination. India did the WTO and the world a favor
by bringing the case that led the EU to modify its supplemental GSP
program, the GSP+.

Still, the requirement set by the EU for eligibility for the GSP+ was
more or less just a "legal" tactic. Some of the conditions for the GSP+
are so nebulous that they can be interpreted in any number of ways.
The EU and other countries that have these additional conditions for
eligibility for preferential treatment can always find a violation by any
of the preference-receiving countries, if they want to. The EU requires
GSP+ beneficiaries to have ratified twenty-seven international conventions and be making a genuine effort to implement them. The EU uses
a scoreboard to determine the efforts those countries are making, but,
of course, that can be highly subjective.

Notwithstanding the self-interest reflected in the conditions dictated by the preference-giving countries, it would be wrong to conclude that they have no positive impact on the preference-receiving
countries. These conditions can be used, for example, to nudge countries to create and enforce labor laws that protect employees.

THE MARGIN OF PREFERENCE

The margin of preference is the difference between the MFN tariff
rates and the nonreciprocal preferential trade tariff rates. Several
factors can cause the margin of preference for a given preference-
receiving country to change, the most obvious ones being the change
in the tariff rates themselves.[13] Notwithstanding the trade skirmishes
that happen every now and then between major economies, the world's
weighted average MFN tariff rate has been decreasing steadily from 10
percent in 1994, when the Uruguay round of GATT was concluded, to
4 percent in 2017.[14]

This trend is not always welcome by preference-receiving countries
who see their margin of preference eroding. This erosion can be less-
ened by reducing preferential tariff rates, but most products from LDCs
have duty-free access to preference-giving countries already. Erosion of

the margin of preference is accelerated when preference-giving countries establish free trade agreements with countries that are outside the nonreciprocal preferential trade arrangements. In other words, simply increasing the number of countries receiving the preference amounts to an erosion of the margin of preference for the original preference-receiving countries. For example, in the U.S. some of the MFN tariff rates on products that are of interest to LDCs and AGOA countries have remained constant for a long time, but the number of countries that can export those products to the U.S. duty-free has increased, as shown by a sample of products in Table 4.3. (Note the tariff rates, for countries not receiving preferences, did not change between 2005 and 2020, but the number of preference-receiving countries did.)

The same can be said about the EU. It has special trade arrangements with most of its trading partners. As of 2018, the EU's MFN tariffs were fully applied to only six of its trading partners—Australia, China, Hong Kong, New Zealand, Taiwan, and the U.S. (World Trade Organization, 2004; Congressional Research Service, 2020; European Union, 2017). In 2022, the EU concluded negotiations with Australia and New Zealand to establish free trade areas with them. Any closer trade relationship between the EU, for example, and its trading partners chips away at the margin of preference for some preference-receiving countries. New Zealand exports meat and wool to the EU. When the New Zealand–EU free trade area goes into effect, the margin of preference for African countries that export meat and wool to the EU will decrease. In fact, the number of free trade areas in the world has increased exponentially, from 47 in 1995 to 356 in 2023 (WTO, 2023).

A number of empirical studies attempt to determine the magnitude of erosion of the margin of preference and its impact, but results naturally come with large margins of error. The margin of preference is a moving target, and it is product- and country-specific. Moreover, there is no agreement on how to measure it and what assumptions should be made with respect to price elasticities of exports, world prices, costs of certification or proof of country of origin, and the utilization of tariff preferences. Furthermore, there are the typical data limitations in these types of studies.

TABLE 4.3. U.S. extension of duty-free access for selected products

Product	2005		2020	
	Duty	Duty Free	Duty	Duty Free—Additional Countries
Meat of bovine animals, veal	4.4¢/kg	AGOA countries, Australia, Bolivia, Canada, Caribbean countries, Chile, Colombia, Ecuador, Israel, Jordan, LDCs, Mexico, Peru, and Singapore	4.4¢/kg	Bahrain, Dominican Republic and Central American countries,* Morocco, Oman, Panama, Singapore, and South Korea (Bolivia and Ecuador removed)
Hides and skins of bovine animals	2.4%	AGOA countries, GSP countries, Australia, Canada, Caribbean countries, Chile, Israel, Jordan, Mexico, Singapore	2.4%	Bahrain, Dominican Republic and Central American countries, Morocco, Oman, Panama, Peru, and South Korea
Cut flowers—roses	6.8%	AGOA countries, Bolivia, Canada, Caribbean countries, Colombia, Ecuador, Israel, Jordan, Mexico, and Peru	6.8%	Australia, Bahrain, Chile, Colombia, Dominican Republic and Central American countries, Morocco, Oman, Panama, Peru, Singapore and South Korea (Bolivia and Ecuador removed)

(continued)

	2005		2020	
Product	**Duty**	**Duty Free**	**Duty**	**Duty Free—Additional Countries**
Avocados	11.2¢/kg	AGOA countries, Bolivia, Canada, Caribbean countries, Colombia, Ecuador, Israel, Jordan, LDCs, Mexico, and Peru	11.2¢/kg	Bahrain, Chile, Dominican Republic and Central American countries, Jordan, Morocco, Oman, Panama, Singapore, and South Korea (Bolivia and Ecuador removed)
Women's dresses of cotton	11.5%	Qualified AGOA countries, Canada, Chile, Israel, Jordan, Mexico, Singapore	11.5%	Australia, Bahrain, Colombia, Dominican Republic and Central American countries, Morocco, Oman, Panama, Peru, Singapore, and South Korea
Men's or boys' shirts of cotton	19.7%	Qualified AGOA countries, Canada, Chile, Israel, Mexico, Singapore	19.7%	Australia, Bahrain, Colombia, Dominican Republic and Central American countries, Morocco, Oman, Panama, Peru, and Singapore

* The U.S. has a free trade agreement with the Dominican Republic and five Central American countries—Costa Rica, El Salvador, Guatemala, Honduras, and Nicaragua.

Source: U.S. International Trade Commission, 2005 and 2020 issues of Harmonized Tariff Schedule of the U.S.

Subramanian (2003) and Alexandraki and Lankes (2004) estimate the impact of preference erosion caused by trade liberalization by the Quad economies—Canada, the EU, Japan, and the U.S.—on LDCs and middle-income countries, respectively. The aggregate losses of exports were estimated to be 1.7 percent for LDCs and 1.2 percent (at most) for middle-income countries. While these results are sensitive to how tariff preference is measured and the assumptions made, the main conclusion of these studies is that LDCs and middle-income countries that had high export concentrations and depended heavily on the Quad economies are at a higher risk of preference erosion. Subsequent studies, including a wide-ranging compilation of empirical cases on trade preference erosion in Hoekman, Martin, and Braga (2009), come to a similar conclusion.

This conclusion withstands intuition, but it is also a conundrum. The uniqueness and structures of preferential trade schemes may themselves lead a beneficiary country to specialize in a narrow range of products and become highly dependent on a given preference-giving country. Lesotho is an example.

In a review of the Lesotho textile industry, Kipling makes the following statement: "It can be said, with little exaggeration, that Lesotho owes the very existence of its fairly substantial clothing and textile industry to AGOA and exports to the U.S." (Kipling 2010: 1). AGOA could not have come at a better time for Lesotho. In 2000, Lesotho had a small textile and apparel industry, but one that was well positioned to take advantage of an open market. Lesotho's response to AGOA was immediate; both production and exports increased. In a span of five years, exports of textiles and apparel to the U.S. increased by more than threefold, from $140 million in 2000 to a peak of $467 million in 2004.[15]

A study by Frazer and Van Biesebroeck (2010) likewise shows a link between AGOA and the growth of the textile and apparel industry in Lesotho. In the 2010s, exports of textiles and apparel contributed about 50 percent of total export revenue, with 60 percent of it coming from AGOA-eligible exports to the U.S.

Lesotho is, therefore, in a situation where even a slight trade prefer-ence erosion in the U.S. market will have a noticeable negative impact in the short run. For example, it is estimated that a free trade area between the U.S. and Vietnam, a major textile and apparel producer, would decrease Lesotho's production, and exports of textile and ap-parel to the U.S., by 1.8 and 3.4 percent, respectively.[16] Respective de-creases resulting from a complete suspension of AGOA are estimated to be 9.3 and 16 percent (Arenas et al., 2018: 44).

Trade preference erosion was one of the arguments used to support the "Aid for Trade" initiative that was launched at the WTO Ministerial Conference in Hong Kong in 2005. That is, developing countries need to be compensated for a decrease in the preferential margin. While a strong case for compensation can be made, the argument is not with-out counterarguments (Tangermann, 2002: Chapter 8). The argument treats preferential trade as if it were obligatory aid that has to be main-tained and, therefore, must be compensated for with other forms of aid when the margin of preference erodes. Interestingly, the argument for compensation has been raised by countries that are able to and also those that have not been able to take advantage of preferential trade (Mshomba, 2009: Chapter 6).

Lawrence and Rosito (2006) proposed a postponement of MFN tariff reductions, with the sole purpose of raising tariff revenues in the preference-giving countries. The idea is for those revenues to be disbursed later to developing countries that would experience erosion in the margin of preference. This proposition is intriguing, but has obvious flaws. It assumes, incorrectly, that developed countries would find it easier to part with money raised specifically through tariffs than with money from the general pool of government revenues. Imagine the EU or the U.S. telling their consumers that they will continue to pay higher prices on imports so that the tariff revenues generated can be sent to developing countries that would face a margin of preference erosion in the future. More importantly, the proposition makes an er-roneous assumption that higher tariff rates put developed countries in a stronger fiscal position to provide aid. The proposition considers only the impact of tariffs on tariff revenue, with no consideration of the loss to domestic consumers in developed countries who are being taxed by higher tariffs. Dardis and Cooke (1984) estimate that in 1980 alone, U.S. consumers incurred consumer surplus losses of $10 to $12 billion due to tariffs and quotas on apparel.[17]

Abrupt and deep erosion of preference margins can be detrimental to some preference-receiving countries, as already suggested with respect to Lesotho and AGOA. However, tariff reductions, whether at the multilateral or regional level, are typically a gradual phenomenon. Given the WTO's mission to reduce MFN tariffs, producers in preference-receiving countries must operate with the awareness that preference erosion is inevitable. They cannot afford to be complacent. Nonetheless, the WTO has a role to play to nudge countries to standardize some elements of their preferential trade programs.

THE ROLE OF THE WTO

While the impetus for the GSP program and similar arrangements came from developing countries, these countries have no meaningful influence on their structures or trajectories. The WTO, which monitors and enforces multilateral trade rules, also has limited influence, given that these programs are voluntary. There seems to be concern on the WTO side that if it tries to limit the autonomy of the "donor" countries, then those countries could simply decide not to offer nonreciprocal, preferential trade arrangements altogether (McKenzie, 2005). However, the WTO should not simply be a bystander and allow each preference-giving country to set its own conditions, which end up limiting the ability of preference-receiving countries to take advantage of them.

Countries register their preferential trade programs with the WTO, the body that authorizes waivers to the MFN principle. The WTO should use this role to prod countries into harmonizing some of the provisions in preferential trade, including conditionalities and the rules of origin.

Given the due diligence taken by the WTO for a country to be granted membership and also considering the surveillance and enforcement exercised by the WTO, other conditions imposed by some preference-giving countries are not warranted. Accession into the WTO involves an arduous process divided into five stages, vetting the applicants' readiness and commitment to abide by multilateral trade rules. The stages are:

1. Submission of the formal application for membership, which triggers establishment of a Working Party for Accession;
2. Submission of the Memorandum of the Foreign Trade Regime by the observant (applicant), describing in detail its economic system and trade policies;
3. Negotiations on terms and conditions of accession—multilateral negotiations, plurilateral, and bilateral discussions;
4. Adoption of the Report of the Working Party for Accession; and
5. Approval of the accession by the General Council or Ministerial Conference.[18]

The process can take more than a decade to complete. The process requires applicants to be very determined. Seychelles and Liberia, which acceded into the WTO in 2015 and 2016, had applied for membership in 1995 and 2007, respectively. Ethiopia has been in the accession process on and off since 2003 (Tura, 2015). After a hiatus of eight years, Ethiopia resumed negotiations for accession in 2020, with the hope of completing the process in 2021 (Tadesse, 2020). As of early 2023, those negotiations had not yet been completed. Moreover, the most recent internal conflict between the Ethiopian government and the Tigray People's Liberation Front (TPLF), which started in 2020, must have taken Ethiopia's attention away from its negotiations with the WTO.

Considering the scrutiny that countries undergo to become WTO members, it appears that the additional conditions set by the EU and the U.S., for example, are more to give them control than for the legitimate advancement of international trade rules. If it can be determined that additional conditions on beneficiaries of GSP and similar programs are necessary, and that they do enhance development in those countries, then conditions should be harmonized to avoid the possibility of being enforced by each preference-giving country arbitrarily. That would reduce the uncertainty associated with these programs and make them more reliable. As discussed in the following chapter, one of the determinants of preference utilization is the reliability of preferential programs themselves.

5   THE EXTENT TO WHICH PREFERENCES ARE USED AND THEIR BENEFITS

NONRECIPROCAL PREFERENTIAL TRADE ARRANGEMENTS ARE beneficial, in large part, to the extent that beneficiary countries can utilize them. The likelihood of taking advantage of preferential trade arrangements depends on a number of external and internal factors. The benefits of preferential trade arrangements to preference-receiving and preference-giving countries are not different from the benefits usually associated with freer trade in general. To the preference-receiving countries, these arrangements, when utilized, can increase export production and revenues, the diversification of exports, and foreign direct investment, thus increasing domestic employment and tax revenues. The extent to which these benefits occur depends on the responsiveness of domestic supply to preferential treatment. It also depends on how the price benefits of reducing or eliminating import duties are shared between the exporters, importers, and intermediaries. While not exclusively, the discussion on preference utilization will focus on African least developed countries (LDCs). In an effort to help them develop, preference-giving countries give LDCs the most generous nonreciprocal preferential market access.

As for the benefits to preference-giving countries, reducing trade barriers increases a country's welfare by fostering competition, a more

efficient allocation of resources, and the importation of inputs at reduced costs. This leads to a reduction in production costs and increases
the purchasing power of consumers. Moreover, these arrangements
also improve relations between trading partners.

Table 5.1 provides information about four companies in three different countries. All of them rely heavily on the U.S. African Growth
and Opportunity Act (AGOA) and/or the EU Everything But Arms (EBA)
program. While they are only a tiny fraction of companies that take
advantage of preferential trade arrangements, the information sheds
light on the utilization of these arrangements, the benefits, and the
risks of relying on a single market. Reference will be made to Table 5.1
throughout this chapter.

DETERMINANTS OF PREFERENCE UTILIZATION

Many factors determine the preference utilization rate. They include:
(i) the margin of preference; (ii) country-of-origin rules; (iii) the cost of
certification; (iv) the dissemination of information; (v) the reliability
of preferential programs; and (vi) cooperation between exporters and
importers. The importance of these factors varies between countries,
sectors, and individual export producers.

i. The Margin of Preference

The cost of using a preference is weighed against the benefits, which
are in part determined by the margin of preference. For there to be
a margin of preference for a given product, the most-favored-nation
(MFN) tariff rate cannot be zero for that product.

However, no particular threshold is needed for the margin of preference, for preference-receiving exporters to be able to utilize the
preference. This is due to a number of factors, including the sector in
which the exporter is operating, the competitive (dis)advantage the
exporter has, and the exporters' familiarity with the foreign market.

Most studies suggest a threshold nominal margin preference (the difference in percentage points between the MFN rate and the preferential

TABLE 5.1. A sample of firms using AGOA and/or EBA

Name of the Company	Isabella Socks Manufacturing PLC	Hela Intimates EPZ Ltd	Tanzania Tooku Garments Company Ltd	Mazava Fabrics and Production E.A.
Location	Hawassa Industrial Park, Hawassa, Ethiopia	Athi River EPZ, Nairobi, Kenya	Export Processing Zone, Dar-es-Salaam, Tanzania	Morogoro, Tanzania
Name of parent company and home country	Isabella (Private) Ltd., Sri Lanka	Hela Apparel Holdings PLC, Sri Lanka	J.P. United Manufacturing Corporation, Changzhou, China	Winds Group of Companies, Hong Kong
Year the company was established	2016	2016	2012	2010
Annual sales (2021)	Not provided	$100 million	$28.2 million	Not provided
Percentage of sales from exports	100	100	100	100
Percentage of exports through AGOA	30	75	100	100
Main buyers in the U.S.	The Children's Place	PVH Corporation, VF Corporation, Michael Kors, and Torrid	Walmart and The Children's Place	SanMar
Percentage of exports through EBA	70	20	zero	zero

(continued)

TABLE 5.1. (*continued*)

Name of the Company	Isabella Socks Manufacturing PLC	Hela Intimates EPZ Ltd	Tanzania Tooku Garments Company Ltd	Mazava Fabrics and Production E.A.
Main buyers in the EU	Nur Die, Lotto, and ESDA	PVH Corporation	none	None
Percentage of exports through other preferential trade arrangements	zero	5	zero	zero
Authority that certifies the "country of origin" requirements	Ethiopia Chamber of Commerce	Kenya Customs Authority	Tanzania Chamber of Commerce	Tanzania Chamber of Commerce
Payment for certification (2021)	$120	N/A	$45 per container (258 containers in 2021—$11,610)	None, except membership fee for the Chamber of Commerce
Number of employees	735	5,000	4,500	2,000
Percentage of women employees	76	85	79	75
Percentage of yarn/ fabric that is imported	100 percent imports of yarn—from India and China	100 percent imports of fabric from Hong Kong, Sri Lanka, China, India, Pakistan, and Tanzania	100 percent imports of fabric from China, India, and Pakistan	100 percent imports of fabric from China

(*continued*)

Name of the Company	Isabella Socks Manufacturing PLC	Hela Intimates EPZ Ltd	Tanzania Tooku Garments Company Ltd	Mazava Fabrics and Production E.A.
Can the company survive without AGOA/EBA	It would be very difficult to survive without both AGOA and EBA.	No	No	No
Other information or suggestions	• Shortage of trucks and high fuel costs. • A shortage of skilled labor leads to defects. • Export control officers need more training to improve efficiency. • Orders from the U.S. dropped when the U.S. terminated AGOA for Ethiopia in January 2022.	• Logistical challenges • Lack of supply chains in Kenya and in Africa in general	• Delayed delivery of imported materials due to the Tanzania Customs Integrated System being inactive quite often • Shortage of skilled labor	

Sources: Phone conversations and email correspondence between the author and the spokespeople for these companies.

tariff rate) of 2 to 6 percent for countries to be able to utilize preference (Bureau et al., 2007; Francois et al., 2006; Manchin, 2006). Reductions of MFN tariffs by preference-giving countries, a phenomenon taking place at a great pace since the establishment of the WTO in 1995, have been eroding the margin of preference, often causing an outcry from the LDCs. A rationale for the WTO's "Aid for Trade" initiative, formally launched in December 2005 at the WTO Ministerial Conference in Hong Kong, was, in part, to help preference-receiving countries adjust to the challenges caused by the erosion of the margin of preference (World Trade Organization, 2005).

However, measuring the margin of preference itself is not a straightforward exercise. An effective margin of preference not only depends on the difference between the MFN rate and the preference rate, but also on nontariff barriers, some of which are very subtle. It also depends on the number and characteristics of other countries that are also eligible for preference.[1]

Producers of apparel in the Caribbean Basin Initiative countries experienced erosion in the effective margin of preference when the North American Free Trade Agreement (NAFTA) was formed in 1994. The erosion was due to competition from Mexico, even though the nominal margin of preference did not change (Ozden and Sharma, 2006). African, Caribbean, and Pacific (ACP) countries had a similar experience when, in 2001, the EU extended preference eligibility to all LDCs, including Bangladesh, an apparel powerhouse. Again, the beneficiaries of the African Growth and Opportunity Act (AGOA) saw their effective margin of preference erode when the Multi-Fiber Agreement (MFA), which developed countries had used since 1974 to set quotas for textiles and apparel from developing countries, ended on December 31, 2004 (UNCTAD, 2006: 45).

ii. Country-of-Origin Rules

Country-of-origin rules are necessary for any preferential trade arrangement to avoid transshipment of goods from nonbeneficiary countries. As discussed in Chapter 4, some of these rules can be very complicated. In general, the rules of origin required for LDCs are less constraining. LDCs are allowed broader cumulation provisions, compared to other developing countries. Other things being equal, this allows them to have reasonable flexibility in using inputs from other countries on which they depend, without losing eligibility for preferential treatment. But things are not necessarily equal. The cost of labor is relatively very low in LDCs. While this is attractive to investors, it keeps the value added attributed to the direct cost of domestic processing low, thus making it harder to meet some of the country-of-origin requirements (WTO, 2014). Official minimum wages in African LDCs in 2019 ranged from $2 to $112 a month (International Labor Organization, 2020, 104). Using the purchasing power parity method, the range is $5 to $297 a month. On average, African LDCs have lower wages compared to other LDCs.

Another nuance is that since country-of-origin rules use percentage criteria, "calculations are easily affected by movements in exchange rates for finished products that have imported raw materials, in that, when a local currency appreciates, the percentage value added tends to decline, and vice-versa" (WTO, 2014:8). To illustrate, suppose a finished product is initially priced at $10, and to be eligible for certain preferential treatment, there is a requirement of a minimum of 35 percent value added, that is $3.5, by the beneficiary country. Suppose the beneficiary country just meets that requirement and that the domestic currency appreciates in a way that only the price of the finished product is affected. Suppose now the price of that product is $11. Then the percent of value added will decrease and the product will no longer be eligible for preference. If there are big fluctuations in exchange rates, exports whose eligibility for preference are at the margin, will be affected; otherwise, this is not a major concern for African LDCs. Moreover, the most likely scenario, considering historical trends, is that of the local currency depreciating, rather than appreciating. Historically, the demand for foreign currency in most African countries has outpaced the supply of foreign currency.

The percentage criterion has another interesting dimension. It makes a difference whether the numerator is the maximum limit on the value of imported materials or the minimum value that must be added in the beneficiary country. A hypothetical numerical example provided by the WTO (2014) shows how calculations based on a maximum value of imported materials (a build-down method) provide easier eligibility for preference, compared to those based on a minimum value added (a build-up method), as shown in Table 5.2. Nonetheless, it is important not to read too much into this numerical illustration because different programs have different cumulation provisions that affect the characterization of foreign materials. Moreover, there could be different ways to establish the final value of a product, which may produce different eligibility outcomes for the same product destined to a given preferential program (World Customs Organization, 2014).

The high preference utilization of AGOA in the apparel sector is credited to the provision that allows the use of U.S. and third-country

TABLE 5.2. Import content versus domestic content requirement for preference eligibility

		Import content (maximum 50% to be eligible for preference)	Domestic content (direct cost of processing) (minimum 35% to be eligible for preference)
(a)	Domestic materials	$1.00	$1.00
(b)	Foreign materials (not substantially transformed)	$4.00	$4.00
(c)	Direct cost of processing	$2.00	$2.00
(d)	General expenses	$1.50	$1.50
(e)	Profit	$1.50	$1.50
(f)	Appraised value	$10.00	$10.00
(g)	Import content/ domestic content	40% (rule satisfied) = (b/f) × 100	30% (rule not satisfied) = [(a + c)/f] × 100

Source: Table 1 in WTO (2014:8).

yarns and fabrics. Most textile firms import 100 percent of the fabric they use, as illustrated by a sample of firms shown in Table 5.1. A survey of producers in East and Southern Africa, conducted by the United Nations Conference on Trade and Development (UNCTAD) in 2010, indicated that most producers could not comply with rules of origin that required double transformation—yarn to fabric to apparel (UNCTAD, 2011). It is not surprising, therefore, that there was a clear boost in preference utilization by LDCs in the EU's EBA program following less restrictive rules of origin, requiring apparel to have undergone only one transformation, fabric to apparel (World Trade Organization, 2014; UNCTAD, 2019). Prior to 2011, the EBA required apparel from beneficiary countries to have undergone double transformation.

iii. The Cost of Certification

All exports require documentation for customs purposes. However, exports that are eligible for preferential treatment require more detailed and specific documentation (World Customs Organization, 2018a). The record-keeping and accounting process can be burdensome for some producers. Some production processes involve obtaining inputs from different parts of the world, with the sources of inputs and their prices constantly changing. These complexities require careful and sophisticated record-keeping and accounting systems whose costs may exceed the benefits of trying to meet eligibility requirements for preference.

Small exporters are more sensitive to these costs. The quantities exported may be too small to justify the detailed record keeping and paperwork necessary to show preference eligibility. An empirical study by Keck and Lendle (2012) shows that preference utilization increases with the export value. Their study suggests that a high percentage of the cost of certification for the purpose of receiving preference is fixed. Thus, for small exporters who cannot spread that cost over large volumes, the average cost of qualifying for preference can easily be too high. Even if the cost of using preference is mostly a one-time expense, such that over a number of years the benefits would outweigh the cost, future volumes of exports are not predictable. Moreover, fees must also be paid to the certifying authority, as shown in Table 5.1.

iv. The Dissemination of Information

We live in a world in which one can access most information by the click of a button. However, without concerted efforts by the Ministry of Trade and business associations to disseminate information, educate producers, and facilitate certification processes, many producers would not know where to begin or how to navigate the systems. Information and deliberate targeted strategies are key to preference utilization. It is not surprising that preference utilization by Sub-Saharan African countries of the U.S. preferential trade arrangements is high. As of 2023, nineteen African countries had documents laying out their national AGOA strategies.[2] These strategies have been developed with direct input from the private sector.

In the process of preparing these strategies, the private sector has become familiar with AGOA and the U.S. GSP program and the requirements for their products to be eligible for duty-free access to the U.S. market. In addition, the Corporate Council on Africa (CCA) organizes regular U.S.-Africa business summits. These summits bring together government leaders and business executives from across the U.S. and Africa to discuss and strategize regarding various important issues, especially to promote U.S.-Africa trade ties and U.S. investment in Africa. They have been held every other year, since 1997.[3] Such summits are not feasible, or even desirable, for all preference-giving countries, but at a minimum internal updates and consultations within the country are very important.

v. The Reliability of Preferential Programs

By their very nature, nonreciprocal preferential programs are temporary and fully controlled by the preference-giving countries. There is always an element of uncertainty about their duration and coverage. Even when the program itself has a declared long-term availability, individual countries can be suspended for a wide range of reasons. This has certainly been the case with AGOA. Table 5.3 shows countries that have experienced full or partial suspension (relating only to specific products) from AGOA at one point or another or are still under suspension as of 2023. Equatorial Guinea and Seychelles graduated from the U.S. GSP in 2011 and 2017, respectively, based on income per capita, thus losing eligibility for AGOA. As of 2023, Somalia, Sudan, and Zimbabwe had never been eligible for AGOA (USTR, 2016 and 2023).

The U.S., much more so than the other preference-giving countries, has used its preference programs to voice its disapproval of beneficiary countries' behaviors. Beneficiary countries are reviewed each year to determine their compliance with the eligibility criteria. AGOA has become a convenient tool because it holds countries accountable to some extent, and, at the same time, it does not hurt diplomatic relationships in any serious way. For countries such as Cameroon, Eritrea, Mali, and Mauritania, for which the U.S. is not an important market, suspension from AGOA, if that is the only punishment, is just a "slap on the wrist." Nonetheless, such suspensions, or even the potential for suspension, can disrupt the production of individual businesses that rely on the U.S. market.

Madagascar depends on the U.S. market for 15 percent of its total exports. Apparel and clothing make up 70 percent of those exports. About 50 percent of Madagascar's exports of textiles are to the U.S. market. Some textile factories were established in export processing zones with plans to produce products primarily or solely destined to the AGOA market. In 2009, textile factories catering to the U.S. market employed about 50,000 people directly. Half of them lost their jobs when, on January 1, 2010, Madagascar was suspended from AGOA (IRIN News, 2010; International Crisis Group, 2010; Brookings, 2014). Madagascar's apparel and clothing exports to the U.S. dropped from an annual average of $254 million for 2006–9 to $33 million for 2010–13.[45] Madagascar was reinstated into AGOA in 2014.

In 2015, the U.S. threatened to suspend Lesotho from AGOA. The U.S. argued Lesotho was not making enough progress in establishing the rule of law. The threat caused a panic in Lesotho. It is hard to overstate the importance of the textiles and apparel industry in Lesotho and the reliance of Lesotho on the U.S. market. In 2016 and 2017, the industry accounted for 90 percent of formal manufacturing jobs (Bureau of Statistics, 2018). Following the threat of suspension, Lesotho's Minister

TABLE 5.3. Countries suspended from AGOA (as of February 2023)

Country	Period	Reason
Burkina Faso	January 2023–present	Political rights violations
Burundi	January 2016–present	Human rights violations
Cameroon	January 2020–present	Human rights violations
Central African Rep.	January 2014–December 2016	Political rights violations
Cote d'Ivoire	January 2005–October 2011	Political rights violations
Dem. Rep. of Congo	January 2011–December 2020	Human rights violations
Ethiopia	January 2022–present	Human rights violations
Eritrea	January 2004–present	Human rights violations
Eswatini	January 2005–December 2017	Worker rights violations
Gambia	January 2005–December 2017	Human rights violations
Guinea	December 2009–October 2011	Political rights violations
	January 2022–present	Political rights violations
Guinea-Bissau	December 2012-December 2014	Political rights violations
Madagascar	January 2010–June 2014	Political rights violations
Mali	January 2013–January 2014	Political rights violations
	January 2022–present	Political rights violations
Mauritania	October 2000–December 2009	Human rights violations
Niger	December 2009–October 2011	Political rights violations
Rwanda	July 2018–present (applies only to apparel)	Barriers on U.S. goods
South Sudan	January 1, 2015–present	Political rights violations

Sources: Various reports by the Office of the U.S. Trade Representative.

of Trade pleaded its case by describing the critical importance of the textile industry and of the U.S. market as follows:

> Lesotho's textiles and apparel manufacturing industry comprises about 50 formal sector firms—29 of these being dependent upon the export of garments to the U.S. using AGOA preferences. If the AGOA privileges are withdrawn, it is highly likely that most firms (if not all) could close. These 50 firms collectively employ approximately 43,000 workers [80 percent of them women]. About 30,000 of these workers are engaged in the manufacture of garments (and some textiles converted into garments) that are exported to the US under AGOA. (Setipa, 2016)

For their part, Lesotho unions held demonstrations pressuring their government to restore democracy and the rule of law (Industrial Global Union, 2016). The Lesotho government made enough progress to avoid suspension from AGOA, but in 2021 it was in the same predicament for what the U.S. deemed Lesotho's inability to address human trafficking concerns (Moyo, 2021). Those fears subsided following the 2022 annual review of country eligibility for AGOA by the Office of the U.S. Trade Representative (2022).

While these cases relate to individual countries, usually there is a general elevated level of uncertainty at the time a program is up for renewal. An empirical study by Edjigu et al. (2023) shows that countries that have been suspended from AGOA have, on average, experienced a 39 percent decline in exports to the U.S. As Table 5.1 reveals, some producers are dependent on just one or two trading partners for their products. Suspensions from AGOA, therefore, can lead to total closure of manufacturing companies for lack of alternate markets. Recovering from suspensions is also a struggle as some employees might be forced to look for other employment.

Even if there is a legitimate reason for removing a country, the impact may not be confined to that country alone. AGOA's rules of origin view inputs imported from other AGOA countries as part of local content. When a country is removed from AGOA, regional linkages, few as they may be, are also disrupted (Schneidman and Lewis, 2012).

AGOA suspensions can, therefore, disrupt and discourage efforts to deepen economic integration in Africa.

The U.S. GSP program has increasingly become less reliable because of the delays in renewing it when it expires. As of mid-2023, it had not been renewed after it had expired in 2020. Although when it is reauthorized, it is usually done retroactively, some small and medium-sized firms are not able to carry the costs of tariffs for an extended period of time (Icso, 2023). It is estimated that between January 2021 and April 2022, U.S. importers paid at least $1.47 billion in tariffs on imports that would have been eligible for duty-free importation under the GSP (Congressional Research Service, 2022).

Since the early 1990s, renewals of the U.S. GSP program have been for very short periods, often coming months after its expiration. However, since the establishment of AGOA, the unpredictability of the U.S. GSP program has not been much of a concern for most Sub-Saharan African countries, as they hardly rely on it. AGOA expires in 2025. Undoubtedly, there will be debates about its renewal. However, it is reasonable to expect its renewal, given its vital role in maintaining and advancing investment and trade relations between the U.S. and Sub-Saharan Africa, especially as China continues to make inroads in Africa. Currently, China's program for LDCs and EU's EBA do not specify an end date. The current GSP program of the EU expires in 2023, but there is no reason not to expect its renewal for another ten years.

vi. Cooperation between Exporters and Importers

The working relations between exporters and importers is important because each side has to do its part. The exporter prepares the "evidence" and goes through the process of obtaining certification and forwarding the documents to the importer. The importer is responsible for applying for preference benefits and providing the documents to the customs authorities in the preference-giving country. These relationships are not necessarily easy to establish. That is part of the reason why some exporters not only export to just a few countries, but also to just a few buyers in those countries, as suggested by the information in Table 5.1.

PREFERENCE UTILIZATION

Preference utilization is measured by the degree to which products that are eligible for preferential treatment actually receive it. In other words, it is the value of a product that received preferential treatment from a preference-giving country divided by the value of total exports of that product to that country. For the EU and the U.S., where there is more than one program through which an African LDC can receive a preference, it is imperative that the preference utilization rate is calculated by combining the programs available to avoid the potential to overstate underutilization.

As UNCTAD (2019) has pointed out:

> Low utilization rates can also result from the existence of competing preference schemes. For example, many exporters from Africa to the U.S. have been utilizing the African Growth and Opportunity Act preference scheme and have established operating processes and accounting systems to comply with the requirements of this scheme. As a result, the utilization rate of the Generalized System of Preferences of the U.S. is rather low. (87)

Since there is wide variation in preference utilization, when data is available, it is best to calculate preference utilization ratios by product category, country of export, specific preference programs, and margins of preference. Among the findings by a World Trade Organization (2021) study that examined the utilization of preference treatment by LDCs for a period of five years (2015–19) is that preference utilization varied greatly among LDCs and between sectors. The analysis that follows here confirms that finding and also provides insight into the difference in preference utilization of preferential programs offered by China, the EU, and the U.S. Based on the IMF's database for Direction of Trade, the annual average of exports by African LDCs, 2014 to 2018, was $112 billion. On average, 29, 12, and 4 percent went to China, the EU, and the U.S., respectively.

China's Preferential Treatment for LDCs

As of 2021, there were 33 African LDCs, all of which were eligible for China's duty-free and quota-free (DFQF) program. However, preference utilization of China's preference has always been understood to be minimal, even though trade between China and LDCs, especially those that produce oil and minerals, has been increasing. The low preference utilization was confirmed by a study by the LDC group in the WTO specifically on the utilization of China's DFQF program by LDCs (World Trade Organization, 2019). While the study revealed wide variation in preference utilization between countries and sectors, on aggregate, the conclusion was that preference utilization was minuscule, irrespective of the margins of preference.

The WTO study provides the value of exports for the top one or two products by LDC beneficiaries to China in 2016. There were 29 African LDCs in the study.[6] The total value of their exports for those products was $17.76 billion. All of those exports were dutiable. That is, the MFN tariff rate was above zero. Of the total exports, 22 percent—$3.91 billion—was eligible for preferential treatment. Of the eligible exports, only 1.62 percent—$63 million—utilized the preference.

Among the African LDCs in the study, Angola was an outlier—its exports alone were worth $13.9 billion. However, excluding Angola barely affects the utilization rate because only a tiny fraction of its exports was eligible for China's DFQF program. Excluding Angola, total exports were $3.86 billion, exports eligible for preference were $3.85 billion, and the utilization rate was 1.64 percent. Of the 29 African countries included in the study, 19 had a zero utilization rate. Some of the low utilization rates can be explained by the small quantities of exports by some countries.

The relative newness of China's DFQF program can potentially be a reason for the preference underutilization. The program started in 2010. Nonetheless, it is still puzzling to see that countries such as the Democratic Republic of the Congo (DRC) and Zambia have not been able to take advantage of preferential treatment. These countries have relatively large exports to China and are familiar with the Chinese market.

Exports of copper and articles thereof (Chapter 74 in the harmonized tariff schedule) from the DRC and Zambia to China in 2016 were worth $0.97 billion and $1.96 billion, respectively. The DRC also exported $0.76 billion worth of cobalt and other base metals (Chapter 81 in the harmonized tariff schedule) to China (World Trade Organization, 2019, 6–8). The margins of preference were 1.8 percent and 4 percent for copper and cobalt, respectively. Yet exports of those minerals had a zero utilization rate. Given the margins of preference, the amount of tariff revenues that could have been avoided was $47.7 million and $35.3 million for DRC and Zambia, respectively.[7]

The inability of countries like the DRC and Zambia to utilize China's preferential trade arrangement is not unique to them. In another study, the WTO made the following observation:

> In the case of minerals and metals, the phenomenon of underutilization is more circumscribed. On the one hand, trade preferences are almost fully used (underutilization rates of 10% or below) in the EU; Japan; Republic of Korea; and the US. On the other hand, preferences are not heavily utilized under the PTA-LDCs of Australia; Canada; Chile; China; Switzerland; Chinese Taipei; and Thailand. China is by far the largest importer of metals and minerals from LDCs so overall utilization rates in this sector are driven by the performance of LDCs in that market. While statistics for China are available only for two years, calculations indicate an underutilization of 96% and 99% (2016 and 2018 respectively). Given that polarization, LDC-PTA-specific features may be influencing underutilization rates, such as specificities related to direct consignment or certification obligations. (World Trade Organization, 2021, 6)

As the quote suggests, the inability to take advantage of preferential treatment may be due to specific features of the LDCs and the preferential trade arrangements themselves. Oftentimes, the complexities of the rules of origin are the main constraints to preference utilization. However, that cannot explain the situation of the DRC and Zambia. Their major exports to China are minerals that can easily be certified as "wholly produced" in the benefit-receiving country and thus qualify for duty-free access. The high underutilization rate may be explained by the dynamics at play between the exporting and importing firms and the incentive structure for taking the trouble to take advantage of preferential trade arrangements. In other words, it is possible that most of the cobalt exports from the Democratic Republic of the Congo and copper exports from Zambia are from Chinese companies that are already subsidized by cheaper loans from the Export-Import Bank of China.

The WTO (World Trade Organization, 2021) shows there are annual variations in preference underutilization and, therefore, warns against making conclusions based on a single year's data. Analyzing data from several years is always a good practice, but data on China's DFQF program is not readily available. For the two years, 2016 and 2018, for which data was available at the time the WTO conducted its study, the overall preference underutilization rate of China's DFQF program increased from 83 to 92 percent (World Trade Organization, 2021, 4).

When considering a given product from a given LDC to a specific preference-giving country, there is no reason to expect large annual variations in preference underutilization rates. The exception would be if there are frequent changes in the ownership or number of firms exporting the product or frequent changes in the country-of-origin rules. None of this is the case for exports of major minerals.

Given the current underutilization of China's DFQF program by African LDCs, the program is of little value to Africa, except to serve as a subject for public and diplomatic relations. Surprisingly, the LDC Group in the WTO seemed casual about the situation in their study of China's DFQF program. Apart from providing evidence for preference underutilization, the LDC Group, whose members one would expect to be informed about the constraints behind such underutilization, could not provide an explanation. Their conclusion was the following:

> This preliminary analysis of the utilization rates of China's DFQF shows that there are significant figures of low or zero utilization rate. . . . The LDC Group is ready to engage in discussions with the Chinese delegation and customs authorities to identify the reasons and possible explanations for these patterns, with a view to seeking remedy at the earliest convenience. (World Trade Organization, 2019, 4)

The EU's Everything But Arms and GSP Program for LDCs

The EU's preferential trade treatment for African countries is inter-twined with colonial history, as discussed in Chapter 2. Its initial motive was not necessarily the economic development of African col-onies, but an assurance of the supply of primary products. Notwith-standing that initial ulterior motive, Europe has been and continues to be an important market for African products. Since the 1960s, when most African countries got their independence, the EU's preference for products from former colonies had a development component, as it was used in conjunction with other assistance programs. In 2001, the EU created the Everything But Arms (EBA) program to give duty-free and quota-free access to all goods, except arms and ammunitions, from the LDCs.

Table 5.4 shows preference utilization by African LDCs of the EU's EBA/GSP for the period 2016–20. Table 5.5 is a synopsis of Table 5.4, to highlight differences in EBA eligibility and utilization. Even with the seemingly generous provisions of the EBA, only 27 percent of exports to the EU were eligible for EBA or GSP, 65 percent of which actually received preference. Exports from African LDCs are mostly primary products; primary products already enter the EU market duty free and, therefore, do not need to use the EBA or any other preferential trade arrangement (Brenton, 2003). On aggregate, 17 percent of all exports by African LDCs to the EU received preference.

The information in Tables 5.4 and 5.5 is also a "cautionary tale" about aggregate data. First, it should be emphasized that since none of the African LDCs export arms and ammunitions to the EU, the prefer-ence eligibility rate for any given country simply reflects exports that are subject to MFN tariff rates. In other words, the "ineligible" portion enters duty free for everyone. Second, there is wide variation in the percentages of preference eligibility and preference utilization rates between countries. Four countries and seven countries, respectively, had a preference utilization rate of less than 5 percent and over 96 percent. It is also worth noting that when all LDCs (not just African LDCs) are considered in aggregate, the preference utilization rate rises to 92 percent and the preference utilized as a percent of total exports

TABLE 5.4. Preference utilization by African LDCs of EU's EBA/GSP programs

			Annual Average, 2016–2020			
African LDCs	Total Exports to EU (€ millions)	Eligible for EBA/GSP (€ millions)	Preference Eligible as a Percent of Total Exports	Preference Utilized (€ millions)	Preference Utilization Rate (Percent)	Preference Utilized as a Percent of Total Exports
(1)	(2)	(3)	(4)	(5)	(6)	(7)
Angola	3,101	48	1.56	29	60.41	0.94
Benin	46	4	7.83	3	85.04	6.60
Burkina Faso	179	19	10.38	17	93.60	9.71
Burundi	26	0.24	0.91	0.16	68.32	0.62
Central African Republic	16	0.46	2.97	0.07	15.95	0.47
Chad	275	1	0.34	0	0	0
Comoros	22	8	37.36	8	93.53	34.95
Congo, Democratic Republic	1,120	13	1.15	9	71.09	0.82
Djibouti	11	4	36.90	0.14	3.64	1.34
Equatorial Guinea[8]	1,076	14	1.29	8	58.71	0.76

(continued)

Annual Average, 2016–2020

African LDCs	Total Exports to EU (€ millions)	Eligible for EBA/GSP (€ millions)	Preference Eligible as a Percent of Total Exports	Preference Utilized (€ millions)	Preference Utilization Rate (Percent)	Preference Utilized as a Percent of Total Exports
Eritrea	8	2	25.22	2	95.61	24.11
Ethiopia	523	289	55.26	247	85.66	47.34
Gambia	11	9	82.62	9	91.15	75.31
Guinea	588	3	0.48	2	56.20	0.27
Guinea-Bissau	16	0.31	1.93	0.15	46.43	0.90
Lesotho	280	6	2	2	30.32	0.61
Liberia	383	3	0.81	2	52.92	0.43
Madagascar	1,030	765	74.25	15	1.98	1.47
Malawi	268	238	88.96	235	98.78	87.87
Mali	44	5	12.22	4	66.83	8.16
Mauritania	549	295	53.77	290	97.47	52.84
Mozambique	1,493	1,090	73.04	1,063	97.47	71.19
Niger	115	4	3.35	3	81.50	2.73
Rwanda	51	9	19	9	91.04	17.06
São Tomé and Principe	9	1	11.22	1	87.18	9.78

(continued)

TABLE 5.4. (continued)

			Annual Average, 2016–2020			
African LDCs	Total Exports to EU (€ millions)	Eligible for EBA/GSP (€ millions)	Preference Eligible as a Percent of Total Exports	Preference Utilized (€ millions)	Preference Utilization Rate (Percent)	Preference Utilized as a Percent of Total Exports
Senegal	428	317	74	306	96.57	71.52
Sierra Leone	239	3	1.13	1	41.59	0.47
Somalia	19	0.44	2.34	0.18	41.44	0.97
South Sudan	5	0.36	7.73	0.02	4.23	0.33
Sudan	199	21	10.63	20	95.24	10.121
Tanzania	527	259	49.16	253	97.45	52.76
Togo	109	21	19	18	86.14	16.56
Uganda	450	138	30.67	136	98.36	30.17
Zambia	354	59	16.55	53	90.92	15.05
Total African LDCs	13,570	3,651	26.90	2,366	64.81	17.44
Bangladesh	15,299	15,280	99.87	14,773	96.68	96.56
Other LDCs	7,383	7,016	95.03	6,637	94.60	89.90
All LDCs	36,252	25,947	71.57	23,776	91.64	65.58

The euro amounts are rounded, but percentages were calculated using unrounded numbers.
Sources: European Commission (2020a) and European Union's database on the utilization of EBA, GSP, and GSP+—EU's GSPhub.un.

TABLE 5.5. EBA eligibility and utilization—annual average, 2016–2020

		Share of Exports Eligible for EBA				
		0–10	11–25	26–50	51–75	76–100
EBA Utilization rate	0–10	Chad		Djibouti	South Sudan	Madagascar
	11–25	Central African Republic				
	26–50	Sierra Leone, Somalia, Guinea, Guinea-Bissau, Lesotho, Liberia				
	51–75	Angola, Burundi, Equatorial Guinea, São Tomé and Principe	Mali			
EBA Utilization rate	76–100	Burkina Faso, Democratic Republic of Congo, Niger	Benin, Eritrea, Rwanda, Sudan, Togo, Zambia	Comoros, Ethiopia, Uganda	Gambia, Mauritania, Mozambique, Senegal, Tanzania	Malawi

Source: Synopsis of Table 5.4.

jumps to 66 percent. The most dominant LDC, by far, is Bangladesh.[9] The value of exports from Bangladesh that utilized preference was six times that of all African LDCs combined.

No generalization can be made regarding the EBA based on Tables 5.4 and 5.5. (See also Gasiorek et al. (2010).) The EBA is hardly of any value for some African LDCs. Yet the EBA is of great value for others, to the extent that a large percentage of their exports to the EU utilizes the preferential advantage. Nonetheless, the relevance of EBA is expected to diminish as the EU (a) continues its efforts to establish Economic Partnership Agreements (EPAs) with the African, Caribbean, and Pacific (ACP) countries, and (b) reduces some MFN tariffs to zero.

U.S. AGOA Program

In 2020, twenty-seven Sub-Saharan African countries, including non-LDC countries, were eligible for benefits under both the general AGOA provision and AGOA's apparel provision.[10] Two of those non-LDC countries are Sub-Saharan Africa's two largest economies, Nigeria and South Africa. Combined, the value of U.S. imports from those two countries was $17.3 billion, which was 90 percent of the total U.S. imports from Sub-Saharan Africa. As shown in Table 5.6, $11.9 billion—68.5 percent of those imports—entered the U.S. under the *most favored nation* zero import duties. That is, the zero customs duties were not due to any special preferential program. Of the remaining $5.4 billion worth of imports, $3 billion entered duty-free under AGOA and $0.9 billion entered duty-free under the U.S. GSP program. Essentially, all U.S. imports from Sub-Saharan Africa that faced custom duties could have taken advantage of AGOA or the GSP program and entered duty-free. Overall, preference utilization was 72.5 percent. However, preference utilization is noticeably higher for certain sectors, such as apparel, live plants and cut flowers, and fruits and nuts. Some countries, such as Kenya, Lesotho, South Africa, Tanzania, and Mauritius, made efforts to expand those sectors precisely to take advantage of the preferential trade arrangements offered by the U.S. While almost

TABLE 5.6. Preference utilization by Sub-Saharan African countries eligible for AGOA's general and apparel benefits (2020)

1	2	3	4	5		6	7
Harmonized Tariff Schedule of the U.S.—Chapter number	Products	Value ($)	Value of products with MFN duty free ($) (percent of the value in parentheses)	Value of products that utilized preferential treatment ($) AGOA	GSP	Value of eligible products to which duty was applied (no program claimed) ($)	Preference utilization—percent (5)/(5+6)
6	Live trees and other plants; bulbs, roots and the like; cut flowers and ornamental foliage	15,614,170	881,900 (5.6)	4,022,627	10,323,330	386,313	97.4
7	Vegetables	28,967,297	2,090,795 (7.2)	14,149,632	4,129,309	8,597,561	68.0
8	Fruit and nuts	278,674,488	36,774,544 (13.2)	208,494,464	9,879,009	23,526,471	90.3
27	Mineral fuels, mineral oils and products of their distillation	1,872,428,760	165,583,556 (8.8)	550,414,750	2,601	1,156,427,853	32.2

(continued)

TABLE 5.6. (*continued*)

1	2	3	4	5		6	7
Harmonized Tariff Schedule of the U.S.—Chapter number	Products	Value ($)	Value of products with MFN duty free ($) (percent of the value in parentheses)	Value of products that utilized preferential treatment ($)		Value of eligible products to which duty was applied (no program claimed) ($)	Preference utilization—percent (5)/(5+6)
				AGOA	GSP		
61, 62, and 63	Textiles and apparel	1,224,704,309	2,238,142 (0.2)	1,175,627,515	678,591	46,160,061	96.2
1–97	All products	17,330,979,094	11,874,964,741 (68.5)	3,026,151,289	876,714,649	1,500,171,676	72.5

Source: U.S. International Trade Commission's database—usitc.gov/trade.

every year there is a slight change in the list of countries eligible for AGOA, the overall utilization rate has remained around 70 percent.

Given the competitive advantage that Asian countries have over African countries in apparel under "a level playing field," the AGOA apparel program has given qualified African countries a "leg up" in competition. In a country such as Lesotho, AGOA has been a catalyst in the growth of its textiles and apparel sector. The most important feature of the AGOA apparel program is the third-country fabric provision that allows qualified countries to use fabric made in any country, as if it were produced in the domestic market. This provision does not apply to South Africa. This provision has made it easier for African countries to attract foreign direct investors who seek to take advantage of it. Approximately 95 percent of U.S. imports of apparel from AGOA-eligible countries are produced using third-country fabric (Schneidman and Lewis, 2012; Lu, 2020). As the information in Table 5.1 suggests, some Asian companies opened subsidiaries in African countries precisely to take advantage of AGOA, and those subsidiaries would not survive without it.

BENEFITS FOR PREFERENCE-RECEIVING COUNTRIES

Among the potential benefits of special and preferential treatment to the benefit-receiving countries are increased export prices, increased foreign direct investment and production, greater export product diversification, and increasing domestic employment and tax revenues. The extent to which those countries will experience these economic benefits depends on a number of factors, discussed below.

Increase in Export Prices

A tariff is a tax on imports. Removal of a tariff may cause the price of the product to increase for the exporter, and the price of the product to decrease for the importer. This is because the amount of import tax (tariff) that was being paid to the government can now be shared by the exporter and the importer.[11] As such, removal of a tariff may be a benefit to both the exporter and the importer. However, the benefit is not necessarily equally distributed. The distribution of this benefit depends on the relative power of each side. In a situation where the exporter has limited bargaining power, most of the benefits will accrue to the importer, that is, the price will decrease for the importer with little or no change in the price received by the exporter.

In their carefully conducted empirical study, Olarreaga and Ozden (2005) measured the price benefit (tariff rent) captured by textiles and apparel preference-receiving countries in the AGOA program. The study focused on apparel exported to the U.S. by seven countries, for a period of six quarters, beginning with the first quarter of 2001. Using a weighted average, there was a 5.3 percent increase in the price for exports of apparel from these countries with AGOA preferential treatment compared to exports that were subject to MFN tariffs. The seven African countries captured a maximum of 30 percent of the increase in price captured. For individual countries, the weighted average increase in price and the percentage of that increase that was captured (in parentheses) were: Eswatini—0.1 (7); Kenya—7.9 (45); Lesotho—5.2 (29); Madagascar—1 (6); Malawi—6 (35); Mauritius—10.2 (66); and South Africa—14.4 (81). According to the study, these were the maximum possible tariff rents captured by those countries because the benefits were measured at U.S. customs. They do not account for the tariff rate that might be captured by trade intermediaries. It is common for small or new exporters to use intermediaries to assist them in accessing foreign markets.

Olarreaga and Ozden's empirical evidence suggests that the most important determinants of the distribution of tariff rents are the relative size of the exporter and importer. Size determines leverage. For example, a large U.S. company such as Walmart, which has diverse sources for its imports, will have substantial leverage over small exporters in Lesotho who rely mostly on the U.S. market for their apparel products. In terms of elasticities, this means Walmart's demand for apparel will be elastic, while Lesotho's supply of apparel to Walmart will be inelastic.

Size disadvantage is a reality for most producers in Africa. Producers in East Africa with whom the author corresponded stated they have no leverage whatsoever with their customers, except to try to produce quality products. To increase their bargaining power, African producers must strengthen domestic and regional producers' associations. Competition among African producers is unavoidable, and it is even good for efficiency. However, that should not prevent cooperation among associations, for mutual benefit. Regional economic blocs provide convenient structures within which to build such regional associations.

Increase in Foreign Direct Investment and Production

Many factors determine the inflow of foreign direct investment, two of which are access to larger markets and friendly investment policies. Preferential trade treatment extended to developing countries is an invitation to companies that want to take advantage of the markets that have reduced or eliminated tariffs. Programs such as AGOA and EBA also encourage (and sometimes require) beneficiary countries to establish friendlier policies for investment.

All national AGOA strategy papers make clear the need to remove barriers and improve the investment climate. African countries such as Ethiopia, Eswatini, Ghana, Kenya, Lesotho, Madagascar, Mauritius, Namibia, South Africa, and Tanzania saw an immediate increase in FDI and more utilization of existing capacity in their textile and apparel industry directly linked to AGOA (Kaplinsky and Morris, 2008; Phelps et al., 2009; Brookings, 2010; Staritz and Morris, 2013; Yeshiwas, 2016).

To further encourage foreign direct investment, African countries have established export processing zones (EPZs), special industrial parks, or other types of special economic zones designed to give incentives to export-oriented production. Table 5.7 provides examples of the incentives in EPZs for a small sample of African countries. Incentives shown in the table are not exhaustive. Of course, the effectiveness of these incentives in any country depends on the institutional

TABLE 5.7. Incentives in EPZs in a sample of African countries

Country	Incentives
Cameroon	• 10-year corporate income tax holiday • Favorable labor laws and an exemption from the standard wage classification scheme
Ethiopia (Industrial Parks)	• 8–15 years income tax exemption • Export tax exemption • Exemption from custom duties • Unlimited repatriation of profits and dividends
Ghana	• 10-year tax exemption on dividends • Exemption from payment of value added tax and import duties on inputs
Kenya	• 10-year corporate income tax holiday • 10-year withholding tax holiday on dividends and other remittances to non-resident parties • Exemption from payment of value added tax and import duties on inputs
Mauritius	• Free repatriation of dividends • Favorable labor laws for termination of employment and overtime
Tanzania	• Exemption from payment of VAT and import duties for inputs • 10-year corporate income tax holiday • Exemption from taxes and levies imposed by local government authorities on products produced in EPZs
Togo	• 10-year corporate income tax holiday • 10-year tax exemption on dividends • Reduced tax on salaries, from 7% to 2%

Sources: Countries' EPZ websites; Madani, 1999; and Trade Law Centre for Southern Africa, 2010.

environment, overall macroeconomic stability, overall infrastructure, political commitment to foreign direct investment, and political stability. Mauritius is often cited as a country that has had all these ingredients, which allowed its EPZs, first created in 1970, to be important in contributing to the country's economic growth (Frankel, 2012).

Many other countries in the world offer similar incentives to attract foreign direct investment. As of 2019, there were 5,383 special economic zones in 147 economies (UNCTAD, 2019a: 136–37).

Foreign direct investment, linked to special and preferential treatment, has been a boost to production and employment, especially of women, in textile and horticulture sectors. AGOA has provided a clear shift in U.S. trade policy by targeting African countries; its impact on investment and production is, thus, easier to see.[12] Studies show that AGOA has caused an increase in production and exports of textiles and apparel in almost all beneficiary countries (Kassa and Coulibaly, 2019; USTR, 2020; World Bank, 2015). Exports of textiles and apparel to the U.S. from AGOA textile beneficiaries whose benefits have never been interrupted increased from an annual average of $246 million (1996–2000) to $765 million (2016–20).[13]

The increase in exports in this sector was mostly due to trade creation rather than trade diversion (Condon and Stern, 2011; Fernandes et al., 2021). However, since foreign investors, no less those in the textiles and apparel industry, are nomadic in nature and practice, a high degree of fragility exists. Foreign investors tend not to make efforts to establish domestic backward linkages that would integrate them firmly into the local economy (Edwards and Lawrence, 2016). Investors are quite sensitive to erosion in the margin of preference and incentives given to them by host governments. When AGOA took effect in 2000, the MFA was still in effect, thus giving African producers of apparel a substantial advantage over their rivals in Asian countries for exports to the EU and the U.S. Biggs et al. (1996: 80) estimated that the quota scheme increased the cost of men's casual shirts exported by India and China to the EU by 14 percent and 24 percent, respectively. This is an important reason why AGOA beneficiaries became immediately attractive to investors. However, no sooner had the MFA ended (on December 31, 2004) than a number of foreign producers closed business in AGOA countries. Production of apparel fell precipitously.

> The value of SSA clothing exports to the US dropped by 26% during 2004–2006. . . . Lesotho experienced a fall in export value of 15%, most of which occurred in 2005; its exports stabilized in 2006. Madagascar fared worse (a decline of 26%), as did [Eswatini] (24%). Kenya saw largely unchanged exports (a fall of only 5%). The biggest casualties were South Africa (a decline of 53%) and Mauritius (a decline of 48%). (Kaplinsky and Morris, 2008: 262)

The closure and departure of firms left thousands of garment workers without employment. The decline in the industry happened even though when the MFA ended, a considerable nominal margin of preference was still left for AGOA countries whose apparel could enter the U.S. market duty-free. In the immediate post-MFA year, the weighted average tariff for U.S. imports of apparel was 11.36 percent (Kaplinsky and Morris, 2008: 261).

With an improvement in the investment climate and productivity in AGOA countries, the production and export of apparel rebounded and even increased over time. Nonetheless, some firms on the margin will not survive when the margin of preference decreases or tax or other government incentives end. Moreover, machines used in the textile and apparel industry can easily be moved from one country to another in response to various factors. It is important, therefore, that producers do not become too reliant on preferential treatment. More importantly, it is important for policy makers to be sure that tax holidays and other incentives are reduced or eliminated gradually. Policy makers must also design systems that integrate foreign producers into the domestic economy through backward and forward linkages. Currently, producers in export processing zones are only allowed to produce for export.

Increase in Export Diversification

Export diversification is an ever-present goal in all long-term economic development programs initiated by or for African LDCs. One of the key priorities of the Africa Union's Agenda 2063 is the promotion of diversification in exports and economic activities in general, to develop resilient economies. Countries that are reliant on a single or just a few export commodities are vulnerable to adverse shocks that cause prices to fall or supply to decrease. Export diversification is often measured by UNCTAD's Export Product Concentration Index, ranging from zero to one. The index provides the degree of concentration of the "basket" of exported products. African countries such as Angola (petroleum), Botswana (diamonds), the Republic of Congo (petroleum), Chad (petroleum), Equatorial Guinea (petroleum), Nigeria (petroleum), and South Sudan (petroleum) that are highly dependent on natural resources have a high concentration index.[14] While natural resources contribute to economic growth, they can also be a barrier to export diversification.

As to be expected, export diversification is determined by many factors. They include, not in any particular order, an abundance of natural resources, human capital, the quality of institutions (governance), infrastructure, the production structure, the degree of development of the financial sector, and access to foreign markets. Abundance of a natural resource predisposes a country to be too reliant on it. The situation is made worse by the fact that, with the exception of Botswana, Sub-Saharan African countries that are endowed with natural resources, especially petroleum, have weak institutions, as reflected by their high levels of corruption. Advancement in human capital, improved infrastructure, production structures that have backward and forward linkages in domestic manufacturing, and a vibrant financial sector increase export diversification (Osakwe and Kilolo, 2018; Giri, at al., 2019). Amurgo-Pachero and Pierola (2008: 21) also found that

> geographical factors (proxied by distance) and the size of the market of the destination nation significantly determine the change in the probability that a country exports a more diversified basket of goods. We also find that trading with a partner in the North increases the probability to export more goods especially for developing countries. Likewise, we also find that signing FTAs [Free Trade Areas] and therefore reducing trade costs helps to boost diversification.

The case is often made that for African countries to be able to take advantage of preferential trade arrangements, the rules of origin should be relaxed to allow these countries to use imported inputs more freely. The openness of the markets of the major trade partners, when not limited to just a few products or only primary products, has the potential to stimulate export diversification (Brenton and Hoppe, 2006). AGOA has enabled some African countries not only to increase their aggregate exports to the U.S., but also to diversify their exports of agricultural and manufactured products. These countries include Botswana, Ethiopia, Kenya, Lesotho, Tanzania, and South Africa (Kassa and Coulibaly, 2019).

It is important to recognize that some rules of origin have provisions that are too accommodating. Some attractive provisions can inadvertently limit production linkages in benefit-receiving countries. Edwards and Lawrence (2016) show that while AGOA's provision to allow the use of U.S. and third-country fabrics is critical to African LDC competitiveness in the U.S. market, it has "caused least developed AGOA recipients to specialize in fabric-intensive products with low value added." African LDCs rely heavily on imported fabric (Balchin and Calabrese, 2019). For example, Kenya imports 93 percent of the fabric used to produce apparel for export (Kenya Investment Authority, 2019). Given that most producers of apparel in African countries are subsidiaries of corporations in Asia, reliance on imported fabric is a "no brainer." It is exactly how the corporations would want it to be, to preserve their vertical integration within the corporation.

Increase in Domestic Employment and Tax Revenues

The increase in employment and tax revenues is linked to increases in investment and production. Increased exports can increase employment opportunities and the quality of jobs. The number and types of jobs created depend on many factors, including the business environment, the quality of public education, and the desired levels of processing of products (to add value). A good business environment attracts investors, good public education produces skilled labor, and various levels of processing of products (to add value) require varying degrees of skilled labor.

Provisions in the preferential trade arrangements call for good working conditions. Although this is not always adhered to, AGOA and other nonreciprocal preferential trade arrangements include language to protect workers. For example, AGOA requires beneficiary countries to respect "internationally recognized worker rights and human rights" (The White House, 2000).[15] A number of African countries have fallen short of ensuring worker rights and human rights, a reason why some have seen their eligibility for AGOA benefits suspended.

AGOA has created thousands of employment opportunities for low-skilled workers in industries such as horticulture and textile and apparel. It has also created jobs for skilled workers in the processing of products and in marketing and sales. In Kenya alone, AGOA has created over 50,000 jobs directly in the textile and apparel industry (Owusu and Otiso, 2021).

It can be expected that increases in production and formal employment will increase tax revenues and valuable foreign exchange. There are hardly any empirical studies that estimate the impact of nonreciprocal preferential trade arrangements on government revenues of the preference-receiving countries. However, a study by Conningarth Economists (2002) suggests that AGOA increased South Africa's government revenue by one percent just one year after AGOA went into effect.

––––––

Special and preferential trade arrangements provide opportunities for developing countries to expand their export sector and, potentially, grow their economies. But they are only opportunities. There is nothing inherent about preferential trade arrangements that guarantees substantial positive outcomes for the beneficiary countries. The utilization of these arrangements and the benefits derived from them depend on many factors, both external and internal. The magnitude of the margins of preference, the reliability of the preferences, and the rule-of-origin provisions are among the key external determinants.

Internally, the domestic capacity to expand the production of exports depends on political stability, investment policies, access to credit, the quality and reliability of infrastructure (electricity, water, transportation), and opportunities for backward and forward linkages in production.

AGOA has been a catalyst that has propelled African countries to expand production of textiles and apparel. Yet some of the production activities linked to preferential trade are like tall buildings built hastily, without strong foundations. They are not grounded and, thus, are quite fragile. In Lesotho, for example, while the textile industry has generated thousands of jobs, most of the factories are owned by foreigners who can easily "jump ship" when the margin of preference erodes.

It is imperative that preferential trade arrangements be seen for what they are—useful, but temporary. Producers taking advantage of them must not be complacent; they must look for ways to reduce production costs and find new markets and new customers.

CONCLUSION

THE WORLD IS FULL OF stark economic inequalities between continents, nations, and even people of the same nation. According to the World Bank, the average GDP per capita (purchasing power parity) in high-income countries, in 2022, was 14 times more than that in Sub-Saharan African countries. Within Sub-Saharan Africa itself, the GDP per capita in Botswana was 22 times higher than that in Burundi. The inequality in the GDP per capita manifests itself in many other measures of in-equality, including access to food and other basic necessities, the pro-vision of social services, shares of exports and imports in the world, access to foreign direct investment, and technological innovation.

Economic inequalities are closely correlated to inequalities in po-litical power. Those with economic and political power shape global trade relations, notwithstanding that each member of the World Trade Organization (WTO), for example, has a single vote. African countries are part of the global economy, but have "mostly been taker[s] rather than maker[s] of the rules in the international system" (Sidiropoulos, 2022: 99). This is mainly because of their relatively small economies. The economic power of the U.S., China, and the EU dwarfs that of most African countries. The competition among the global powers for African resources, markets, investment projects, and strong diplomatic ties is a double-edged sword for African countries.

On the one hand, African countries do not have to rely as heavily on the U.S. and European countries for investments, loans, and manufactured products as they did before China became an economic power. Competition between global powers gives African countries alternatives and some negotiating power. China is increasingly becoming an important lender to African countries, with, supposedly, fewer conditions than those imposed by the World Bank. Chinese lending to African governments and regional institutions increased from an annual average of $1.5 billion between 2001 and 2005 to $14 billion between 2016 and 2020. Total Chinese loans to Africa from 2002 to 2020 amounted to $170 billion. In the same period, the World Bank and African Development Bank loans to Africa amounted to $264.15 billion and $36.85 billion, respectively (Boston University Global Development Policy, 2023). Having alternative lenders, for example, gives African countries some leverage and the courage to refuse loans that come with potentially tough conditions.

On the other hand, some of the competition tactics used by these competing economic powerhouses are harmful to African economic development, especially in countries with poor governance and weak democratic institutions that are easily manipulated. The tactics used by global powers include giving personal favors to African leaders to approve large construction projects that lack transparency and paying for expensive, ostentatious conferences where promises of aid are ceremoniously made. Of course, African countries must be cautious not to become "prey" to these charms and find themselves in a debt trap.

If African countries could unite and negotiate as a coalition, they would have some leverage even when negotiating with global powers. However, that type of unity is not present. It is too early to determine whether or not the African Continental Free Trade Area (AfCFTA) will bring African countries together to the point of giving the continent noticeable power in global negotiations.

As Sidiropoulos (2022: 99) describes it:

Africa's agency [negotiating power] has grown over the last decade or so, as the institutions that the continent created in the early twenty-first century have become more effective at coordinating Africa's voice in multilateral forums. However, that voice is still marginal—a problem compounded by the fact that the continent's fifty-plus countries do not all share the same interests, making a common voice difficult to achieve or subject to the lowest common denominator.

To build a strong coalition, AfCFTA needs, first and foremost, to become a genuine free trade area. AfCFTA claims to be what it is not. Part of the challenge is that many African leaders make promises about a continental free trade area and unity lightly. Moreover, African leaders, in general, do not hold each other accountable. This is partly because very few of them have the moral authority to criticize others.

As to the root causes of economic and political power inequalities between African and developed countries, that is beyond the scope of this book. However, to the extent that the colonial economic system was repressive and exploitative by its very design, it can be argued that colonialism is one cause of the vulnerabilities of some African countries—economies that are too specialized and overly dependent on other countries for manufactured products.

But most African countries have been independent for over sixty years. While that is a relatively short time for a country, colonialism cannot be used, indiscriminately, as an excuse for slow growth in development. Domestic policies and political stability play a vital role in determining the trajectory of a country's economic development. Moreover, each country's economy has many parts that are intricately connected, requiring thoughtful domestic policies.

The trade arrangements whereby richer countries give preferential market access to products originating from developing countries are a means through which economies of developing countries can be helped to grow faster and a way to deal with economic disparities between countries. At their best, they are meant to be staircases on which developing countries can climb to be more productive and develop diverse and resilient economies. When successful, preferential trade arrangements can help reduce the economic inequality between rich and poor countries. They can be a contributing factor in promoting human development in developing countries.

Historically and practically, the preferential market access devised by European countries to favor the African, Caribbean, and Pacific (ACP) countries was meant, on the one hand, to support those countries and, on the other hand, to preserve the colonial pattern of trade that had worked favorably for the Europeans during the colonial era. That is, to put it in general terms, Europe wanted to import unprocessed raw materials and export processed and manufactured products. This pattern was reinforced by the European tariff escalation scheme under which the effective rate of protection (barriers) was lower for unprocessed goods than for processed and manufactured products.

The side effect of these arrangements was that African countries specialized narrowly in a few products, regardless of whatever the intentions of these programs may have been. This was the case despite the potentially positive impact of STABEX and SYSMIN, programs established to stabilize the export earnings of agricultural crops and mineral products. In fact, STABEX and SYSMIN became an incentive to specialize in order to meet the threshold for assistance through these programs. A vicious cycle is often associated with these types of programs. The longer they are implemented, the longer they lock a country into narrow specialization and, thus, the more the programs are needed to stabilize export earnings. This pattern was reinforced internally after independence. Many African countries embraced and expanded the roles of agricultural marketing boards, which acted with nearly absolute monopoly and monopsony powers for the crops they were assigned to promote.

International commodity agreements for products such as cocoa, coffee, tea, rubber, sugar, and tin, established in the 1950s and 1960s, were viewed as ways to stabilize and support the world prices of commodities originating from developing countries. But, again, one of their side effects was to push countries to become too dependent on a few commodities for export revenue. While the collapse of these agreements at the end of the Cold War was not welcomed by countries that had become reliant on them, the silver lining was that it forced those countries to become less dependent on a single commodity.

Many African countries are eligible for the GSP programs and, more importantly, for the EU's EBA and the U.S.'s AGOA programs. For all these programs, the rules regarding the country of origin of products are critical, both for customs purposes and to help prevent the transshipment of goods, that is, trade deflection. Yet the autonomy exercised by preference-giving countries has created a multitude of different specifications for domestic content requirements and cumulation provisions for imported inputs and intermediate products. Even a slight variation in these rules, places logistical and practical constraints on the ability of preference-receiving countries to diversify their markets for their products. As Barceló III (2006:12) explained:

> When multiple [Rules of Origins (ROOs)] vary or conflict, producers and traders cannot be sure that a single production run, with a certain make-up of components and value added, will satisfy all relevant ROOs. If more than one production run is needed to satisfy different sets of ROOs, returns to scale are lost.

Nonreciprocal preferential trade arrangements are a tool for economic development. However, it is a tool whose strength diminishes over time as the margin of preference decreases. In addition, since it is a "borrowed" tool, its life span is not always certain. Long-run development plans cannot be made based on it, at least not without discounting its future value. Yet, when available, these preferential trade arrangements can be used in conjunction with other development tools to expand and diversify the export sector and, in turn, be a source of economic development. Here are recommendations for different entities—international organizations, preference-giving countries, producers in preference-receiving countries, preference-receiving countries, regional economic blocs, and the African Union.

KEY INTERNATIONAL ORGANIZATIONS

The key international organizations in this area are the WTO, the United Nations Conference on Trade and Development (UNCTAD), and the Economic Commission for Africa (ECA). The WTO should work with preference-giving countries to standardize domestic content requirements and cumulation provisions. Bilateral cumulation can still apply to each country or region giving trade preferences. Inputs imported by Tanzania from the EU, for example, should count in the bilateral cumulation (donor country content) of Tanzania's exports to the EU.

The value of preferential trade agreements is significantly diminished by the high level of uncertainty about their renewals. GSP and other preferential trade programs are periodically reviewed to reexamine eligibility, product coverage, depth of tariff cuts, and the duration of the programs. Because of the unilateral nature of the decisions about these programs and the domestic politics in the preference-giving countries, there is always uncertainty when they come up for renewal. The U.S. GSP program is one that has become of particular concern, since it is often not renewed on time (and then renewed retroactively) and renewed only for short periods (just two years). AGOA has not yet suffered that degree of uncertainty, but there are no guarantees that it would not be in the same predicament in the future.

Here again, the WTO, as the issuer of the waiver to the MFN principle, should require a minimum period of at least ten years for extensions of these programs. That would allow both importers and exporters to make medium-term investment decisions with a higher degree of certainty about market access.

With respect to the ongoing negotiations on Economic Partnership Agreements (EPAs), UNCTAD and the ECA should provide technical expertise to African countries. Negotiations between developed countries and most African countries are usually asymmetrical due to the disparity in technical capacity. For any area of negotiation, developed countries are equipped with a slew of specialists, whereas African countries might be represented by just a few generalists. UNCTAD and the ECA can help bridge the technical capacity gap and enable African countries to negotiate minute details of agreements with clear understanding and full knowledge.

PREFERENCE-GIVING COUNTRIES

A key feature of preferential trade arrangements is that they are unpredictable. Clearly, the margin of preference is always changing, mostly decreasing, but not in the most predictable way. Preference-giving countries could increase the stability of these programs by renewing them at least a year before their expiration and avoiding ambiguous conditions on eligibility that can be used arbitrarily to disqualify a country. To enable preference-receiving countries to engage in at least medium-term planning, these programs should be extended for at least ten years, each time they are renewed.

PRODUCERS IN PREFERENCE-RECEIVING COUNTRIES

Producers of export products in preference-receiving countries are the ones that are directly affected by any changes in nonreciprocal preferential trade programs. They need to stay abreast of all the nuances of program provisions to ensure their products are not ineligible due to some technical shortcomings. That requires them to work closely among themselves through their respective manufacturers' associations and with their Ministry of Trade. They must also maintain close ties with their importers to be sure products are meeting the requirements of their importers.

To the extent possible, producers must avoid being too dependent on one market for their products and/or a single supplier for their inputs. They also need to have contingency plans in case of abrupt changes in policies or margins of preference. Finally, producers must adhere to labor laws as required by their respective governments.

PREFERENCE-RECEIVING COUNTRIES

Preference-receiving countries can do a lot to help their producers benefit from preferential trade arrangements. Moreover, these arrangements are not imposed on them. If they think they are harmful, they can choose not to take part in them. It has been made clear that the renewals of these arrangements are never guaranteed and a beneficiary country can be terminated from a given program by a preference-giving country for a variety of reasons. Therefore, no matter how friendly the conditions might be, preference-receiving countries must always operate with the mind-set that these programs are temporary, regardless of how long they have been in existence.

It is to be expected that preference-receiving countries will ask for rules of origin that more readily accommodate inputs from other countries, that is, rules of origin that are less restrictive. The third-party provision in the AGOA and EBA programs, for which LDCs pushed, is considered a key feature for African countries to be able to take advantage of these programs. While this provision has enhanced exports of fabric-intensive apparel from Sub-Saharan Africa to the U.S. and the EU, it has, inadvertently, also limited the motivation to produce fabric domestically (Edwards and Lawrence, 2016). Thus, in this case, AGOA and EBA may not foster the backward and forward linkages that one might have expected. Moreover, foreign investors would prefer to import fabric from their home parent companies in Asia or elsewhere. By producing fabric in one or a few locations, they can take full advantage of economies of scale.

The third-party provision provides an advantage, but African countries must not be too reliant on imported fabric. Trade becomes an important source of development when production is spread to various sectors and geographical regions through backward and forward linkages. The supply chain of the textile industry goes from cotton production, ginning, weaving and knitting, and fabric production, all the way to apparel production.

As Calabrese and Balchin (2022:42) show in their study, the degree of embeddedness of investors in the domestic economy is highly dependent on the types of investment incentives available to them. They conclude:

> Beyond the initial stages of development in a sector, it is important to incentivize investors to contribute to upgrading and be willing to relocate some of the investment decisions in the country. This can be done through specific policies that support the development of the necessary skills and networks to upgrade the sector.

Most of the investment incentives offered by African countries have been rather generic, aiming simply at the broad goals of increasing foreign direct investment and the volume of exports. With the exception of South Africa and Mauritius, production in the textile industry is dominated by the downstream processes of cutting and sewing.

Investment incentives must be deliberate in their application to maximize foreign direct investment spillovers that can occur through (i) an increase in demand for domestic inputs; (ii) domestic firms hiring workers who have acquired experience from foreign firms; (iii) domestic workers with experience from foreign firms opening their own operations; and (iv) learning new management and operating practices (Brussevich and Shawn, 2019: 5).

Tax and other financial incentives must be structured so as to encourage the use of domestic raw materials, thereby building backward linkages. Specific examples include corporate tax and value added tax exemptions contingent on buying local materials and providing low-interest loans to domestic suppliers of raw materials and other inputs.[1] In addition, regulations for foreign direct investment should mandate a minimum requirement for local employees in managerial positions. This will require the training of local managers and create a pool of people with transferable skills.

Incentives must be carefully spelled out to reduce ambiguity and avoid being taken advantage of. For example, it is not sufficient to require a minimum number of local managers, without specifying what roles constitute a managerial position. Without such specifications, every employee could be labeled a manager. Likewise, if there is a tax holiday for ten years, for example, safeguards need to be in place to prevent nomadic firms from simply coming to operate during those ten years and then moving to a different country. A safeguard could be that a foreign direct investor cannot bring in used machines from another plant, that is, machines that can easily be abandoned or discarded at no major loss after the grace period is over.

Some countries are encouraging the processing of raw materials by taxing or banning exports of those materials. These policies have been applied to agricultural products and natural resources. Because the benefits of adding value seem so obvious, it is, mistakenly, very easy to justify any means. However, this is a case where good intentions do not necessarily justify the means. A tax on cashew nuts or ban on exports of them, for example, would amount to an implicit subsidy for processors and an implicit tax on farmers. Processors operate in an oligopolistic market structure and, therefore, have considerable control over the price they pay farmers. Cashew nut producers are small subsistence farmers who are price takers. By limiting the market for their product, producer prices fall, removing the benefits that trade could bring them.[2] Setting producer price floors is not a solution either. They negate the whole idea of encouraging domestic processing.

If the main objective is to promote the domestic processing of raw materials, a direct production subsidy for processors of those materials would be less distortionary than an export tax or a ban on exports. Note that an export tax is the same as giving a production subsidy (to domestic buyers and domestic processors of raw materials) and imposing a production tax (to producers of the raw materials) combined. Domestic processors could be subsidized by being exempted from paying import duties on the machinery and equipment they need. That is what Cameroon did in conjunction with its restrictions on log exports (Business in Cameroon, 2022).

Although some investment decisions are made with a clear target market based on a particular program such as AGOA or EBA, preference-receiving countries should devise incentives to encourage producers to diversify their markets. The tax incentives that are used to attract investors to export processing zones can be structured in ways that promote such diversification. As discussed in Chapter 5, some firms depend solely on one market and on just one or two buyers in that market. That is very risky.

More broadly, African countries must improve the long-term determinants of investment, so that the specific incentives used to attract investment have full effect. These determinants include: (i) macroeconomic stability; (ii) political stability; (iii) a good education system; (iv) a regulatory environment that encourages the operation of private enterprises and overall good governance; (v) good and reliable infrastructure; and (vi) increased regional economic integration.

Specifically, macroeconomic stability and political stability allow economic actors to make long-term plans and projections. Without them, most economic activities become speculative and highly risky. An educated labor force is productive and relatively mobile between industries. The global economy, of which African countries are a part, is dynamic. The relative demand for goods and services is constantly shifting, requiring labor that is adaptable to changes in demand and technology. While economic diversification may require targeted industrial policies, what is necessary is a regulatory environment that is conducive to opening and conducting business. This requires good governance. Some countries, especially oil-rich countries, have become too dependent on just one or two export commodities. Many of these countries are also burdened by corrupt governments whose leaders have enriched themselves with proceeds from natural resources.

Infrastructure is vital for economic development. Given the high cost of infrastructure projects and budget constraints, projects must be chosen carefully to ensure that rural areas are integrated into the economy. Infrastructure must also be developed in ways that foster economic diversification, both within an industry and across industries. In addition, economic blocs should work on joint projects to increase linkages between countries in a regional bloc.

REGIONAL ECONOMIC BLOCS AND THE AFRICAN UNION

Regional economic blocs in Africa need to commit to their agreements and avoid being split apart by the negotiations under way to establish Economic Partnership Agreements (EPAs) with the EU. There is unanimity among African leaders about the importance of economic integration, as demonstrated by an array of regional economic blocs and the establishment of the African Continental Free Trade Area (AfCFTA) in 2018. Regional economic integration in Africa is key to attracting investment and increasing intraregional trade. Most African economies are too small to attract productions that need to take advantage of economies of scale to operate profitably.

However, the depth of integration in most of the regional blocs, let alone the AfCFTA, which is relatively new, is way below the commitments member countries have made. For example, the Economic and Monetary Community of Central Africa (CEMAC) and the East African Community (EAC) are supposedly custom unions. In a customs union, member countries remove trade barriers among themselves and maintain common external tariffs. Members of a customs union usually first negotiate among themselves to establish a common position before they negotiate with nonmembers. Yet Cameroon and Kenya, members of the CEMAC and the EAC, respectively, have been able to successfully conclude EPA negotiations with the EU and the UK, individually. This clearly shows that the CEMAC and the EAC are not genuine custom unions. In fact, the EAC does not even function as a full-fledged free trade area, considering various nontrade barriers on intraregional trade (TradeMark Africa, 2022).

The EPA negotiations have heightened the differences between countries in each bloc, and each country seems to be focusing just on its own interests. That is not the way to build viable economic integration.

The AGOA and EBA programs, the two most important preferential trade programs for Sub-Saharan African countries, have provisions that enhance regional economic integration. The country-of-origin rules in these programs allow regional cumulation and even cross-regional cumulation, thus treating neighboring regional blocs as one. These provisions add opportunities for vertical integration within regions. To take advantage of such provisions, regional economic blocs must actually function as free trade areas, customs unions, or whatever level of integration they claim to be. The African Continental Free Trade Area (AfCFTA) came into effect in 2021. However, regional blocs are not even operating as full-fledged free trade areas yet. A genuine continental free trade area requires countries first to honor their commitments to free trade at the regional level.

The AU is limited in what it can do because it does not have the resources or the power needed to direct the course of action of any individual economic bloc (Mshomba, 2017). Ideally, the AU should be given the mandate to establish certain guidelines with respect to economic integration. For example, the AU should establish the minimum requirements of openness and operations for an economic bloc, and the AfCFTA, for that matter, to be officially considered a free trade area, a customs union, a common market, or a monetary union. If the labels for these phases of integration were used with a common meaning, it would be easier, for example, for two free trade areas that want to merge to do so. In fact, a genuine continental free trade area would, in effect, consolidate a number of existing regional blocs.

———

Preferential trade arrangements expand export markets for preference-receiving countries. Thus, they can be important instruments through which to promote human development in those countries. Increased exports, and trade in general, can lead to an improvement in people's lives through increased incomes, access to technology, and a reduction in inequality.

Trade increases the prices of a country's export goods, thereby increasing incomes of the people who are providing the resources to produce those goods. Increased incomes allow people to have access to better nutrition, health services, and education. Increased incomes can also bring and enhance political stability, which is often threatened by poverty. These improvements, together with access to technology, increase the productivity of labor, which, in turn, increases incomes.

African countries can and have used preferential trade arrangements as springboards for economic diversification and economic growth, especially by increasing economic opportunities for women. Horticulture and textiles and apparel are clear examples of industries that have developed and expanded to take advantage of AGOA and EBA programs.

But it is important to remember that these benefits are not necessarily automatic. They require, for example, governments to have and enforce labor laws that protect workers. Countries must also invest in health care and education services, as well as programs that specifically empower women, to address economic inequality. Women in Africa face many barriers to access capital and own property. These barriers must be dismantled in order for preferential trade arrangements to support African countries in producing much-needed gender equality in the economic sphere.

There is no reason to suggest that AGOA, EBA, and GSP programs will be discontinued anytime soon, especially given that the global powers are competing for strong diplomatic and economic relations with African countries. However, the hope is that the number of countries that qualify for these programs will decrease over time, as their economies grow and they no longer need special consideration. Non-reciprocal preferential trade arrangements are only one tool, albeit an important one, in the development toolbox. On their own, the positive impact of these arrangements can be limited. However, when used in conjunction with other development programs and with rules and laws that protect employees and reduce income inequality, they can accelerate economic growth and, in turn, human development.

NOTES

Introduction

1. See also Kragelund and Carmody (2015).

2. This is also the challenge African countries face in negotiations in the World Trade Organization (Mshomba, 2009).

3. The World Bank (1998) makes rather revealing observations about the dynamics of aid during the Cold War era.

Chapter 1

1. For more extended theoretical discussions of these models, see any international economics textbook.

2. First published in 1817.

3. This is a simplification to avoid unnecessary confusion. Assuming that labor is immobile is in effect saying that there are two types of labor in each country: labor that can only produce cotton and labor that can only produce corn. The simplification made here does not change the qualitative results of this hypothetical example.

4. In fact, production subsidies do not reduce the actual opportunity cost, but they reduce the effective opportunity cost borne by producers.

5. Deardorff (1982) showed that the Heckscher-Ohlin theorem is valid even in a model with multiple factors of production, goods, and countries.

6. Chapter 3 focuses on the negotiations to establish Economic Partnership Agreements.

7. Paul Krugman won a Nobel Prize in Economic Sciences in 2008 "for his research on international trade and economic geography. By having shown the effects of economies of scale on trade patterns and on the location of economic activity, his ideas have given rise to an extensive reorientation of the research on these issues" (National Science Foundation, 2008).

8. Real interest rate = $\dfrac{1 = nominal\ interest\ rate}{1 + inflation\ rate}$ − 1. When dealing with low inflation rates, real interest rates can be approximated by the Fisher equation: real interest rate = nominal interest rate—inflation rate. The Fisher equation tends to underestimate the real interest rate, especially when the inflation rate is high, as it was in many African countries at the time.

9. The sources are the International Monetary Fund's *International Financial Statistics*, various issues of International Currency Analysis's *Pick's Currency Yearbook* and *World Currency Yearbook*, and the World Bank's *Commodity Price Data*.

10. The parallel market exchange rate premium in Ghana was highest in 1982 when it reached between 2,100 and 4,500 percent (Kapur, 1991; Maehle et al., 2013).

11. For a very insightful discussion about Tanzania's agricultural policy in the 1970s and 1980s, see Lofchie (1994).

12. Price floors have been used and continue to be used in the EU and the U.S. to support farmers at a very high cost. African countries cannot sustain such policies.

13. Very easy—Mauritius and Rwanda; easy—Kenya, Tunisia, South Africa, Zambia, Botswana, and Togo, listed in order, according to the index.

Chapter 2

1. Namibia was a colony of South Africa.

2. For details of the negotiations by the six EEC members regarding overseas territories, see Djamson (1976), Ravenhill (1985), Zartman (1971), Twitchett (1978), and van Benthem van den Bergh (1963).

3. Associate countries could apply tariffs on products from the EEC bloc, but they had to apply them uniformly to all EEC countries.

4. West Germany and East Germany unified in 1990, and Czechoslovakia split into the Czech Republic and Slovakia in 1993.

5. The Brazzaville Group consisted of Cameroon, Central African Republic, Chad, Dahomey (Benin), Gabon, Ivory Coast (Côte d'Ivoire), Madagascar, Mauritania, Niger, Congo Brazzaville (Republic of Congo), Senegal, and Upper Volta (Burkina Faso).

6. Zartman (1971, 80–115) provides an interesting narrative and analysis of the negotiations by the EEC members with Nigeria and East African countries (Kenya, Tanzania, and Uganda).

7. These were: Francophone—Benin, Burkina Faso, Côte d'Ivoire, Guinea, Mali, Niger, Senegal, Togo; Anglophone—Gambia, Ghana, Liberia, Nigeria, and Sierra Leone; Arab—Mauritania; Lusophone—Guinea-Bissau. Cape Verde (a Lusophone country) joined ECOWAS in 1977. Mauritania withdrew from ECOWAS in 2000.

8. *Associables* were countries that were former British colonies, that is, Commonwealth countries. Associates were former colonies of the other European countries. Associates had already been negotiating with the EEC.

9. Asian Commonwealth countries such as India and Pakistan were left out as they were seen to be more competitive, did not offer any key raw materials, and, at the same time, would have required the EDF to be increased substantially (Lecomte, 2001).

10. The Lomé conventions also had provisions for industrial, financial, and technical cooperation.

11. It is not clear whether the price comparison was to be done in nominal terms or in real terms, that is, taking into account inflation. World inflation in the 1970s and 1980s was in double digits with an annual average of 12 percent (International Monetary Fund, 1980; Boughton, 2000).

12. For extended discussions on international commodity agreements, see U.S. International Trade Commission (1975) and Mshomba (2000, 139–74).

Chapter 3

1. The ACP countries are mentioned together to provide context. However, the chapter focuses on African countries in the ACP. The ACP countries work together as a group as members of the Organization of African, Caribbean, and Pacific States (OACPS). The headquarters of the OACPS are in Brussels, Belgium.

2. Somalia joined the EAC officially on December 15, 2023, when this book was in the production stage (The East African, 2023).

3. France is a member of the IOC because of Reunion, which is considered a region of France.

4. Democratic Republic of the Congo was in the Central Africa Group, but it joined the EAC in 2022.

5. Krapohl and Van Huut (2020) provide a very good discussion about these privileges.

6. EU's GSP and GSP+ are discussed in detail in Chapter 4.

7. The IMF's Government Financial Statistics database on Direction of Trade Statistics and the World Bank database on Taxes on International Trade.

8. Calculated using data from the IMF's Direction of Trade database.

9. Sources of data shown in this section are: European Union reports on EU trade with its trading partners (a typical title of a report would be,

"European Union, Trade in goods with Gabon," as an example); the European Union database on the utilization of EBA, GSP, and GSP+—EU's GSPhub.un; the IMF database for Direction of Trade Statistics; and UNCTAD's database on trade—UNCTADstat.

10. The higher the ranking, the more corrupt the country is perceived to be.

11. According to World Bank data, in 2021, Kenya and Tanzania accounted, respectively, for 37 and 23 percent, of the GDP of the EAC.

12. For a comprehensive discussion about the EAC, see Mshomba (2017).

13. SADC usually refers to all sixteen members of the Southern African Development Community. In the context of EPA negotiations with the EU, SADC refers only to seven of those members.

14. Calculated using data from the European Union database on the utilization of EBA, GSP, and GSP+—EU's GSPhub.un.

15. This data is for the period 2017–20.

16. The IMF database on Government Financial Statistics.

17. Since the study assumes imports of products that are not produced domestically, there is no loss in producer surplus.

18. For a comprehensive discussion on economic integration in Africa, see Mshomba (2017).

Chapter 4

1. All African countries, except Eritrea, are either members of the WTO or have observer status.

2. It was not until 1995, when the World Trade Organization replaced GATT, that the agricultural and textile sectors came under that multilateral jurisdiction.

3. The counterargument to the infant-industry argument for protection is that the industry may remain infant and it can be politically difficult to remove protection.

4. Although Armenia, Belarus, Kazakhstan, Kyrgyzstan, and Russia are listed individually, they are members of the Eurasian customs union and, therefore, give identical preferential market access to GSP-eligible countries.

5. China-Africa Research Institute, Johns Hopkins School of Advanced Studies: http://www.sais-cari.org/data-china-africa-trade.

6. Dispute settlement (DS) cases are numbered in chronological order by the WTO's database on disputes cases. DS246 is on "European Communities—Conditions for the Granting of Tariff Preferences to Developing Countries."

7. For a legal analysis of the case, see McKenzie (2005).

8. The *combined nonmenclature* (CN) is a coding system used to identify similar products for the purpose of tariff rates and other trade barriers and also for trade statistics. It consists of eight digits, derived from a narrowing

of the definition of products. For example, according to the harmonized tariff system codes of the EU:

- Chapter 61 (2 digits) in the Harmonized System (HS) has a broad classification of "articles of apparel and clothing accessories, knitted or crocheted."
- HS 6105 (4 digits) classifies men's or boys' shirts.
- HS 610590 (6 digits) classifies men's or boys' shirts of textile material.
- CN 61059010 (8 digits) classifies men's or boys' shirts of wool or fine animal hair.

9. The Uruguay Round of GATT, from which the WTO was born, was launched in 1986 and concluded in 1993.

10. The main source for the discussion on the rules of origin for the EU GSP is the European Commission (2016).

11. Qualifying member countries of the Southern African Development Community are Botswana, Mauritius, and Tanzania. Qualifying member countries of the West African Economic and Monetary Union are Benin, Burkina Faso, Côte d'Ivoire, Guinea-Bissau, Mali, Niger, Senegal, and Togo.

12. According to the Department of Commerce Office of Textiles and Apparel (OTEXA) website, U.S. textiles and apparel that qualify for duty-free benefits under AGOA include:

1. apparel made of U.S. yarns and fabrics;
2. apparel made of SSA (regional) yarns and fabrics, subject to a cap;
3. apparel made in a designated lesser-developed country of third-country yarns and fabrics (also subject to a cap);
4. apparel made of yarns and fabrics not produced in commercial quantities in the U.S.;
5. textile or textile articles originating entirely in one or more lesser-developed beneficiary SSA countries;
6. certain cashmere and merino wool sweaters; and
7. hand-loomed, handmade, or folklore articles and ethnic printed fabrics.

Under a "special rule" for lesser-developed beneficiary countries, SSA LDCs (with a per capita gross national product of less than $1,500 a year in 1998, as measured by the World Bank) enjoy an additional preference in the form of duty-free and quota-free access for apparel made from fabric originating anywhere in the world.

13. World Bank's database on tariff rates.

14. The average simple MFN tariff rate decreased from 20 percent in 1994 to 9 percent in 2017. There is no measure of average tariff rate without shortcomings. The average simple tariff rate gives all imported products equal weights, regardless of the different values of imports. The weighted average takes into account different weights of imports, but it can be downward biased

since the volume of imports depends, among other things, on the tariff rate. If, for example, a tariff was high enough to eliminate imports of a product altogether, that tariff would not be included in calculating the weighted average tariff.

15. Trade Law Centre for Southern Africa (2023).

16. Before Donald Trump became president, the U.S. and eleven other countries (including Vietnam) were negotiating the establishment of a free trade area to be called the Trans-Pacific Partnership (TPP). Trump withdrew the U.S. from the negotiations and, effectively, killed the prospects for a TPP. The U.S. and Vietnam have had a bilateral trade agreement since 2000, but not one that comes to the level of a free trade area.

17. That is equivalent to about $37 to $44 billion in 2023.

18. World Trade Organization (2007, Chapter 4). See also Marković (2009) and Amadeo (2019).

Chapter 5

1. For an extensive discussion, see Low et al. (2005).

2. Botswana, Burundi, Eswatini, Ethiopia, Ghana, Kenya, Lesotho, Madagascar, Malawi, Mali, Mauritius, Mozambique, Namibia, Rwanda, Senegal, Sierra Leone, Tanzania, Togo, and Zambia. Reports are available at the Trade and Law Centre of Southern Africa's website on "National AGOA Strategies."

3. In 2019, following the 12th U.S.-Africa Business Summit held in Maputo, Mozambique, the CCA announced that starting in 2020, it will hold the U.S.-Africa Business Summit annually. As it happened, the CCA could not hold a summit in 2020 because of the COVID-19 pandemic (Corporate Council on Africa, 2020). However, they resumed in 2021.

4. Calculations based on data from the U.S. International Trade Commission's database—usitc.gov/trade.

5. Andriamananjara and Sy (2015) provide an interesting hypothesis that the rapid growth of the textiles industry may have hurt other sectors by "sucking" labor and other resources out of other sectors. They also suggest a possibility of the "Dutch disease," where growth in the textiles industry caused an appreciation of the ariary (the local currency), leading other export sectors to be less competitive in the world market.

6. Data for Burkina Faso, Gambia, São Tomé and Principe, and South Sudan were not included.

7. Calculated using information in Table 2 in World Trade Organization (2019, 6–8).

8. Equatorial Guinea graduated from LDC status in 2021.

9. Bangladesh is scheduled to graduate from the LDC category in 2026. It will then have three years as a transition period before it loses its eligibility for the EBA program (Dhaka Courier, 2021).

10. Benin, Botswana, Burkina Faso, Cabo Verde, Chad, Cote d'Ivoire, Eswatini, Ethiopia, Ghana, Guinea, Kenya, Lesotho, Liberia, Madagascar, Malawi, Mali, Mauritius, Mozambique, Namibia, Nigeria, Senegal, Sierra Leone, South Africa, Tanzania, Togo, Uganda, and Zambia. Not all AGOA-eligible countries have duty-free access for textiles and apparel to the U.S. market. In 2020, the following eleven countries were eligible for the general AGOA provisions, but not for the special textile and apparel preferences: Angola, Central African Republic, Comoros, Congo (Republic), Djibouti, Gabon, Gambia, Guinea-Bissau, Niger, Rwanda, and São Tomé and Príncipe (U.S. States Trade Commission, 2023).

11. Exporters pay tariff revenues indirectly through reduced prices for their products. UNCTAD (2023:7) estimates that annually, on average, from 2001 to 2021, "AGOA has relieved exporters in sub-Saharan Africa from paying approximately $250–300 million in tariffs." The program's beneficiaries, all other things being equal, would have paid approximately $5–6 billion in tariffs during 2001–21.

12. The EBA program is also of unique importance to African LDCs, but the EU has had special and preferential treatment for African imports since colonial times.

13. Calculations based on data from the U.S. International Trade Commission's database—usitc.gov/trade.

14. A country that exported only one commodity (that is, the opposite of diversification) would have an index of 1. The export product concentration indices for these countries in 2022 were as follows: Angola—0.84, Botswana—0.79, the Republic of Congo—0.6, Chad—0.69, Equatorial Guinea—0.59, Nigeria—0.70, and South Sudan—0.84 (UNCTADSTAT database).

15. Internationally recognized worker rights include "(A) the right of association; (B) the right to organize and bargain collectively; (C) a prohibition on the use of any form of forced or compulsory labor; (D) a minimum age for the employment of children, and (E) acceptable conditions of work with respect to minimum wages, hours of work, and occupational safety and health." (U.S. Department of State, 1987)

Conclusion

1. For an extended discussion on how to promote backward linkages, see Sabha et al. (2020).

2. See Food and Agriculture Organization (2014).

BIBLIOGRAPHY

ACP-EEC (1975). *ACP-EEC Convention signed [in] Lomé on 28 February 1975, ACP-EEC Courier,* No. 31, March.

ACP-EEC (1979). *The Second ACP-EEC Convention signed in Lomé on 31 October 1979, ACP-EEC Courier,* No. 58, November.

ACP-EEC (1985). *The Third ACP-EEC Convention signed [in] Lomé on 8 December 1984 and related documents.* Brussels: European Commission.

ACP-EEC (1992). *Fourth ACP-EEC Convention signed [in] Lomé on 15 December 1989.* Brussels: European Commission.

ACP-EU (1996). "Special Issue on the Revised Lomé Convention." *ACP-EU Courier,* No. 155, January–February.

ACP Secretariat (2000). *Partnership Agreement Between the Members of the African, Caribbean, and Pacific Group of States of the One Part, and the European Community and Its States, of the Other Part.* Geneva: Organization of the ACP States.

African Business Portal (2022). "Emerging Flower Exporters in Africa." African Business Portal.

African Development Bank (2012). *Cape Verde: The Road Ahead.* Abidjan: African Development Bank.

African Development Bank (2016). "Why AGOA Remains Critical to Lesotho's Development." October 3, African Development Bank Group.

African Union Commission (2015). Agenda 2063: The Africa We Want. Addis Ababa: African Union Commission.

Aiello, Francesco (1999). "The Stabilisation of LDCs' Export Earnings: The Impact of the EU STABEX Programme." *International Review of Applied Economics,* 13, no. 1: 71–85.

Akuo, Jacob (2021). "Cameroon Resumes the Implementation of Progressive Elimination of Customs Duties Under the EU-Cameroon Economic Partnership Agreement (EPA)." Dayspring Law Firm, Douala, Cameroon.

Alexandraki, Katerina, and Peter Lankes (2004). "The Impact of Preference Erosion on Middle-Income Developing Countries." *IMF Working Papers,* WP/04/169.

Alston, Julian, et al. (2007). *Impacts of Reductions in US Cotton Subsidies on West African Cotton Producers.* Washington, DC: Oxfam America.

Amadeo, Kimberly (2019). "How Does a Country Become a WTO Member: Six Steps to Accession." *The Balance,* May 14.

Amurgo-Pachero, Alberto, and Martha Pierola (2008). "Patterns of Export Diversification in Developing Countries: Intensive and Extensive Margins." World Bank Policy Research Paper 4473.

Anami, Luke (2020). "Tanzania's Inward-Looking Policies Unlikely to Change." *East African* (Kenya), November 7.

Andriamananjara, Soamiely, and Amadou Sy (2015). "AGOA and Dutch Disease: The Case of Madagascar." *Africa in Focus,* Brookings, February 15.

Arenas, Guillermo, et al. (2018). *Supporting Lesotho's Economic Diversification and Trade Integration: Structural Transformation Through Greater Export Competitiveness.* Washington, DC: World Bank.

Aschheim, Joseph, and Y. S. Park (1976). "Artificial Currency Units: The Formation of Functional Currency Areas." *Essays in International Finance* 114, Princeton University.

Balchin, Neil, and Linda Calabrese (2019). *Comparative Country Study of the Development of Textile and Garment Sectors: Lessons for Tanzania.* London: Overseas Development Institute.

Barceló III, John (2006). "Harmonizing Preferential Rules of Origin in the WTO System." *Cornell Law Faculty Publications,* December 19.

BBC (2015). "Zimbabwe Dollars Phased Out." BBC News, June 12.

BBC (2018). "Tanzania's Magufuli Deploys Military Amid Cashew Nut Crisis." BBC News, November 12.

BBC (2023). "US to Remove Uganda and Three Other African Countries from AGOA Trade Deal." BBC News, October 31.

Beck, Thorsten, and Robert Cull (2014). "Small- and Medium-sized Enterprise Finance in Africa." *African Growth Initiative.* Working Paper 16, Brookings, July.

Belay, Seyoum (2007). "Export Performance of Developing Countries under the Africa Growth and Opportunity Act: Experience from US Trade with Sub-Saharan Africa." *Journal of Economic Studies,* Glasgow, 34, no. 6: 515–33.

Biggs, Tyler, et al. (1996). *Africa Can Compete! Export Opportunities and Challenges for Garments and Home Products in the European Market*. World Bank Discussion Paper 300, Africa Technical Department Series. Washington, DC: World Bank.

Bilal, San (2021). "EU-Africa Trade Relations and the EPA Process: Ratification and Sustainable Development Perspectives for Cameroon, Côte d'Ivoire and Ghana." Discussion Paper 304, European Centre for Development Policy Management.

Borrell, Brent, and Maw-Cheng Yang (1992). *EC Bananarama 1992*, WPS 523, International Economics Department. Washington, DC: World Bank.

Boston University Global Development Policy Center (2023). *A New State of Lending: Chinese Loans to Africa*. Boston: Boston University Global Development Policy.

Boughton, James (2000). *The IMF and the Silent Revolution: Global Finance and Development in the 1980s*. Washington, DC: International Monetary Fund.

Bown, Chad, and Melina Kolb (2020). "Trump's Trade War Timeline: An Up-to-Date Guide." *Peterson Institute for International Economics*, February 14.

Brenton, Paul (2003). "Integrating the Least Developed Countries into the World Trading System: The Current Impact of EU Preferences under Everything but Arms." World Bank Policy Research Working Paper 3018, April.

Brenton, Paul, and Mombert Hoppe (2006). "The African Growth and Opportunity Act, Exports, and Development in Sub-Saharan Africa." World Bank Policy Research Working Paper 3996, August.

British High Commission, Nairobi (2021). "UK-Kenya Economic Partnership Agreement enters into Force." March 24, British High Commission, Nairobi.

Brookings (2010). "AGOA at 10: Challenges and Prospects for U.S.-Africa Trade and Investment Relations." *African Growth Initiative*, Brookings, July.

Brookings (2014). "Africa in the News: Swaziland Loses and Madagascar Regains AGOA Status, African Union Summit, and U.S. Export Import Bank Debate Could Impact U.S.-Africa Trade." *Africa in Focus*, Brookings, June 27.

Brussevich, Mariya, and Tau Shawn (2019). "Encouraging FDI Spillovers." Washington, DC: World Bank.

Bureau, Jean-Christopher, et al. (2007). "The Utilization of Trade Preferences for Developing Countries in the Agri-food Sector." *Journal of Agricultural Economics* 58, no. 2: 175–98.

Bureau of Statistics—Lesotho (2018). *Statistical Report No. 02: 2018 Performance of the Manufacturing Sector in Lesotho*. Maseru: Bureau of Statistics.

Business in Cameroon (2021). "Timber Traceability: CEMAC Postpones Log Export Ban to 2023 to Allow Local Processing Projects to Mature." *Business in Cameroon*, August 9.

Business in Cameroon (2022). "Cameroon Plans to Raise Log Export Duties to 60% to Stimulate Local Processing." *Business in Cameroon*, November 22.

Calabrese, Linda, and Neil Balchin (2022). "Foreign Investment and Upgrading in the Garment Sector in Africa and Asia." *Global Policy* 13, no. 1: 34–44.

Campbell, Colin (2009). "Distinguishing the Power of Agency from Agentic Power: A Note on Weber and the 'Black Box' of Personal Agency." *Sociological Theory* 27, no. 4: 407–18.

Canada Gazette (2013). "General Preferential Tariff Withdrawal Order (2013 GPT Review)." In *Canada Gazette*, Part II, 147(21): 2120–2206.

Casacuberta, Carlos, and Néstor Gandelman (2010). "Reallocation and Adjustment in the Manufacturing Sector in Uruguay." Chapter 4 in Porto, Guido, and Bernard Hoekman, eds., *Trade Adjustment Costs in Developing Countries: Impacts, Determinants and Policy Responses.* Washington, DC: Centre for Economic Policy Research and World Bank and CEPR.

Central Bank of Lesotho (2011). "Africa Growth and Opportunities Act (AGOA): Economic Impact and Future Prospects." *Economic Review*, Central Bank of Lesotho.

Chang, Ha-Joon (2002). *Kicking Away the Ladder: Development Strategy in Historical Perspective.* London: Anthem Press.

Chimanikire, Donald (2019). "EU-Africa and Economic Partnership Agreements (EPAs)—Revisited." *L'Europe en Formation,* no. 388: 51–67.

The Citizen (2017). "Govt Insists a Ban on Maize Export Won't Be Lifted." *Citizen* (Tanzania), June 29.

The Citizen (2019). "Cashew Nuts Ban Affects BoPs [Tanzania's Balance of Payments]." *Citizen* (Tanzania), January 15.

The Citizen (2023). "Moody's Gives Tanzania Favourable Credit Rating." *Citizen* (Tanzania), April 23.

Commission of the EC (1984). *Community and STABEX*, DE 49, X/174. Brussels: Commission of the EC.

Condon, Niall, and Matthew Stern (2011). *The Effectiveness of African Growth and Opportunity Act (AGOA) in Increasing Trade from Least Developed Countries.* London: EPPI-Centre, Social Science Research Unit, Institute of Education, University of London.

Congressional Budget Office (2018). *CBO Estimate for Divisions of Rules Committee Print 115–66—Consolidated Appropriations Act, 2018*, March 22. Washington, DC: Congressional Budget Office.

Congressional Research Service (2015). *Trade Adjustment Assistance for Workers and the TAA Reauthorization Act of 2015.* Washington, DC: Congressional Research Service.

Congressional Research Service (2019). *Generalized System of Preferences (GSP): Overview and Issues for Congress,* November 7. Washington, DC: Congressional Research Service.

Congressional Research Service (2020). *EU-Japan FTA: Implications for U.S. Trade Policy,* June 16. Washington, DC: Congressional Research Service.

Congressional Research Service (2022). *Generalized System of Preferences (GSP): Overview and Issues for Congress,* July 20. Washington, DC: Congressional Research Service.

Congressional Research Service (2023). "African Growth and Opportunity Act (AGOA)." *In Focus,* May 5. Washington, DC: Congressional Research Service.

Conningarth Economists (2002). *Macroeconomic Impact on the South African Economy of Duty-Free Exports to the United States Which Fall under GSP and Its Extension to AGOA.* Pretoria: Conningarth Economists.

Corporate Council on Africa (2020). "2020 U.S.-Africa Business Summit Announced," Press release, October 30.

Cranenburgh, Oda van (2009). "Restraining Executive Power in Africa: Horizontal Accountability in Africa's Hybrid Regimes." *South African Journal of International Affairs* 16, no. 1: 49–68.

Curran, Louise, et al. (2008). "The Economic Partnership Agreements: Rationale, Misperceptions and Non-trade Aspects." *Development Policy Review* 26, no. 5: 529–53.

CUTS International. "The Most Favoured-Nation Provision in the EC-EAC EPA and Its Implications." Geneva: CUTS International.

D'Alfonso, Alessandro (2014). "European Development Fund: Joint Development Cooperation and the EU Budget: Out or In?" European Parliamentary Research Service, November. Brussels: European Union.

Dardis, Rachel, and Katherine Cooke (1984). "The Impact of Trade Restrictions on U.S. Apparel Consumers." *Journal of Consumer Policy* 7: 1–12.

Davenport, Michael, et al. (1995). *Europe's Preferred Partners? The Lomé Countries in World Trade.* London: Overseas Development Institute.

Deardorff, Alan (1982). "The General Validity of the Heckscher-Ohlin Theorem." *American Economic Review* 72, no. 4: 683–94.

Deaton, Angus (1992). "Saving and Income Smoothing in Côte d'Ivoire." *Journal of African Economies* 1, no. 1: 1–24.

Department of the Treasury (2019). *Financial Report of the U.S. Government.* Washington, DC: Department of the Treasury.

Dhaka Courier (2021). "The Graduate." *Dhaka Courier,* March 5.

Diao, Xinshen (2013). "Economywide Impact of Maize Export Bans on Agricultural Growth and Household Welfare in Tanzania: A Dynamic Computable General Equilibrium Model Analysis." International Food Policy Research Institute Discussion Paper, 01287.

Djamson, Eric (1976). *The Dynamics of Euro-African Co-operation*. The Hague: Martinus Nijhoff.

Dunlop, Adam (1999). "What Future for Lomé's Commodity Protocols?" ECDPM Discussion Paper. Maastricht: European Centre for Development Policy Management.

EAC Secretariat (2021). "EAC Working with EU Technical Groups on Economic Partnership Agreements (EAPs)." Press release, February 24, East African Community.

EAC Secretariat (2022). "EAC Ministers Adopt 35% as the EAC CET 4th Band." Press release, May 6, East African Community.

EAC Secretariat (2023). "EAC officially launches the Verification Mission to assess Somalia's readiness to join the Community." Press release, January 25, East African Community.

The East African (2015). "Miners Lobby Uganda to Lift Ban on Mineral Export." *East African* (Kenya), July 25.

The East African (2022). "Kenya Rattled as Britain Rejects New EAC Tariffs." *East African* (Kenya),. September 15.

The East African (2023), "Somalia Signs Accession Treaty to Join EAC." *East African* (Kenya), December 15.

East African Community (2004). *EAC Common External Tariff* (Annex I to Protocol on the Establishment of the East African Customs Union). Arusha, Tanzania: East African Community.

Easterly, William (2001). "The Lost Decades: Developing Countries' Stagnation in Spite of Policy Reforms, 1980–1998." *Journal of Economic Growth* 6, 2: 135–57.

ECA (2007). "Aid for Trade: Emerging Issues and Challenges." E/ECA/COE/26/7, March 1. Addis Ababa: Economic Commission for Africa.

Economic Commission (2019). "Report from the Commission to the European Parliament, the European Economic and Social Committee and Committee on the Regions on Implementation of Free Trade Agreements 1 January 2018–31 December 2018," October 14. Brussels: European Union.

Edjigu, Habtamu, et al. (2023). "Uncertainty in Preferential Trade Agreements Impact of AGOA Suspensions on Exports." Research Policy Working Paper, 10424, World Bank.

Edwards, Lawrence, and Robert Lawrence (2016). "AGOA Rules: The Intended and Unintended Consequences of Special Fabric Provisions," in Sebastian Edwards, Simon Johnson, and David N. Weil, eds., *African Successes*, vol. 3 *Modernization and Development*, 343–93. Chicago: University of Chicago Press.

European Commission (1997). *The Stabex System and Export Revenues in ACP Countries*. Brussels: European Commission.

European Commission (2005). *GSP: The New EU Preferential Terms of Trade for Developing Countries.* MEMO/05/43, February 10. Brussels: European Commission.

European Commission (2015). *Generalized System of Preferences: Handbook on the Scheme of the European Union.* Brussels: European Commission.

European Commission (2016). *The European Union's Rules of Origin for the Generalized System of Preferences: A Guide to Users.* Brussels: European Commission.

European Commission (2017). *EU Grants Sri Lanka Improved Access to Its Market as Incentive to Reform,* May 17. Brussels: Economic Commission.

European Commission (2019). *European Union's GSP+ Scheme,* May 23. Brussels: European Commission.

European Commission (2020). *EU-Central Africa (Cameroon) Economic Partnership Agreement Creating Opportunities for EU and African Businesses,* October. Brussels: European Union.

European Commission (2020a). *Joint Report to the European Parliament and the Council: Report on the Generalised Scheme of Preferences covering the Period 2018–2019,* February 10. Brussels: European Union.

European Commission (2022). "European Union, Trade in Goods with Equatorial Guinea," August 2. Brussels: European Union.

European Commission (2022a). "European Union, Trade in Goods with Gabon," August 2. Brussels: European Union.

European Commission (2022b). "European Union, Trade in Goods with Nigeria," August 2. Brussels: European Union.

European Economic Community (1957). *The Treaty of Rome,* March 25. Brussels: European Economic Community.

European Parliament (2021). "Signature and Conclusion of the New Agreement Between the EU and the Countries of Sub-Saharan Africa, the Caribbean and the Pacific (ACP-EU Post-Cotonou)." January. Brussels: European Union.

European Union (2002). "Council Common Position of 18 February 2002 concerning Restrictive Measures against Zimbabwe." *Official Journal of the European Communities,* 50. Brussels: European Union.

European Union (2011). "Commission implementing regulation (EU) No 439/2011 of 6 May 2011 on a derogation from Regulation (EEC) No 2454/93 in respect of the definition of the concept of originating products used for the purposes of the scheme of generalised tariff preferences to take account of the special situation of Cape Verde regarding exports of certain fisheries products to the European Union." *Official Journal of the European Union,* 119. Brussels: European Union.

European Union (2012). *Regulation (EU) No 978/2012 of the European Parliament and of the Council of 25 October 2012: Applying a Scheme of Generalized Tariff Preferences and Repealing Council Regulation (EC) No 732/2008*. Brussels: European Union.

European Union (2012a). "Interim Agreement Establishing a Framework for an Economic Partnership Agreement between the Eastern and Southern Africa States, on the One Part, and the European Community and Its Member States, on the Other Part." *Official Journal of the European Union*, European Union.

European Union (2017). "Comprehensive Economic and Trade Agreement (CETA) between Canada, of the One Part, and the European Union and Its Member States, of the other part." *Official Journal of the European Union*, European Union.

Federal Deposit Insurance Corporation (2015). *Supervisory Insights*, 12(2). Washington, DC: Federal Deposit Insurance Corporation.

Fernandes, Ana Margarida, et al. (2021). "The Longer-Term Impact of the African Growth and Opportunity Act." Center for Economic Policy and Research, Washington, DC.

Financial Times (2015). "The Doha Round Finally Dies a Merciful Death." *Financial Times*, December 21.

Fontagne, Lionel, et al. (2010). "An Impact Study of the Economic Partnership Agreements in the Six ACP Regions." *Journal of African Economies* 20, no. 2: 179–216.

Food and Agriculture Organization (2014). "Technical Note: Analysis of Price Incentives and Disincentives for Cashew Nuts in the Republic of Mozambique for the Time Period 2005–2013." Rome: Food and Agriculture Organization of the United Nations.

Food and Agriculture Organization (2022). "The Cotton-4 (C-4) Countries in the Context of the Global Cotton Market: Situation and Short- and Medium-Term Outlook." Rome: Food and Agriculture Organization of the United Nations.

Francois, Joseph, et al. (2006). "Preference Erosion and Multilateral Trade Liberalization." *World Bank Economic Review* 20, no. 2: 197–216.

Frankel, Jeffrey (2012). "Mauritius: African Success Story." Mossavar-Rahmani Center for Business and Government Faculty, Harvard Kennedy School, Working Paper 2012–06.

Frazer, Garth, and Johannes Van Biesebroeck (2010). "Trade Growth under the African Growth and Opportunity Act." *Review of Economics and Statistics* 92, no. 1.

Frederik, Stender, et al. (2021). "The Trade Effects of the Economic Partnership Agreements between the European Union and the African, Caribbean and Pacific Group of States: Early Empirical Insights from Panel Data." *Journal of Common Markets Studies* 59, no. 6: 1495–1515.

French Ministry for Europe and Foreign Affairs (2022). "France and the Indian Ocean Commission." Paris: French Ministry for Europe and Foreign Affairs.

Gasiorek, Michael, et al. (2010). *Mid-term Evaluation of the EU's Generalised System of Preferences*. Sussex: Centre for the Analysis of Regional Integration at Sussex.

GATT (1962). "Report of Committee III on Its Future Programme of Work." L/1732, February 23. Geneva: General Agreement on Tariffs and Trade.

GATT (1979). "Differential and More Favourable Treatment, Reciprocity and Fuller Participation of Developing Countries (L/4903)." December 3. Geneva: General Agreement on Tariffs and Trade.

GATT (1994). "Understanding on the Interpretation of Article XXIV of the General Agreement on Tariffs and Trade 1994." Geneva: General Agreement on Tariffs and Trade.

Gelan, Ayele, "Economic Commentary: Ethiopia's Low Wage Is a Curse, Not a Blessing." *Addis Standard* (Ethiopia), April 25.

Ghosh, Atish, and Jonathan Ostry (1994). "Export Instability and the External Balance in Developing Countries." *IMF Staff Papers* 41, no. 2.

Giri, Rahul, et al. (2019). "Understanding Export Diversification: Key Drivers and Policy Implications." IMF Working Paper, Strategy, Policy and Review Department, WP/19/105.

Gumede, William (2013). "Paper 2: Power and Inequality Is Africa." Democracy Works Foundation, South Africa.

Gustafsson, Marcus, et al. (2017). "The EAC-EU EPA and Brexit: Legal and Economic Implications for EAC LDCs." Institute of International Economic Law, Georgetown University Law Center.

Hallaert, Jean-Jacques (2006). "A History of Empirical Literature on the Relationship Between Trade and Growth." *Mondes en développement* 135: 63–77.

Hamadeh, Nada, et al. (2022). *New World Bank Country Classifications by Income Level: 2022–2023*. Washington, DC: World Bank.

Hendrik, Van den Berg, and Joshua Lewer (2007). "Trade and Growth: The Empirical Evidence." Chapter 2 in Hendrik, Van den Berg, and Joshua Lewer, eds., *International Trade and Economic Growth* (New York: Routledge).

Herrero, Alisa, et al. (2015). "Implementing the Agenda for Change: An Independent Analysis of the 11th EDF Programming." Discussion Paper 180, European Centre for Development Policy.

Herrmann, Roland (1982). "On the Economic Evaluation of the Stabex System." *Intereconomics* 17, no. 1: 7–12.

Hoekman, Bernard, Will Martin, and Carlos A. Primo Braga, eds. (2009). *Trade Preference Erosion Measurement and Policy Response*. Washington, DC: World Bank, and Hampshire: Palgrave Macmillan.

Hoekstra, Quint (2019). "Conflict Diamonds and the Angola Civil War (1992–2002)." *Third Quarterly* 40, no. 7: 1322–39.

Howard, Audrie (2015). "The Successes and Failures of the Kimberley Process Certification Scheme in Angola, Sierra Leone, and Zimbabwe." *Washington University Global Studies Law Review* 15, no. 1: 136–59.

Hsiang, Evan (2023). "Chinese Investment in Africa: A Reexamination of the Zambian Debt Crisis." *Harvard International Review*.

Human Rights Watch (2011). *"You Will Be Fired If You Refuse": Labor Abuses in Zambia's Chinese State-Owned Copper Mines*. New York: Human Rights Watch.

ICAC (2001). *Survey of the Cost of Production of Raw Cotton*. Washington, DC: International Cotton Advisory Committee.

ICAC (2002). *Production and Trade Policies Affecting the Cotton Industry*. Washington, DC: International Cotton Advisory Committee.

Icso, Isabelle (2023). "How Tariffs Hit Small Business (and Why Congress Needs to Renew GSP)." U.S. Chamber of Commerce.

Idris, Jamilah, et al. (2016). "Trade Openness and Economic Growth: A Causality Test in Panel Perspective." *International Journal of Business and Society* 17, no. 2: 281–90.

Ighobor, Kingsley (2022). "One Year of Free Trading in Africa Calls for Celebration despite Teething Problems," *Africa Renewal*. New York: United Nations.

Iimi, Atsushi (2007). "Infrastructure and Trade Preferences for Livestock Sector: Empirical Evidence from Beef Industry in Africa." WPS 4201, Finance, Economics and Urban Development. Washington, DC: World Bank.

The Independent (2022). "Miners in Crisis as Ban on Unprocessed Minerals Bites" *Independent* (Uganda), March 7.

Industrial Global Union (2016). "Lesotho: Unions Demonstrate to Save AGOA." Industrial Global Union, December 1.

International Crisis Group (2010). *Madagascar: Crisis Heating Up?* Africa Report No. 166, November 18. Brussels: International Crisis Group.

International Labor Organization (1996). *Globalization Changes the Face of Textile, Clothing and Footwear Industries*. Geneva: International Labor Organization.

International Labor Organization (2020). *Global Wage Report 2020–21: Wages and Minimum Wages in the Time of COVID-19*. Geneva: International Labor Organization.

International Monetary Fund (1980). *Annual Report 1980*. Washington, DC: International Monetary Fund.

International Monetary Fund and World Bank (2018). *The Bali Fintech Agenda: Chapeau Paper*. Washington, DC: World Bank Group.

IRIN News (2010). "Textile Industry Unravels." *IRIN News*, February 24.

Jacobsen, Reinhard (2022). "OACPS-European Union Post-Cotonou Negotiations Process in a Stalemate." *UN Insider*, July.

Kaplinsky, Raphael, and Mike Morris (2008). "Do the Asian Drivers Undermine Export-Oriented Industrialization in SSA?" *World Development* 36, no. 2: 254–73.

Kapur, Ishan (1991). *Ghana: Adjustment and Growth, 1983–91*. Washington, DC: International Monetary Fund.

Kassa, Woubet, and Souleymane Coulibaly (2019). *Revisiting the Trade Impact of the African Growth and Opportunity Act: A Synthetic Control Approach*. World Bank Policy Research Working Paper 8993, Africa Region. Washington, DC: World Bank.

Keck, Alexander, and Andreas Lendle (2012). "New Evidence on Preference Utilization." Staff Working Paper ERSD-2012–12, World Trade Organization Economic Research and Statistics Division.

Kennedy, Kevin (2011). "The Generalized System of Preferences after Four Decades: Conditionality and the Shrinking Margin of Preference." *Michigan State International Law Review* 20, no. 3: 521–668.

Kenya Investment Authority (2019). "Cotton, Textile, and Apparel Sector Investment Profile—Kenya." Kenya Investment Authority.

Kilimo News (2021). "State of the Horticulture Industry in Kenya." *Kilimo News* (Kenya), July 13.

Kim, Jeonghoi (2010). "Recent Trends in Export Restrictions on Raw Materials." Chapter 1 in OECD, *The Economic Impact of Export Restrictions on Raw Materials*. Paris: OECD.

Kimani, Mary (2012). "Women Struggle to Secure Land Right: Hard Fight for Access and Decision-Making Power," *Africa Renewal*, United Nations.

Kipling, Jack (2010). *Impact of AGOA on the Lesotho Clothing & Textile Sectorsy*. Nairobi, Kenya: African Cotton and Textile Industries Federation.

Kokole, Omari (1981). "STABEX Anatomized." *Third World Quarterly* 3, no. 3: 441–59.

Kołodzejski, Marek (2018). "Economic, Social and Territorial Situation of France–La Réunion." August. Brussels: European Union.

KPMG [Klynveld Peat Marwick Goerdeler] (2017). "China Tax Alert: China Customs Released the Rules of Origin of Imported Goods from the Least Developed Countries." Issue 8, March.

Kragelund, Peter, and Pádraig Carmody (2015). "Who Is in Charge? State Power and Agency in Sino-African Relations." *Cornell International Law Journal* 49: 1–24.

Krapohl, Sebastian, and Sophie Van Huut (2020). "A Missed Opportunity for Regionalism: The Disparate Behaviour of African Countries in the EPA-Negotiations with the EU." *Journal of European Integration* 42, no. 4: 565–82.

Krugman, Paul. (1979). "Increasing Returns, Monopolistic Competition and International Trade," *Journal of International Economics* 9: 469–79.

Krugman, Paul (1980). "Scale Economies, Product Differentiation and the Pattern of Trade." *American Economic Review* 70: 950–59.

Krugman, Paul (1981). "Intra-Industry Specialization and the Gains from Trade." *Journal of Political Economy* 89: 959–73.

Krugman, Paul (1989). "Industrial Organization and International Trade." In Richard Schmalensee and Robert Willig, eds., *Handbook of Industrial Organisation*, vol. 2, 1179–1223. Amsterdam: North-Holland.

Kyatusiimire, Sharon (2015). "Uganda Mines Close as Export Ban Hurts." *East African Business Week* (Uganda). July 21.

Laaksonen, Kalle, et al. (2007). "Mauritius and Jamaica as Case Studies of the Lomé Sugar Protocol." Working Paper 06/21, TRADEAG, Agricultural Trade Agreements.

Lanktree, Graham (2020). "UK-Kenya Deal Triggers East African Trade Tensions." *Politico*, October 27.

Lawrence, R. (1971). "Primary Products, Preferences, and Economic Welfare: The EEC and Africa." In P. Robson, ed., *International Economic Integration*, 262–384. Baltimore: Penguin Books.

Lawrence, Robert, and Tatiana Rosito (2006). "A New Compensation Mechanism for Preference Erosion in the Doha Round." Faculty Research Working Papers Series, Harvard University, John F. Kennedy School of Government.

Le Billon, Philippe (2008). "Diamond Wars? Conflict Diamonds and Geographies or Resource Wars." *Annals of the Association of American Geographers* 98, no. 2. 345–72.

Lecomte, Henri-Bernard (2001). "Effectiveness of Developing Country Participation in ACP-EU Negotiations." Working Paper, Overseas Development Institute.

Lesotho Times (2009). "Hell on Earth for Factory Workers," *Lesotho Times*, November 4.

Liuima, Justinas (2022). "Uzbekistan to Benefit from EU GSP+ Trade Scheme." *Euromonitor International*, May 19.

Lloyd, Peter (2011). "The Discovery of the Heckscher-Ohlin Model of International Trade." *International Journal of Development and Conflict, Gokhale Institute of Politics and Economics* 1, no. 3: 241–64.

LMC International and Overseas Development Institute (2012). *The Impact of EU Sugar Policy Reform on Developing Countries*. London: UK Department of International Development.

Lofchie, Michael (1994). "The Politics of Agricultural Policy." in Joel Barkan, ed., *Beyond Capitalism vs. Socialism in Kenya and Tanzania*, 129–73. Boulder: Lynne Rienner.

London School of Economics (2021). Sustainability Impact Assessment in Support of Negotiations with Partner Countries in Eastern and Southern Africa in View of Deepening the Existing Interim Economic Partnership Agreement. London: London School of Economics.

Low, Patrick, et al. (2005). "Multilateral Solutions to the Erosion of Non-Reciprocal Preferences in NAMA." WTO Research and Analysis Working Paper, ERSD-2005-05.

Lu, Sheng (2020). "USITC Report: U.S. Apparel Sourcing under African Growth and Opportunity Act (AGOA)." U.S. International Trade Commission.

Luke, David, and Heini Suominen (2019). "Towards Rethinking the Economic Partnership Agreements." In San Bilal and Bernard Hoekman, eds., *Perspectives on the Soft Power of EU Trade Policy*, 143–50. London: Center for Economic Policy and Research.

Lusaka News (2016). "Government Bans Maize Export." *Lusaka News* (Zambia), April 5.

Luxembourg Centre for Contemporary and Digital History (1957). "Treaty establishing the EEC - Annex IV: Overseas countries and Territories to Which the Provisions of Part IV of the Treaty Apply (Rome, 25 March 1957)." University of Luxembourg.

Madani, Dorsati (1999). "A Review of the Role of the Export Processing Zones." Policy Research Working Paper 2238, World Bank.

Maehle, Nils (2013). "Exchange Rate Liberalization in Selected Sub-Saharan African Countries: Successes, Failures, and Lessons." IMF Working Paper, WP/13/32.

Mail and Guardian (2002). "Zambia Bans Maize Export." *Mail & Guardian* (South Africa), January 1.

Manchin, Miriam (2006). "Preference Utilization and Tariff Reduction in EU Imports from ACP Countries." *World Economy* 29, no. 9: 1243–66.

Manger, Mark, and Kenneth Shadlen (2014). "Political Trade Dependence and North-South Trade Agreements." *International Studies Quarterly* 58, no. 1: 79–91.

Mankiw, Gregory (2015). "Economists Actually Agree on This: The Wisdom of Free Trade," *New York Times*, April 24.

Marković, Ivan (2009). "How to Join the World Trade Organization: Some Aspects of the Accession Process." *Economic Annals*, 54, no. 180 (January–March).

May, Ernesto (1985). "Exchange Controls and Parallel Market Economies in Sub-Saharan Africa: Focus on Ghana." World Bank Staff Working Papers, SWP711.

Mbodiam, Brice, and Sylvain Andzongo (2020). "EPA: Cameroon Set on Suspending Tariff Dismantling till the end of 2020 despite the EU's Protests," *Business in Cameroon Magazine*, November 12.

McKenzie, Michael (2005). "Case Note: European Communities—Conditions for the Granting of Tariff Preferences to Developing Countries," *Melbourne Journal of International Law* 6, no. 1.

McQueen, Matthew (2002). "EU Preferential Market Access Conditions for the Least Developed Countries," *Intereconomics* 37, no. 2: 101–9.

Mkandawire, Thandika, and Charles Soludo, eds. (2003). *African Voices on Structural Adjustment*. Asmara: Africa World Press.

Mkapa, Benjamin (2016). "Why EPA Is Not Beneficial to Tanzania." November 1, South Centre, Bulletin 95.

Morse, Yonathan (2019). *How Autocrats Compete: Parties, Patrons, and Unfair Elections in Africa*. New York: Cambridge University Press.

Moss, Brandon (2020). "Zambia Bans Exports of Maize." *Agrifocus African Market* (South Africa), September 7.

Moss, Kevin (2006). "The Consequences of the WTO Appellate Body Decision in the EC Tariff Preferences for the African Growth and Opportunity Act and Sub-Saharan Africa." *New York University Journal of Law and Politics* 38, no. 3: 665–706.

Mourlon-Druol, Emmanuel. (2015). "The UK's EU Vote: The 1975 Precedent and Today's Negotiations." *Bruegel Policy Contribution*, Issue 2015/08: 1–10.

Moyo, Herbert (2021). "Lesotho: 45,000 Textile Jobs at Severe Risk." *Lesotho Times*, January 29.

Mshomba, Richard (1993). "The Magnitude of Coffee Arabica Smuggled from Northern Tanzania into Kenya." *Eastern Africa Economic Review* 9, no. 1: 165–75.

Mshomba, Richard (2000). *Africa in the Global Economy*. Boulder, CO: Lynne Rienner.

Mshomba, Richard (2009). *Africa and the World Trade Organization*. New York: Cambridge University Press.

Mshomba, Richard (2017). *Economic Integration in Africa: The East African Community in Comparative Perspective*. New York: Cambridge University Press.

Muendler, Marc-Andres (2010). "Trade Reform, Employment Allocation and Worker Flows." Chapter 7 in Guido Porto and Bernard Hoekman, eds., *Trade Adjustment Costs in Developing Countries: Impacts, Determinants and Policy Responses*. Washington, DC: Centre for Economic Policy Research and World Bank.

Mugabi, Isaac (2022). "Ghana and Uganda Ban Grain and Food Exports." AllAfrica.com, May 27.

National Science Foundation (2008). "National Science Foundation Congratulates 2008 Nobel Laureates in Physics, Chemistry and Economics." October 17, news release 08-185.

Ndofor, Herman, and Charles Ray (2022). "Cameroon: Africa's Unseen Crisis." May 9, Foreign Policy Research Institute.

Ngo-Eyok, Suzanne (2013). "Advocacy for Free Trade." *Rural 21: The International Journal of Rural Development,* February, 16–17.

Ngounou, Boris (2022). "Central Africa: Log Export Ban Postponed Indefinitely." *Afrik 21* (France), November 2.

New Times (2016). "Tanzania Backs Out of EAC Deal with EU over Brexit." *The New Times* (Rwanda), July 10.

New York Times (2020). "U.K. Leaves E.U., Embarking on an Uncertain Future." *New York Times*, December 31.

Nippon Express (2020). "Cold Chain Development for Flower Exports in East Africa." *Nippon Express* (Japan).

Obiukwu, Onyedimmakachukwu (2014). "Africa's Richest Presidents: Why Jonathan's Position Is Not the Biggest News." *Ventures* (Africa), October 8.

O'Connell, Stephen, and Lindsay Renée Dolan (2012). "Development and Aid in Sub-Saharan Africa." *Journal of Catholic Social Thought* 9, no. 2: 245–64.

O'Donnell, Jefcoate, and Robbie Gramer (2018). "Cameroon's Paul Biya Gives a Master Class in Fake Democracy." *Foreign Policy*, October 22.

Odyek, John (2019). "Mining Companies Cry Out Their Exports Are Banned," *New Vision* (Uganda), November 10.

OECD (2005). "Trade-Adjustment Costs in OECD Markets: A Mountain or a Molehill?" Chapter 1 in OECD *Employment Outlook*. Paris: OECD,

Office of the U.S. Trade Representative, Executive Office of the President (2018). *U.S. Generalized System of Preferences Guidebook*. Washington, DC: Office of the U.S. Trade Representative, Executive Office of the President.

Okeowo, Alexis. "China, Zambia, and a Clash in a Coal Mine." *New Yorker*, October 9.

Olarreaga, Marcelo, and Caglar Ozden (2005). "AGOA and Apparel: Who Captures the Tariff Rent in the Presence of Preferential Market Access?" *World Economy* 28, no. 1: 63–77.

Osakwe, Patrick, and Jean-Marc Kilolo (2018). "What Drives Export Diversification: New Evidence from a Panel of Developing Countries." UNCTAD Research Paper No. 3, October.

Otondi, Sekou Toure (2016). "Tanzania's Refusal to Sign EU Trade Pact Gives East Africa Time to Rethink," *The Conversation*, July 21.

Owusu, Francis, and Kefa Otiso (2021). "Twenty Years of the U.S. African Growth and Opportunity Act (AGOA): Policy Lessons from Kenya's Experience." *Kenya Studies Review* 9, no. 1: 16–34.

Oxfam (2002). *Stop the Dumping: How EU Agricultural Subsidies Are Damaging the Livelihoods in the Developing World.* Nairobi: Oxfam International.

Ozden, Caglar, and Gunjan Sharma (2006). "Price Effects of Preferential Market Access: Caribbean Basin Initiative and the Apparel Sector." *World Bank Economic Review* 20, no. 2: 241–59.

Park, Young-Il, and Kym Anderson (1991). "The Rise and Demise of Textiles and Clothing in Economic Development: The Case of Japan." *Economic Development and Cultural Change* 39, no. 3: 531–48.

Phelps, Nicholas, et al. (2009). "Broken Chain? AGOA and Foreign Direct Investment in the Kenyan Clothing Industry." *World Development* 37, no. 2: 314–25.

Pichon, Eric (2022). *Economic Partnership Agreement with the East African Community.* May. Brussels: European Union.

Piermartini, Roberta (2004). "The Role of Export Taxes in the Field of Primary Commodities." WTO Discussion Papers, No. 4. Geneva: WTO Economic Research and Statistics Division.

Pouwels, Alexandra (2021). "The Integration of the European Development Funds into the MFF 2021–2027." June. Brussels: European Union.

Press, Daniel, and Iain Murray (2017). "Economic Freedom Is Key to African Development: Secure Property Rights, Institutional Reform, and Affordable Cnergy Can Unlock Prosperity for Africa." *OnPoint*, 227. Competitive Enterprise Institute.

Property Rights Alliance (2023). *International Property Rights Index 2022.* Washington, DC: Property Rights Alliance.

Rahhou, Jihane (2023). "Morocco Bans Vegetable Exports to West Africa to Stabilize Domestic Prices." *Morocco World News*, February 12.

Ravenhill, John (1985). *Collective Clientelism: The Lomé Conventions and North-South Relations.* New York: Columbia University Press.

Reuters (2018). "Tanzania Seeks Buyers for Surplus Cashew Nut Output—Minister." December 28.

Reuters (2021). "European Parliament Gives Green Light to Huge Farm Subsidies Deal." November 23.

Ricardo, David (2001). *On the Principles of Political Economy and Taxation.* London: Electric Book.

Rodney, Walter (1989). *How Europe Underdeveloped Africa.* Nairobi: East African Educational Publishers.

Runde, Daniel, et al. (2021). "Supporting Small and Medium Enterprises in Sub-Saharan Africa through Blended Finance." Center for Strategic and International Studies.

Sabha, Yassin (2020). "Promoting Technology Transfer and Productivity Spillovers for Foreign Direct Investment (FDI)." Washington, DC: World Bank.

Sachs, Jeffrey, and Andrew Warner (1995). "Economic Reform and the Process of Global Integration." *Brookings Papers on Economic Activity* 1, no. 1: 118.

Schneidman, Witney, and Zenia Lewis (2012). *The African Growth and Opportunity Act: Looking Back, Looking Forward.* Washington, DC: Brookings Institution.

Schor, Adriana (2016). "Is Trade Good for Development? The Elusive Question." *Brazilian Political Science Review* 10, no. 2: 1–21.

Schulz, Nicolai (2020). "The Politics of Export Restrictions: A Panel Data Analysis of African Commodity Processing Industries." *LSE Research Online Documents on Economics,* 103779.

Setipa, Joseph (2016). "Why AGOA Remains Critical to Lesotho's Development." Africa Development Bank Group, October 3. London School of Economics and Political Science.

Sharpe, Andrew, and Shahrzad Mobasher Fard (2022). "The Current State of Research on the Two-Way Linkages between Productivity and Well-being." ILO Working Paper 56. Geneva: International Labor Organization.

Singer, H. (1989). "The 1980s: A Lost Decade—Development in Reverse?" In H. Singer and S. Sharma, eds. *Growth and External Debt Management.* London: Macmillan.

Sidiropoulos, Elizabeth (2022), "Africa: Aspiring to Greater Global Agency." Chapter 7 in Sinan Ülgen, ed., *Rewiring Globalization.* Washington, DC: Carnegie Endowment for International Peace, 2022.

Sixtus, Mbom (2016). "Cameroon Goes It Alone with Controversial EU Trade Deal, Angers Regional Partners." September 26. Royal African Society.

Soumitra Sharma, eds. *Growth and External Debt Management* (46–56). London: Macmillan.

South Centre (2007). *Aid for Trade and Financial Assistance to Implement the EPAs.* May. Geneva: South Centre.

South Centre (2007a). *Fact Sheet NB.1: Understanding the Economic Agreements (EPAs).* March. Geneva: South Centre.

South Centre (2014). *Africa's Acute Problems with the EPAs.* June. Geneva: South Centre.

Staritz, Cornelia, and Mike Morris (2013). "Local Embeddedness, Upgrading and Skill Development: Global Value Chains and Foreign Direct Investment in Lesotho's Apparel Industry." Capturing the Gains Working Paper 20, University of Manchester.

Subramanian, A. (2003). "Financing of Losses from Preference Erosion." Prepared for the WTO WT/TF/COH/14.

Tadesse, Fasila (2020). "Ethiopia Resumes WTO Negotiations with New Offer." *Fortune News* (Ethiopia), February 1, 20, no. 1031.

Tahir, Muhammad (2014). "Trade Openness and Economic Growth: A Review of the Literature." *Asian Social Science* 10, no. 9: 137–43.

Tangermann, Stefan (2002). *The Future of Preferential Trade Arrangements for Developing Countries and the Current Round of WTO Negotiations on Agriculture.* Rome: Food and Agriculture Organization of the United Nations.

Tati, Gabriel (2014). "Reaping the Benefits of Preferential Trade Arrangement: Asian FDI in the Lesotho and Swaziland." *Presses de Sciences Po* 69: 111–30.

Taylor, Ian (2011). *The Forum on China-Africa Cooperation (FOCAC).* New York: Routledge.

Trade Law Centre for Southern Africa (2010). "Africa: Export Zones to Boost Africa's Manufacturing Industry." May 15. Jamestown, South Africa: Trade Law Centre for Southern Africa.

Trade Law Centre for Southern Africa (2023). "Country Information: Lesotho." Jamestown, South Africa: Trade Law Centre for Southern Africa.

TradeMark Africa (2022). "How Non-tariff Barriers Affect Trade in the EAC." TradeMark Africa, August 29.

Transparency International (2023). *Corruption Perception Index 2022.* Berlin: Transparency International.

Tröster, Bernhard, et al. (2020). "Delivering on Promises? The Expected Impacts and Implementation Challenges of the Economic Partnership Agreements between the European Union and Africa." *Journal of Common Market Studies* 58, no. 2: 365–83.

Tura, Hussein Ahmed (2015). "Ethiopia's Accession to the World Trade Organization: Lessons from Acceded Least Developed Countries." *Oromia Law Journal* 4, no. 1: 125–52.

Twitchett, Carol (1978). *Europe and Africa: From Association to Partnership.* Farnborough, England: Saxon House.

U.K. Department of Trade (2021). *International Treaty: Memorandum of Understanding between the UK and Cameroon.* April 21. London: UK Government.

U.K. Secretary of State for Foreign, Commonwealth and Development Affairs (2021). *Interim Agreement establishing an Economic Partnership Agreement be-*

tween the United Kingdom of Great Britain and Northern Ireland, of the one part and the Republic of Cameroon, of the other part. London: UK Government.

U.S. Congress (2000). H. R. 434. *Trade and Development Act of 2000*. Washington, DC: U.S. Congress.

U.S. Congressional Research Service (2022). "Generalized System of Preferences (GSP): Overview and Issues for Congress." July 20. Washington, DC: Congressional Research Service.

U.S. International Trade Commission (1975). *International Commodity Agreements*. Washington, DC: U.S. Government Printing Office.

U.S. International Trade Commission (1979). *Operation of the Trade Agreements Program—31st Report*. Washington, DC: U.S. International Trade Commission.

U.S. International Trade Commission (1997). *Likely Impact of Providing Quota-Free and Duty-Free Entry to Textiles and Apparel from Sub-Saharan Africa*. Publication 3056. Washington, DC: U.S. International Trade Commission.

U.S. International Trade Commission (2013). *Andean Trade Preference Act: Impact on U.S. Industries and Consumers and on Drug Crop Eradication and Crop Substitution, 2013—Sixteenth Report*. Washington, DC: U.S. International Trade Commission.

U.S. International Trade Commission (2014). *AGOA: Trade and Investment Performance Overview*. Washington, DC: U.S. International Trade Commission.

U.S. International Trade Commission (2020). *Harmonized Tariff Schedule of the U.S. (2020) Revision 7*. February. Washington, DC: U.S. International Trade Commission.

U.S. International Trade Commission (2023). *African Growth and Opportunity Act (AGOA): Program Usage, Trends, and Sectoral Highlights*. No. 5419. Washington, DC: U.S. International Trade Commission.

U.S. State Department (1987). *Country Reports Human Rights Practices for 1986*. Washington, DC: U.S. State Department.

U.S. Trade Representative (2016). *International Trade Data System Visa Requirements Under the African Growth and Opportunity Act*. Washington, DC: U.S. Trade Representative.

U.S. Trade Representative (2019). *U.S. Generalized System of Preferences Guidebook*, December. Washington, DC: U.S. Trade Representative.

U.S. Trade Representative (2022). *Annual Review of Country Eligibility for Benefits Under the African Growth and Opportunity Act*. May. Washington, DC: U.S. Trade Representative.

UNCTAD (1994). *Trade and Development Report 1994*. Geneva: UNCTAD.

UNCTAD (2006). *World Investment Report United Nations New York and Geneva 2006—FDI from Developing and Transition Economies: Implications for Development*. Geneva: UNCTAD.

UNCTAD (2011). *An Assessment of the Impact of Reference Erosion and Rules of Origin in Eastern and Southern Africa: A Study and Survey of Eastern and Southern African Exporters.* Geneva: UNCTAD.

UNCTAD (2013). *Generalized System of Preferences: Handbook of the Scheme of Canada.* Geneva: UNCTAD.

UNCTAD (2015). *Explanatory Notes on the Generalized System of Preferences Scheme of the European Union.* Geneva: UNCTAD.

UNCTAD (2016). *A Brief on International Commodity Bodies (ICBs): Updated on 1 February 2016.* Geneva: UNCTAD.

UNCTAD (2016a). *Handbook on the Special and Preferential Tariff Scheme of China for Least Developed Countries.* Geneva: UNCTAD.

UNCTAD (2016b). *Generalized System of Preferences: Handbook on the Scheme of the U.S. of America.* Geneva: UNCTAD.

UNCTAD (2017). *State of Commodity Dependence 2016.* Geneva: UNCTAD.

UNCTAD (2017a). *Generalized System of Preferences: Handbook on the Scheme of Japan.* Geneva: UNCTAD.

UNCTAD (2018). *Key Statistics and Trends in Economic Integration in ACP Region.* Geneva: UNCTAD.

UNCTAD (2018a). *Generalized System of Preferences: Handbook on the Scheme of Australia.* Geneva: UNCTAD.

UNCTAD (2019). *Economic Development in Africa Report 2019: Made in Africa—Rules of Origin for Enhanced Intra-African Trade.* Geneva: UNCTAD.

UNCTAD (2019a). *World Investment Report 2019: Special Economic Zones.* Geneva: UNCTAD.

UNCTAD (2020). *Handbook of Preferential Tariff Scheme of the Republic of Korea in Favour of Least Developed Countries.* Geneva: UNCTAD.

UNCTAD (2022). *Economic Development in Africa Report 2022: Rethinking the Foundations of Export Diversification in Africa—the Catalytic Role of Business and Financial Services.* Geneva: UNCTAD.

UNCTAD (2023). *The African Growth and Opportunities Act Limitations, Utilization, and Results.* Geneva: UNCTAD.

UNDP Regional Bureau for Africa (2021). *Graduation of African Least Developed Countries (LDCs): Emerging Issues in a New Development Landscape.* New York: UNDP Regional Bureau for Africa.

United Nations (1964). *Towards a New Trade Policy for Development: Report by the Secretary-General of the United Nations Conference on Trade and Development.* New York: United Nations.

United Nations (2020). *The World Economic Situation and Prospects 2020.* New York: United Nations.

United Nations Development Program (2022). *Human Development Report 2021/2022: Uncertain Times, Unsettled Lives—Shaping Our Future in a Transforming World.* New York: United Nations Development Program.

United Nations Department of Economic and Social Affairs (2017). *Reflections on Development Policy in the 1970s and 1980s.* UN-DESA Policy Brief #53, July. New York: United Nations.

United Nations Economic and Social Council (2021). "Resolution Adopted by the General Assembly on 11 February 2021: Extension of the Preparatory Period Preceding the Graduation of Angola from the Least Developed Country Category." New York: United Nations.

United Nations Economic Commission for Africa (2018). "A Comparison of the Provisions of the Economic Partnership Agreements." Working paper. Addis Ababa: Economic Commission for Africa.

Usman, Zainab, and David Landry (2021). *Economic Diversification in Africa: How and Why It Matters.* Washington, DC: Carnegie Endowment for International Peace.

USTR (2014). "President Obama Removes Swaziland, Reinstates Madagascar for AGOA Benefits." Press release, June 26.

USTR (2016). *2016 Biennial Report on the Implementation of the African Growth and Opportunity Act.* Washington, DC: U.S. Trade Representative.

USTR (2020). *2020 Biennial Report on the Implementation of the African Growth and Opportunity Act.* Washington, DC: U.S. Trade Representative.

USTR (2023). *2023 AGOA Eligible Countries.* Washington, DC: U.S. Trade Representative.

van Benthem van den Bergh, Godfried (1963). "The New Convention of Association with African States." *Common Market Law Review* 1, no. 2: 156–82.

Vanzetti, David, et al. (2005). "Banana Split: How EU Policies Divide Global Producers." *Policy Issues in International Trade and Commodities Study Series,* No. 31. Geneva: UNCTAD.

Vásquez, Ian, et al. (2021). *The Human Freedom Index 2021: A Global Measurement of Personal, Civil, and Economic Freedom.* Washington, DC: Cato Institute.

Vernon, Raymond (1966). "International Investment and International Trade in the Product Cycle." *Quarterly Journal of Economics* 80, no. 2: 190–207.

Voice of America. (2023). "Central African States Fail to Honor Timber Export Ban." Voice of America, February 2.

Vollmer, Sebastian, et al. (2009). "EU-ACP Economic Partnership Agreements: Empirical Evidence for Sub-Saharan Africa." *Proceedings of the German Development Economics Conference,* Verein für Socialpolitik, Research Committee Development Economics.

Weil, Gordon (1965). ed. *A Handbook on the European Economic Community.* New York: Frederick A. Praeger.

Wells, Sidney (1969). "The Developing Countries: GATT and UNCTAD." *International Affairs* 45, no. 1: 64–79.

Wessel, Marius, and Foluke Quist-Wessel (2015). "Cocoa Production in West Africa, a Review and Analysis of Recent Developments." *NJAS-Wageningen Journal of Life Sciences*, 74–75, 1–7.

White House (2000). "Details of the Trade and Development Act of 2000." May 17.

White House (2015). "Presidential Proclamation: To Modify Duty-Free Treatment Under the Generalized System of Preferences and for Other Purposes." Press release, September 30, The White House, Washington, D.C.

Wickizer, Vernon (1943). *The World Coffee Economy*. Stanford, CA: Food Research Institute, Stanford University.

Worker Rights Consortium (2018). *"Ethiopia Is a North Star": Grim Conditions and Miserable Wages Guide Apparel Brands in Their Race to the Bottom*. Washington, DC: Worker Rights Consortium.

Worker Rights Consortium (2019). *Gender-Based Violence and Harassment at Nien Hsing Textile Co., LTD (Lesotho): Findings, Recommendations, and Status*. Washington, DC: Worker Rights Consortium.

World Bank (1994). *Adjustment in Africa: Reforms, Results, and the Road Ahead*. New York: Oxford University Press.

World Bank (2015). *Kenya Apparel and Textile Industry: Diagnosis, Strategy and Action Plan*. Washington, DC: World Bank.

World Customs Organization (2014). *Guidelines on Certification of Origin*. Brussels: World Customs Organization.

World Customs Organization (2018). *Guide to Customs Valuation and Transfer Pricing*. Brussels: World Customs Organization.

World Customs Organization (2018a). *Guidelines on Certification of Origin*. Brussels: World Customs Organization.

World Trade Organization (2004). *The Future of the WTO: Addressing Institutional Challenges in the New Millennium*. Geneva: World Trade Organization.

World Trade Organization (2005). *Doha Work Programme: Ministerial Declaration*, WT/MIN(05)/DEC, December 12. Geneva: World Trade Organization.

World Trade Organization (2007). *Handbook on Accession to the WTO*. Geneva: World Trade Organization.

World Trade Organization (2014). *Challenges Faced by LDCs in Complying with Preferential Rules of Origin under Unilateral Preference Schemes*. Geneva: World Trade Organization.

World Trade Organization (2015). *African Growth and Opportunity Act (AGOA as Amended): Request for a Waiver* (G/C/W/713). Geneva: World Trade Organization.

World Trade Organization (2019). *Further Evidence from Utilization Rates: Utilization by LDCs of China's Preference*. Geneva: World Trade Organization.

World Trade Organization (2021). *Utilization of Trade Preferences by Least Developed Countries: 2015–2019 Patterns and Trends*. Geneva: World Trade Organization.

World Trade Organization (2022). *World Trade Statistical Review 2022*. Geneva: World Trade Organization.

World Trade Organization (2022a). *World Tariff Profiles*. Geneva: World Trade Organization.

World Trade Organization (2023). *Regional Trade Agreements (Database)*. Geneva: World Trade Organization.

Yeshiwas, Woderyelesh (2016). "The Impact of AGOA Related Foreign Direct Investment Inflows on Employment in Sub-Saharan Africa: The Case Study of Ethiopia." Master's thesis, Addis Ababa University.

Zafar, Ali (2011). "Mauritius: An Economic Success." In Punam Chuhan-Pole and Manka Angwafo, eds., *Yes, Africa Can: Success Stories from a Dynamic Continent*, 91–106. Washington, DC: World Bank.

Zartman, William (1971). *The Politics of Trade Negotiations between Africa and the European Economic Community: The Weak Confront the Strong*. Princeton, NJ: Princeton University Press.

INDEX

Note: Page numbers in *italics* refer to tables.

Printed in the USA
CPSIA information can be obtained
at www.ICGtesting.com
JSHW081459140724
66375JS00001B/1